Rhetoric Across Borders

Rhetoric Across Borders

Edited by Anne Teresa Demo

Parlor Press
Anderson, South Carolina
www.parlorpress.com

Parlor Press LLC, Anderson, South Carolina, USA

© 2015 by the Rhetoric Society of America
All rights reserved.
Printed in the United States of America

S A N: 2 5 4 - 8 8 7 9

Library of Congress Cataloging-in-Publication Data

Rhetoric across borders / edited by Anne Teresa Demo. -- First edition.
    pages cm
  Includes bibliographical references and index.
    ISBN 978-1-60235-737-2 (pbk. : acid-free paper) -- ISBN 978-1-60235-738-9 (hardcover : acid-free paper)
  1. Rhetoric. I. Demo, Anne Teresa, 1968- editor.
  P301.R425 2015
  808--dc23
                                        2015024861

Cover design by David Blakesley.
Cover image by Nuno Silva at Unsplash.com. Used by permission.
RSA 2014 logo designed by Lori Klopp.
Copyediting by Jared Jameson.
Printed on acid-free paper.

1 2 3 4 5
First Edition

Parlor Press, LLC is an independent publisher of scholarly and trade titles in print and multimedia formats. This book is available in paper, hardcover, and digital formats from Parlor Press on the World Wide Web at http://www.parlorpress.com or through online and brick-and-mortar bookstores. For submission information or to find out about Parlor Press publications, write to Parlor Press, 3015 Brackenberry Drive, Anderson, SC 29621, or e-mail editor@parlorpress.com.

CONTENTS

Remapping the Political

Contesting Boundaries: Science, Technology, and Nature

Teaching Across Divides

In Conversation: Fragments and Provocations

Rhetoric Across Borders

INTRODUCTION

Anne Teresa Demo

The location and timing of the sixteenth Biennial Rhetoric Society of America (RSA) Conference made "Border Rhetorics" a relevant and generative theme for the over twelve-thousand attendees who convened in San Antonio, Texas from May 22-26, 2014. San Antonio's history reflects the constructed and contested nature of boundary-work at all levels—geographic, cultural, and communal—and inspired conversations that addressed the realities of material divisions while also recognizing the potential of intersectionality. Held during a year that marked the centennial of an organizational division between English and Communication (when public speaking teachers broke away from the National Council of Teachers of English in 1914), the conference featured twelve "In Conversation" panels that paired prominent scholars from Composition/English and Communication. These panels addressed concepts foundational to rhetorical inquiry such as agency, activism, and publics as well as issues with such shared investments as the status of rhetorical education and the role of journals in the future of rhetorical scholarship. To be sure, such conversations predate the 2014 conference; however, these panels (and the selected excerpts included herein) sought to provoke new dialogues and cultivate the flow of inquiry and collaboration across the disciplinary borders of rhetoric.[1] As RSA President Kendall Phillips noted, "RSA was formed in large part as a bridge across this border and that is still one of the driving forces of the association" (5).

Conference participants engaged the theme of "Border Rhetorics" in ways that not only reinvigorated the border as a conceptual metaphor but also challenged boundaries within rhetorical scholarship. In addition to panels on contemporary geo-political borders, panelists leveraged the sense of movement and divergent cultures that define a borderland, whether formed by nation-states or academic disciplines. From Ancient Greece and the Ching Dynasty to modern classrooms and social media, the conference provided an opportunity for sustained reflection on the rhetorical nature of borders across periods, cultures, and sites while prompting dialogue on our role in contesting boundaries through our scholarship and pedagogy. The diverse subjects and methodological orientations covered in the 425 conference sessions document how rhetorical scholarship is refiguring the theory/praxis divide.

With over 1,300 papers presented at the conference, this volume features only a select representation of essays and excerpts from the "In Conversation" panels. The organizational groupings reflect thematic through-lines in the submissions as well as a confidence in Burke's perspective by incongruity as a method fitting the exploration of various borderlands. Accordingly, sections juxtapose essays that approach themes such as materiality and politics from different periods and genres. As Burke notes in the prologue to *Permanence and Change*, "perspective by incongruity could be likened to the procedure of certain modern painters who picture how an object might seem if inspected simultaneously from two quite different positions" (lv). Each section also features scholars at diverse stages in their careers and work that approaches rhetoric from the range of perspectives offered in Composition/English and Communication with the hope that such "planned incongruity" cultivates a wrenching loose of disciplinary borders. Finally, the volume concludes with fragments and provocations excerpted from "In Conversation" panels to goad further dialogue, collaboration, and debate.

The selected essays in the first section, *Between Materiality and Rhetoric*, explore points of interface between rhetoric and materiality. Peter Goggin's essay opens with an epigraph that provides an apt orientation to the shared assumption animating the work across this section: "Discursive practices and material phenomena do not stand in a relationship of externality to each other; rather *the material and discursive are mutually implicated in the dynamics of intra-activity* . . . Neither is articulated or articulable in the absence of the other; matter and meaning are mutually articulated" (Chapter Two). Working from diverse periods and disciplinary orientations, the authors illuminate how attending to the mutuality between materiality and rhetoric engenders a productive revision and/or expansion of our approaches to essential aspects of rhetorical inquiry.

First, Bruce McComiskey examines two forms of material rhetoric in the Dead Sea Scrolls *Purification Rules* A and B (4Q*Tohorot* A, fragment 4Q274, and 4Q*Tohorot* B, fragments 4Q275, 4Q276, and 4Q277). McComiskey designates discursive embodiment and ritual erasure as forms of material rhetoric based on a reading of the "communicative nature of physical bodies and persuasive function of material practices" informed by Kenneth Burke's theory of entitlement and J. L. Austin's speech act theory. Next, Peter Goggin considers the materiality of place in the ecologies of small oceanic and continental islands. He analyzes how localized controversies over domestic, wild, and feral animals in "fringe places," such as the Isles of Scilly and Bermuda, reveal not only the mutuality between materiality and place but also telling "frictions" between the local and global. Goggin argues that attending to the intersection of material and place-based rhetoric complicates homogeneous notions of globalization and sustainability. Lisa Phillips also engages the relationship between materiality and environments but illuminates their mutuality through an analysis of controversies over smellscapes. Phillips identifies a persistent gap in rhetorical scholarship across Communication and Composition/English related to "how sensory categories of smell, taste, and touch impact our rhetorical understanding of communication, people, and material embodiment" (Chapter Three). Concluding that contemporary social and environmental justice issues require an attentiveness to the full realm of sensate embodiment, Phillips calls for work that explores our experience of odor and how it sensitizes us to otherness. Finally, Jeffrey B. Holmes examines the role of materiality in the embodied meaning-making process that occurs in videogames. Drawing from James Paul Gee's work in games studies, Holmes develops the concept of "projective embodiment" to account for "the relationship between the player and the tools of the game (including the virtual gameplay system and the material interface), and the way they must work together to make gameplay meaningful" (Chapter Four). His approach has implications beyond gaming, as digital meaning-making increasingly shapes our relationship to others.

The second section, *Crossing Cultures: Refiguring Audience, Author, Text, and Borders*, explores how various forms of translation, migration, and liminality can refigure our understanding of the interplay between audience, author, and text. Maha Baddar examines the eroding boundary between audience and author during the Medieval Arabic Translation Movement. Focusing on "A Statement on the Soul" by Arabic philosopher Abu Yaqoub al-Kindi, Baddar shows how al-Kindi functioned as an "audience-author" in his introduction of pagan philosophies by Plato, Pythagoras, and Aristotle into a monotheistic discourse community. Baddar's analysis suggests that cultures are crossed not only by individuals but also by texts as they move across time and geographies to refigure rhetorical inquiry. Keith Miller also traces the migration of texts by examining the transatlantic circulation of *Acts* 17:26 ("God hath made of one blood all the nations for to dwell on all the face of the earth") in Abolitionist and civil rights rhetoric from 1676 to 1976. Miller introduces the term *interargumentation* to account for a diachronic system of argument that operates via "appeal-by-citation." He finds that "the formidable intertext" created by the web of citation challenges "the longstanding and largely unquestioned practice of dividing British and American culture and history into distinct conceptual and chronological units" (Chapter Six). The cultural journeys examined by Elizabethada Wright address a different form of interplay between text and audience. Examining a popular travel guide by Victor H. Green, *The Negro Travelers' Green Book: The Guide to Travel and Vacations,* Wright approaches the text as a representative anecdote that functions aspirationally. She argues that the *Green Book* not only advises African American motorists how to safely negotiate interstate travel under Jim Crow but also acculturated readers to a "middle-class conservative consumerism" through editorial commentary about the tourist locations, advice on travel decorum, and appeals to sell the *Green Book* as a means to offset travel costs (Chapter Seven). Also addressing the boundaries of identity, Patrick Shaw explores the liminal moments in Gertrude Stein's work, *The Autobiography of Alice B.* According to Shaw, "Stein's epistemological rhetoric is constituted by a dialectic of identity that constructs relations among writer, reader, and texts, and constructs a negative dialectic between written text and spoken text and between the writer and the verbal image" (Chapter Eight). His analysis reveals how cultures and otherness are inscribed in the dialectics that form identity. Finally, co-authors Antonio Tomas De La Garza, D. Robert DeChaine, and Kent A. Ono call for a renewed focus on border rhetorics but encourage approaches that emphasize the dynamic process of "bordering" as "an act of power . . . that refigures not only physical but also intellectual and social space" (Chapter Nine). The authors outline four organizing principals for rhetorical border scholarship including the obligation to (1) destabilize boundaries, (2) account for the role of power and agency in divisions between self/other and inside/outside, (3) emphasize the affective and performative dimensions of bordering, and (4) engage the pedagogical imperative underwriting rhetorical border studies.

Essays in the third section, *Remapping the Political*, examine the diverse genres that broaden our understanding of the *res publica* and the tactics employed to circumscribe politics. The section opens with Rasha Diab's analysis of peacemaking rhetoric enacted outside the confines of Greco-Roman and

Judeo-Christian traditions. Focusing on medieval Arab-Islamic peacemaking practices, Diab analyzes "Essay Nine" of a fourteen-volume medieval encyclopedia by Egyptian scholar Al-Qalqashandī. She argues that the text "demonstrates a multi-dimensional understanding of peacemaking and provides examples of how . . . peacemaking can manifest as a document, a performative act, and a rhetorical expression" (Chapter Ten). Diab concludes with a call to explore texts and archives that expand the frontiers of traditional rhetoric and, in so doing, reframe the past and future of peacemaking. Shifting to an epideictic genre, Rosemary Williamson compares motion of condolence speeches presented to Australian parliaments in the aftermath of natural disasters occurring in 2011, 1974 and 1893. In addition to delineating characteristics that define the condolence motion as a form of epideictic rhetoric, Williams reveals the evolving regional imprint on narratives of belonging and identity. In the context of the condolence motion, Williams finds that the rhetoric of resilience expressed in 2011 articulates a "regional singularity" that coheres with longstanding populist narratives in Australia even as the expression of the "resilient Queenslander" contributes to "distinctive political, economic, and social histories for the nation's states and territories" (Chapter Eleven). Jeffrey A. Kurr also addresses an evolving speech genre, but within a U.S. context. Surveying digital enhancements employed in Barack Obama's State of the Union addresses delivered between 2011 and 2014, Kurr considers how these modifications shape public deliberation and contribute to the emergence of a "digital presidency." Kurr concludes by discussing how the enhanced State of the Union exemplifies key facets of the digital presidency and finds that "the digital presidency is not limited to this singular address but rather a new way to understand the ways in which the president reaches the public, one that warrants further study across all genres of presidential rhetoric" (Chapter Twelve). Finally, Lora Arduser and Amy Koerber trace a shift in Republican campaign rhetoric on women's issues following the 2012 presidential election. In contrast to GOP rhetoric on reproductive rights that provoked charges of a "Republican War on Women" in 2012, Arduser and Koerber assert that that the messaging recalibration after the election disarticulated reproductive rights as a concern for women voters. Instead, party rhetoric emphasized the economic life of women as family CFOs and breadwinners and, in so doing, "begin[s] to etch in political borders that would seem to transform reproductive issues such as contraception and abortion into 'non-issues'" (Chapter Thirteen).

In the fourth section, *Contesting Boundaries: Science, Technology, and Nature*, authors consider how shifting notions of expertise and competing epistemologies alter our conceptions of science and the environment. Ron Von Burg addresses a foundational constraint in public debates over scientific

questions: how to facilitate participation by nonscientists in civic deliberations that hinge on scientific expertise. His analysis of a 2012 open letter
from TEDx Director Lara Stein and TED.com Editor Emily McManus iso-
lates key strategies for evaluating scientific expertise based on "the rhetorical
performance of expertise" (Chapter Fourteen). Von Burg argues that such
knowledge "empowers non-scientists as sentinels protecting the boundaries
of legitimate science" and thereby enriches public debates in which pseudoscience circulates. John Angus Campbell also addresses the relationship
between citizens and science by tracing the emerging expertise of the Lower
Hood Canal Watershed Coalition (LHCWC)—a group of citizens and representatives from businesses, state agencies, and the Skokomish Tribe who
sought "corrective actions" related to improving water quality and protecting
natural resources between 1985 and 2005. Campbell distinguishes between
a citizen *scientist* (when citizens employ scientific tools such as empirical observation to enrich scientific knowledge) and *citizen* scientist (when citizens
rely on tools of rhetoric such as audience adaptation to facilitate civic deliberation on issues related to science). According to Campbell, "Whereas citizen *science* is guided by the concerns of particular disciplines, and written in
a technical language, *citizen* science is motivated not by a desire to advance
knowledge but by the need to translate it into the vernacular, adapt it to
local conditions and realize its potential for the common good" (Chapter
Fifteen). Read together, Campbell and Von Burg illuminate how boundaries between science and civic life are being remapped. Alexis F. Piper also
examines environmental rhetoric but focuses on American nature writing
as a borderland genre where science, history, and autobiography merge and
anthropocentric and ecocentric worldviews overlap. Piper argues that nature
writing from Thoreau forward features Native American eco-orientations
as a commonplace but rarely engage indigenous writers directly. To realize
the transformative potential of nature writing, Piper calls for direct engagement with indigenous authors such as Winona LaDuke, Linda Hogan, and
Jeanette Armstrong. Finally, Amy D. Propen examines the evolving decision
calculus used to evaluate environmental risk in debates over seismic testing at
California's Diablo Canyon. Propen argues that "the dissolving boundaries
between human and nonhuman animals reflect a qualitative, palpable shift
in the form and scope of the discussion—of what counts as perceived risks
and for whom" (Chapter Seventeen). Her analysis concludes by considering
the implications of using invasive tracking and visualization technologies on
nonhuman animals in the process of advocating on their behalf.

The selected essays in the final section, *Teaching Across Divides*, explore
the different boundaries that shape teaching in rhetoric and composition.
Here, the authors reflect on the challenges and rewards gained by explic-

itly engaging the borders and boundary-work that often remains invisible to our students. Amy Milakovic describes a four-day field trip in her undergraduate "Art of War" class that offers students an experiential engagement with design norms shaping the memorial landscape in Washington, DC. Focusing on the Women in Military Service for America Memorial, Milakovic considers the "publicness of memory" as experienced by her students in their reactions to the memorial and their role in perpetuating or contesting gaps in national narratives. Susan Garza also examines how students experience learning outside classroom borders but focuses on the race and class dynamics of service-learning as an Anglo instructor. Garza's essay reflects on two experiences as a white service-learning teacher leading projects in South Texas colonias by considering her legitimacy, intention, and practice. Her essay concludes by addressing how such experiences have informed not only changes in her own teaching but also the development of a writing studio model at Texas A&M University-Corpus Christi that allows for service learning projects that extend across courses. In contrast, the teaching divide analyzed by Kathleen Baldwin emerges from the turn toward digital and multimodal writing instruction. Surveying how the boundary between rhetoric and design is being refigured across diverse literatures, Baldwin argues that the "unresolved" relationship between rhetoric and design compounds the "assessment challenges" faced by writing teachers tasked with evaluating multimodal assignments. Finally, co-authors Jane Detweiler, Margaret R. LaWare, Thomas P. Miller, and Patti Wojahn respond to key challenges outlined in the 2013 Commission on the Humanities and Social Sciences report, *The Heart of the Matter*, by arguing for the centrality of rhetorical training and expertise to contemporary civic life. Their map for "advancing the value of rhetorical study" encourages us to "leverage our disciplinary power toward changing how academic work can be envisioned" (Chapter Twenty-One). As the preceding contributions underscore, rhetorical pedagogy and scholarship is in the vanguard on issues central to strengthening the humanities.

The volume concludes with fragments from select "In Conversation" panels. The excerpts cover a range of issues from activism and intersectionality to publishing and rhetorical theory.[2] Capturing the spirit of the conference and mission of the Rhetoric Society of America, the fragments highlight not only the theoretical, political, and ethical commitments shared by scholars in Communication and Composition/English but also the value of crossing boundaries to engage them. I hope that the dialogue and provocations found in these conversations and the calls to expand rhetorical inquiry in new directions issued across the volume encourage the continued pursuit of rhetoric across borders.

NOTES

1. See for example, "The Mt. Oread Manifesto on Rhetorical Education 2013," *Rhetoric Society Quarterly* 44 (2013): 1-5, which was drafted by William Keith and Roxanne Mountford (with editorial and conceptual contributions from participants in their seminar at the 2013 Rhetoric Society of America Institute). Keith and Mountford also led the "In Conversation" panel "Rhetoric between English and Communication: Looking Back, Looking Forward" at the conference.

2. Unfortunately, technical difficulties and space constraints made it impossible to include excerpts from all the panels.

WORKS CITED

Burke, Kenneth. *Permanence and Change: An Anatomy of Purpose.* 3rd ed. Berkeley: U of California P, 1984. Print.

"The Mt. Oread Manifesto on Rhetorical Education 2013." *Rhetoric Society Quarterly* 44.1 (2013): 14. Print.

Phillips, Kendall. "Howdy." *Rhetoric Society of America.* Rhetoric Society of America, 2014. Web. 2 March 2015.

Between Materiality and Rhetoric

1 Material Rhetoric and the Ritual Transfiguration of Impure Flesh in the Purification Rules (Dead Sea Scrolls 4QTohorot A and 4QTohorot B)

Bruce McComiskey

Material rhetoric is a relatively new feature in the communication-theory landscape. One central problem with articulating a material theory and practice of rhetoric is that, throughout their disparate histories, materialists and rhetoricians have viewed themselves as fundamentally opposed, making it difficult for them to integrate their interests. Karl Marx and Frederick Engels, icons of materialist methodology, are no help. In *The German Ideology*, for example, they viewed language either as a meaningless material object ("agitated layers of air, sounds" [44]) or as a representation of false consciousness ("*language* is the immediate actuality of thought" [446]). However, the whole point of dialectical materialism is to descend "from the world of thoughts to the actual world" and thus to descend "from language to life" (446). Dialectical materialism is "a question of revolutionizing the existing world, of practically coming to grips with and changing the things found in existence" (38), but neither "language-as-object" nor "language-as-false-consciousness" has any potential to revolutionize the world or change existence. Thus, for Marx, Engels, and generations of Marxists to follow, the term "material rhetoric" would have been viewed as an oxymoron. Writing in 1982, Michael Calvin McGee explained, "With the possible exception of Kenneth Burke, no one I know has attempted formally to advance a material theory of rhetoric" (38). And it would still be several years before McGee would witness any such attempts.

More recent rhetorical theorists, perhaps influenced by social Marx-*isms* rather than by Marx and Engels, have challenged both materialism's *pragma*-centrism and rhetoric's *logo*-centrism, integrating the concerns of both into a powerful synthesis. (*Pragma* is the Greek term for things, matter; it is similar in meaning to the Latin term *res*). Communication is always embodied in some medium; material rhetorics explore the (social) semiotic force of each medium and the actual affordances that each offers in any given situation. The objects and images that surround us every day communicate complex meanings; material rhetorics interpret these meanings and consider ways to communicate using both material itself and visual representations of material. Language does more than just generate mental effects (instruction, conviction, persuasion); material rhetorics consider the tangible results of rhetorical acts and the linguistic effects of corporeal conditions. Since there are myriad ways in which rhetoric is material and matter is rhetorical, each individual articulation of material rhetoric selects salient aspects of this integrated approach and applies them situationally.

This essay examines two specific symbolic actions, discursive embodiment and ritual erasure, as forms of material rhetoric in the Dead Sea Scrolls *Purification Rules* A and B (4Q*Tohorot* A, fragment 4Q274, and 4Q*Tohorot* B, fragments 4Q275, 4Q276, and 4Q277), which date to the middle of the second century BCE (Harrington 57). Throughout the sectarian Dead Sea Scrolls, but especially in the *Purification Rules*, sacred texts construct material conditions of impurity in the flesh through discursive embodiment, and ritual speech acts erase impure discursive embodiments, materially transfiguring flesh from impure back to pure. In order to theorize discursive embodiment and ritual erasure as material symbolic actions, I draw from two perspectives that directly challenge (and offer alternatives to) the representational model of the linguistic sign in which words represent things and concepts. First, Burke's theory of entitlement reverses the traditional structure of the linguistic sign, arguing that words inspirit things with meaning so that things represent words (not the other way around). In the *Purification Rules*, entitlement explains how sacred texts inspirit (or embody) flesh with material conditions of impurity. Second, J. L. Austin's speech act theory describes utterances as intentional actions (not arbitrary representations) that create material effects in the world. In the *Purification Rules*, speech act theory explains how actions and utterances in purification rituals erase embodied impurities from flesh.

As I will explain, the Israelites' status as either pure or impure was high stakes, since this status actually determined their fate in the end of days. Material purity of sacred objects and Israelite bodies was a condition of the Mosaic covenant, and purity guaranteed inheritance of the covenantal blessings described in the Torah. The discursive embodiment of material impurity violated the Mosaic covenant, which could result in subjection to covenantal curses, and it required ritual erasure as a means of material purification. Since discursive embodiment and ritual erasure are both verbal and physical processes, material rhetoric is the best method available for explaining their effects in the Dead Sea Scrolls.

PURITY AND THE MOSAIC COVENANT

Many of the sectarian Dead Sea Scrolls (including the *Purification Rules*) were written during the Second Temple period by a group of pious Jewish priests who led a community of Israelites in a compound called Qumran near the northern shores of the Dead Sea, where most of the scrolls were discovered. The members of this community dedicated (and re-dedicated) themselves to maintaining their purity, thus fulfilling the conditions of the Mosaic covenant, which they believed had been violated by all other Israelites. A covenant is a conditional promise between God and another entity (usually an individual, such as Abraham, or a collective, such as the Nation of Israel), and this promise comes with blessings if the conditions of the covenant are upheld and curses if they are neglected or violated. After the Babylonian exile and the reconstruction of the Temple (thus inaugurating the Second Temple period), the centrality of covenantal theology in ancient Judaism was reaffirmed and deepened with a renewed commitment to the divine promise and an increased emphasis on the legal requirements of the covenant (Bright 356-58, 430). In the case of the Mosaic covenant, God promised Moses that he would be Lord to the Israelite nation, conferring upon them material blessings, in exchange for their purity by means of the strict observance of Torah law. This covenant's nature as a promise with conditions and consequences is most clearly articulated in Deuteronomy 26.18–19: "[And the LORD has promised today that you are his people, his treasured possession, as he promised yo]u, and that you are to keep [all his commandments.] And he shall set you h[igh above all the nations tha]t he has made, [for fame and] for praise and for ho[nor; and for you to be a holy people to the LOR]D your

God, just as [he] has sp[oken] to you" (Abegg, Flint, and Ulrich, trans., *Dead Sea Scrolls Bible* 181).

In order to insure their own purity in the face of rampant impurity, the Qumran community became stricter in the observance of Torah law than even the Torah itself required (Harrington 12). According to Hannah K. Harrington, "Among all of the Jewish groups of the Second Temple era, the Qumran community was the most rigorous in the maintenance of purity. The laws of purity and impurity were a central concern for the authors of the Dead Sea Scrolls" (7). If the community at Qumran could succeed in remaining pure, then upon God's return to earth in the end of days, they would stand with Him against the forces of evil, and once these forces are defeated, they would live forever with God in everlasting glory and redemption. But if they were impure upon God's return, they would be destroyed along with all other wickedness in the world. To say the least, the stakes were high to remain pure, but unfortunately the ancient Israelite world was absolutely rife with sources of impurity.

Jonathan Klawans distinguishes two kinds of impurity in ancient Judaism, moral impurity and ritual impurity. Moral impurity is acquired through sin. Although the Torah provides sacrifices and punishments as means to remove certain moral impurities, punishing only the most egregious sins with permanent exile (*karet*), the Dead Sea Scrolls provide no such method of removal. The only response to moral impurity in the Qumran community is *karet*. Ritual impurity, on the other hand, is not the result of sin but is a natural byproduct of life in ancient Israel. Ritual impurity is acquired through experiencing or contacting signs associated with the cycle of birth and death, the condition of human existence after Adam and Eve were expelled from Eden. Such signs include semen, menstrual fluid, and actual dead bodies. Not only were most of these sources of ritual impurity unavoidable, but also some of the most important biblical injunctions actually necessitate exposure to ritual impurities. The commandment to be fruitful and multiply requires contact with semen and a woman who experiences a menstrual cycle, and the traditional practice of burying the dead requires contact with corpses. However, once acquired, ritual impurities must be purified as quickly as possible, since all forms of impurity are highly contagious.

Throughout the Dead Sea Scrolls, and particularly in the *Purification Rules*, discursive embodiment inscribes material impurities onto Israelite flesh, and ritual erasure purifies Israelite flesh through specific utterances and material practices, transfiguring impure bodies back to a state of purity. In both of these cases (discursive embodiment and ritual erasure), the effect of rhetoric is material and the force of material is rhetorical.

IMPURITY: DISCURSIVE EMBODIMENT

Discursive embodiment results from what Burke calls entitlement, a process through which material things come to stand for words and their related concepts, reversing the traditional structure of the linguistic sign in which words stand for things. Burke talks about entitlement in *The Rhetoric of Religion* and in his essay "What Are the Signs of What?" which appears in *Language as Symbolic Action*. According to Burke, entitlement includes both abstracting and inspiriting. In the process of entitlement, terms are repeatedly abstracted from increasingly wide ranges of situations and their discourses until an ultimate term (or a god-term) is reached. These god-terms then become abstract titles for collections of discourses. But god-terms are not the signifiers of the things they name (as traditional semiotics would have it). Instead, the things named by god-terms become the signifiers of all of the discourses that have been abstracted in the process of entitlement. According to Burke, "in mediating between the social realm and the realm of nonverbal nature, words communicate to things the spirit that the society imposes upon the words which have come to be the 'names' for them. The things are in effect the visible tangible material embodiments of the spirit that infuses them through the medium of words" ("What" 362). Thus, the discourses that are abstracted through the process of entitlement actually inspirit material things with meaning so that these things become the signs of words.

Material impurity is inscribed on Israelite bodies through a process of discursive embodiment in which the flesh is recognized to have met the conditions of ritual impurity described in sacred texts, especially the priestly books of the Torah (including Leviticus, Numbers, and Deuteronomy) and the purity texts among the sectarian Dead Sea Scrolls (including the *Damascus Document*, the *Temple Scroll*, the *Rule of the Community*, and, of course, the *Purification Rules*). Discursive embodiment occurs when powerful discourses (priestly books in the Torah and purity texts in the Dead Sea Scrolls) inspirit flesh with qualities that are understood as materially present when certain conditions arise. One function of material rhetoric is to reconnect objects in the physical world with the discourses that inspirit them.

Although God is the ever-present god-term throughout the entire corpus of the Dead Sea Scrolls, there are other terms that are nearly as universal, though they result from the abstraction of a smaller number of discourses through entitlement. I call these demi-god-terms, since they float between the most abstract god-terms and the less abstract terms whose descriptive capacities are limited to concrete situations. In the *Purification Rules*, although God is the universal god-term, purity and impurity are demi-god-terms that describe the material condition of Israelite bodies, signifying their value to

God in the end of days. Thus, all of the discourses in the priestly books of the Torah and in the purity texts among the Dead Sea Scrolls actually inspirit Israelite flesh as either pure or impure, and materially so.

There are degrees in the contaminating power of ritual impurities requiring degrees in the purifying power of ritual erasure. Among ritual impurities, coming into contact with a man who is impure from seminal emission or a woman who is impure from menstruation would result in relatively low-level impurities and low-level requirements for purification. A higher level of impurity would be acquired by actually experiencing seminal emission or menstruation, and the duration of purifying rituals for these more-direct impurities is longer and slightly more complicated. The highest level of ritual impurity comes from direct contact with a corpse (the ultimate sign of death, which is anathema to God). According to Harrington, "corpse impurity is the most potent of any ritual impurity discussed in the Bible, at Qumran, or in Rabbinic literature" (72). Corpse contact requires, according to the *Purification Rules*, a level of purification that is similar to rituals described in the Torah for the purification of moral impurity. 4Q*Purification Rules* B (especially fragment 4Q277) explains that corpse contamination can only be purified by sprinkling the contaminated Israelite with *me niddah*, or the ash of a red heifer sin offering mixed with pure water, red wool, and hyssop.

Although not a formal symbolic act in the purification process, the first speech act following the discursive embodiment of ritual impurity is to entitle oneself as impure, since many ritual impurities are not marked by outwardly visible signs (one cannot see corpse contamination). So that there would be no doubt about their status, impure members of the Qumran community were required to declare their impurity publicly and loudly: "For this is what it says: [Leviticus 13:45-46] "Unclean, unclean, he will shout, all the days that [the con]dition la[sts] him" (4Q*Purification Rules* A, fragment 4Q274 1.4). Here we have an intentional act of self-entitlement in which impure Israelites shout out the title of their affliction so that other Israelites will not become impure by contact or association, and through this symbolic act, all of the discourses that are abstracted in the process of entitlement inspirit the Israelite with a material quality of impure flesh. Since impurity is anathema to God, and since impurity is highly contagious, all forms of ritual impurity, especially the most potent ones, needed to be purified through ritual erasure as soon as possible. Ritual erasure then, like discursive embodiment, is a form of material rhetoric because its effects are derived from the dialectical integration of verbal and physical signification.

PURIFICATION: RITUAL ERASURE

Once physical bodies become materially impure (by means of entitlement or discursive embodiment), only specific ritual acts of purification, correctly and completely performed, can erase this inscription. These ritual acts are both verbal and physical processes that result in material changes, transfiguring impure Israelite flesh into pure flesh by means of material rhetoric. In *How to Do Things with Words*, Austin describes speech acts as a kind of material rhetoric in which words make things happen in reality. Although Austin himself did not apply his theory of speech acts to non-verbal communication, it is not difficult to describe non-verbal ritual acts as *locutions, illocutions*, and *perlocutions*. For example, ritual locutionary acts are the material performances of the ritual purification procedures themselves, including prescribed periods of isolation, methods of bathing and laundering, and requirements of sprinkling with *me niddah*. Ritual illocutionary acts (specifically, bathing, laundering, and sprinkling in this case) carry the force of intent to purify the impure, and these acts, carried out correctly and completely, actually transfigure impure flesh into pure flesh. Ritual perlocutionary acts account for the material and behavioral effects that these ritual procedures have on those who are newly purified, such as a renewed access to communal meals, worship, and study.

The discursive embodiment (entitlement, inscription) of material impurities onto Israelite flesh requires material rituals of purification in order to erase these discursive inscriptions, and the ritual acts intended to purify ritual impurities have a relatively limited range: first, isolation; second, bathing in a *miqveh* (or purification pool), laundering contaminated clothes, and waiting until sunset on a prescribed day; and third, sprinkling with *me niddah*. At Qumran, isolation was prescribed to "[a]nyone suffering from any form of ritual impurity" (Toews 81), and it served two primary functions: to separate impure people from pure people and objects (especially food), limiting the contagion of impurity, and to provide the opportunity for impure Israelites to confess their sins and repent, even sins that may have been committed unknowingly. The opening lines of 4Q*Purification Rules* A highlights the critical importance of initial isolation following the acquisition of impurity: "he shall begin to lay down his [re]quest; he shall lie down in the bed of sorrows, and in the residence of lamentation he shall reside; he shall reside apart from all the impure, and far from the pure food, at twelve cubits; he shall dwell in the quarter reserved for him, to the north-east of every dwelling, at the distance of this measure . . . ." (fragment 4Q274 1.3-4). Isolation was a precursor to purification but was not itself an active form of ritual erasure.

As performative material rhetoric, then, isolation was certainly a locutionary act but it lacked illocutionary and perlocutionary force.

Following isolation, bathing in a *miqveh* (or a purification pool), laundering impure clothes, and waiting until sunset on a prescribed day are the most basic means of purification among the Qumran community (Harrington 22), and all of these ritual acts have the full complement of locutionary, illocutionary, and perlocutionary forces, the building blocks of performative material rhetoric. The least potent ritual impurities (such as contacting someone who has experienced seminal emission or menstruation) can be completely erased from the flesh by this process in just one day, allowing the newly purified Qumranite to then eat pure communal food and participate in communal worship. Recent excavations at Qumran reveal an aqueduct connecting ten *muqva'ot*, one of which was located just outside of the compound and may have been used for purification following routine, though impure, activities. Other ritual impurities required a more extended time for purification, such as the seven-day process required to erase the impurity caused by the direct experience of seminal emission or menstruation. In these cases, isolation, bathing, and laundering were required each day for seven days, and the impure Israelite was declared pure at sunset on the seventh day. These performative ritual acts of purification transfigured Israelite flesh from impure to pure, in keeping with the primary condition of the Mosaic covenant, and this performative kind of material rhetoric enabled the Qumran community to engage in certain everyday activities that were impure but also necessary and inevitable.

Not all sources of impurity were acquired in the course of everyday life in the Second Temple world. Corpse-contact was a particularly potent source of ritual impurity that required potent material rhetoric for purification. Like the purification of everyday impurities, corpse-contact also required seven-days of ritual erasure in order to achieve purification. The seven days required to purify corpse-contact included the same rituals of erasure that were used to purify other impurities (isolation, bathing, laundering, and waiting till sunset on the last day), with one important addition. On the third and seventh days, those undergoing ritual erasure for corpse impurity were sprinkled with *me niddah*. Joseph M. Baumgarten points out that in 4Q*Purification Rules* B*c* (fragment 4Q277), the Qumran community adds further requirements to the Torah specifications, including that the priest who gathers ashes from the red heifer purification offering must be pure and of mature age, and the recipient of this potent purification ritual must bathe before sprinkling in order to reduce the level of impurity present and allow the *me niddah* to purify all impurities, even those that the impure/purifying Israelite may be unaware of (481). I do not believe that the Qumran community considered it a sin to come into contact with a corpse, since a cemetery was excavated just outside of the compound, and some members of the community must have buried their dead and must not have been exiled for doing so. However, the fact that *me niddah* was made from the ashes of a sin offering indicates that a certain admission of guilt may have been involved, though perhaps only indirectly, as a condition of human existence in the cycle of life and death after Eden, not as the direct result of corpse contact. Either way, the discursive embodiment of corpse contamination is a potent impurity requiring an equally potent means of ritual erasure.

As a form of material rhetoric, ritual performative utterances and acts erase impurities from Israelite bodies, transfiguring impure flesh back to pure flesh, which was one of the primary conditions of the Mosaic covenant. Bathing, laundering, and waiting for a prescribed period before reengaging in communal activities were not only persuasive acts (changing minds) but also material acts (changing reality), together forming a complex practice of material rhetoric.

CONCLUSION

Material rhetoric is a useful methodology for exploring the covenantal demand for ritual purity and the Qumran community's procedures for purification because material rhetoric accounts for the communicative nature of physical bodies and the persuasive functions of material practices. As Jack Selzer points out, "material, nonliterate practices and realities—most notably, the body, flesh, blood, and bones, and how all the material trappings of the physical are fashioned by literate practices—should come under rhetorical scrutiny" (10). Throughout the Dead Sea Scrolls, material practices, ritual procedures that take material form, are rhetorical, and the rhetorical effects they have are material. Material rhetoric in the Qumran *Purification Rules* is manifest in two particular forms: first, the discursive embodiment of ritual impurity as a material quality of flesh, and second, the ritual purification of flesh as the erasure of impure discursive embodiments. Successful and complete purification erases ritual impurities and re-inscribes (or re-embodies) the material status of purity in flesh, making the purity texts (including the *Purification Rules*) vital to a more general understanding of the Dead Sea Scrolls. Burke's theory of entitlement and Austin's speech act theory contribute to an understanding of the discursive embodiment and ritual erasure of impurity as crucial aspects of a material rhetoric that is relevant to the Dead Sea Scrolls.

Works Cited

The Dead Sea Scrolls Bible. Trans. Abegg, Martin G., Jr., Peter Flint, and Eugene Ulrich. New York: HarperCollins, 1999. Print.

Austin, J. L. *How to Do Things with Words.* 1962. Cambridge: Harvard UP, 1975. Print.

Baumgarten, Joseph M. "The Use of הדנ ימ for General Purification." *The Dead Sea Scrolls: Fifty Years After Their Discovery. Proceedings of the Jerusalem Congress, July 20–25, 1997.* Eds. Lawrence H. Schiffman, Emanuel Tov, and James C. VanderKam. Jerusalem: Israel Exploration Society, 2000. 481–85. Print.

Bright, John. *A History of Israel.* 4th ed. Louisville: Westminster John Knox P, 2000. Print.

Burke, Kenneth. *The Rhetoric of Religion: Studies in Logology.* 1961. Berkeley: U of California P, 1970. Print.

—. "What Are Signs of What? (A Theory of 'Entitlement')." *Language as Symbolic Action: Essays on Life, Literature, and Method.* Berkeley: U of California P, 1966. 359–79. Print.

Harrington, Hannak K. *The Purity Texts.* New York: Clark, 2004. Print.

Klawans, J. *Impurity and Sin in Ancient Judaism.* New York: Oxford UP, 2000. Print.

Marx, Karl, and Frederick Engels. *The German Ideology.* 1846. Trans. Clemens Dutt, W. Lough, and C. P. Magill. *Karl Marx, Frederick Engels: Collected Works.* Vol. 5. New York: International, 1976. 19–539. Print.

McGee, Michael Calvin. "A Materialist's Conception of Rhetoric." *Explorations in Rhetoric: Studies in Honor of Douglas Ehninger.* Ed. Ray E. McKerrow. Glenview, IL: Scott, Foresman, 1982. 23–48. Print.

Purification Rules A. Trans. Florentino García Martínez. *The Dead Sea Scrolls Translated: The Qumran Texts in English.* 2nd ed. Leiden: Brill, 1996. 88–89. Print.

Purification Rules B. Trans. Florentino García Martínez. *The Dead Sea Scrolls Translated: The Qumran Texts in English.* 2nd ed. Leiden: Brill, 1996. 89–90. Print.

Selzer, Jack. "Habeas Corpus: An Introduction." *Rhetorical Bodies.* Eds. Jack Selzer and Sharon Crowley. Madison: U of Wisconsin P, 1999. 3–15. Print.

Toews, Casey. "Moral Purification in 1QS." *Bulletin for Biblical Research* 13.1 (2003): 71–96. Print.

2 RHETORICAL AND MATERIAL BOUNDARIES: ANIMAL AGENCY AND PRESENCE IN SMALL OCEANIC ISLANDS

Peter Goggin

Discursive practices and material phenomena do not stand in a relationship of externality to each other; rather the material and discursive are mutually implicated in the dynamics of intra-activity. The relationship between the material and the discursive is one of mutual entailment. Neither discursive practices nor material phenomena are ontologically or epistemologically prior. Neither can be explained in terms of the other. Neither is reducible to the other. Neither has privileged status in determining the other. Neither is articulated or articulable in the absence of the other; matter and meaning are mutually articulated.

—Karen Barad

This paper connects three key concepts involving rhetorical and material boundaries—*place, islands,* and *animals*—while expanding on what these concepts mean in terms of the material and how they are rhetorically constructed and relationally situated.

In accordance with the epigraph above from feminist theorist, Karen Barad, I begin with the premise that each "thing" and each concept—*animal* and human interaction, *island* ecology, and *place*—is richly complex and interrelated in terms of boundaries. The purpose of the essay is to establish a context for viewing these concepts as they relate to discourse on sustainability and globalization, and conclude with some thoughts on islands and animal material presence.

I want to start with a brief sketch on place-based rhetoric. Broadly speaking, place is conceived as a concept of human value where globalization is seen and welcomed for many as a signifier of the redundancy of the "local." In such a context geospatial identity becomes increasingly irrelevant to communication and commerce, and as transnational corporations replace nation-states as the source of power, security, and leadership in the world (Orr). One would be hard pressed to identify any place on the earth's land surface that has been untouched physically by humans and unmapped by aircraft and satellite systems. It would be a challenge to identify any human settlement, no matter how remote or "lost," where inhabitants are not impacted in some way by global development. An outcome of such global interconnection and influence is the perception of a supra-territorialized, borderless, "flattened" world (Christopherson, Garretsen, and Martin, 343) Impacts of the global, from climate change to commerce to communications to population movements, are always located somewhere and in some place that is real and discrete. "Within complex global systems, the islands, neighborhoods, apartment blocks, villages, farms, forests, savannas, and so forth while enmeshed in the global network of commerce, politics, communication, and ecologies, are, in fact, places in their own right." (Goggin 4) The idea here is not to dismiss the notion of boundaries or to reinscribe them, but to encounter them. I am particularly taken by Anna Lowenhaupt Tsing's notion of friction—that realm where the global and local meet with the fringes and the mainstream and where material and rhetorical praxis occur, in those liminal spaces and places. These, she says are the places of encounter, "where the rubber meets the road," and that, "as a metaphorical image, friction reminds us that heterogeneous and unequal encounters can lead to new arrangements of culture and power" (5). These places of encounter, rhetorical and material, I would argue, are where islands and our connections with animals reside and encounter global and local universals.

Complementing Tsing's focus on fringe places in global contexts, relatively recent scholarship into socio-geographic places that have mostly been skipped over or generally ignored in the humanities offers further critique of homogenous global discourses in such fields of inquiry as island studies and rural literacies (for example: Donehower, Hogg, and Schell, *Rural Literacies*,

Mimi Sheller, *Consuming the Caribbean*, and Krista Thompson, *Eye for the Tropics*). Such studies serve to disrupt predominantly urban and mainland perspectives and discourses on literacy education, rhetoric, communication, history, colonial and post-colonial studies, media studies, and so forth. In a prior publication I wrote:

> Drawing on Pratt's study of imperial travel, for example, Sheller observes that such uncontested urban and mainland worldviews constitute a "rhetoric of presence" that fixes "the mastery of the seer over the seen" (50). In these cases, the perception of rural and island people, places, and ecosystems constitutes a form of "world making" that reinforces a sense of timeless dissonance for the mainland & mainstream worldview (Goggin 4).

In a 2012 special issue of *RSQ* that focused on regional rhetorics, guest editor, Jenny Rice, echoes Christopherson, Garretsen, and Martin's concern of a globalized, flattened world perspective and invokes architectural theorist, Kenneth Frampton's argument that the "flat data" view of a generic "Walgreening" sameness that erases topography and regional identity is rooted in "a modernist preference for earth-moving equipment used to create rational planes of construction" (202). She observes that "what is particularly insidious about flat data is that it smoothes over the tectonics of place. The light, the air, the stubbornness of any given landscape is eradicated by a construction that makes everything level" (202). For scholars who situate themselves as proponents of the significance of places and locales, the accepted and unreflexive constructs of globalization perpetuate a perspective that diminishes the existence of places and those that dwell there that otherwise offer alternative or, at least, subtly nuanced viewpoints on the world (Goggin, 4).

A reframing of world-making through place-based rhetoric recognizes the complexities of competing ideologies that inform the discourses of globalization, localization, and glocalization as well as the confluences, divergences, collisions, and fusings that occur in the liminal spaces and places where technological and ecological systems intersect and interact, whether through natural or human-caused events. Geologist Steve Semken illustrates this particularly succinctly in ecological terms in his definition of "sense of place":

> Place is distinguished from space by being socially constructed and local rather than quantitatively described and universal.... In other words, people make places out of space..., and a given locality or

landscape can hold widely divergent meanings for different individuals or cultures . . . (149).

As Semken's words suggest, materiality and discursive practice are mutually
and dynamically interactive. Hence, the concept of space and the discourses
that construct it are interrelated. Philosophy historian Edward Casey observes that while the concept of place has been subsumed in Western thought
by an obsession with space since the spread of Christianity, place as a subject of resistance and reflexivity has found new vitality and significance in
response to the discourses of globalization, flat data, and presumptions of
sameness.

More recently, Thomas Rickert asserts in his book, *Ambient Rhetoric*, that
rhetoric informs and transforms "how we are in the world, how we dwell,"
and that dwelling is how people "come together in the continual making of
a place," and that "place is interwoven in to the way they have come to be as
they are." For Rickert, rhetoric informs and transforms "how we are in the
world, how we dwell," and that dwelling is how people "come together in the
continual making of a place," and that "place is interwoven in to the way they
have come to be as they are." [. . .] "the affects [. . .] and the role of material
environment are elevated in priority; they are no longer simply *complementary* to rhetorical theory, but rather absolutely *integral* to it" (xiii)

Islands then, as physically discrete ecologies that are likewise intermeshed
with global ecologies, can provide insight into the fluid materiality and
boundaries of place through the interactions of people and other animals
in a locale. At this juncture, I should clarify that while there are hundreds
of thousands of islands in the world and that what constitutes an "island"
both materially and metaphorically is relative and essentially limitless, for the
purpose of this essay, I am limiting my discussion of islands to mostly small
oceanic and continental islands with relatively small human populations between one thousand and one hundred thousand residents and employing the
generic definition of an island as, a small body of land completely surround-
ed by water. Within this context, I explore the question; do animals have a
sense of place? Even to ask this question invokes the animal/human binary
and presupposes that the answer is ambiguous at best depending on our perspectives on consciousness, language, and agency. As Carey Wolfe discusses
on Wittgenstein's observation on animals and language, "if a lion could talk,
we could not understand him," thus we have a conundrum that allows for
multiple interpretations. To illustrate, I offer examples of just two studies
that have recently inspired my thinking on this issue: Amy Propen's cartographic analysis of animal agency and presence via the Wandering Albatross
and Elephant Seals in the satellite tracking and conservation mapping of the

Patagonian Sea, and Sean Morey's analysis of the Great White Shark, Mary Lee, as an avatar through networked web presence, and raw satellite tracking data. In the conservation mapping example Propen states, "the seal becomes a co-author of a map of its own existence; the researcher becomes, as Benson has suggested, a mediator of a sort of 'virtual intimacy' between human and nonhuman animals." She concludes thusly:

> Within the context of the *Atlas*, remote tracking technologies allow marine species to illustrate their own paths and tell their own conservation stories. These stories, and the technological mediation that enables them, also have rhetorical implications for how we understand our relationships to nonhuman animals and how we perceive their status as autonomous beings in the world. (138-39)

Propen's work with rhetorical analysis of interactions between humans and oceanic species underscores the significance of place in reconceiving notions of agency and challenges the ocean/land (and I would include here island/mainland) conceptual and material boundaries. Morey likewise contributes to a reimagining of rhetorical and material boundaries in the places and zones where humans and non-human animals encounter each other. In his presentation on the shark's online presence, he posits the following:

> While Mary Lee doesn't have the same register of avatar that we do, she has the networked trappings of one as she becomes co-composed with co-networked agents of fishermen, scientists, site visitors, web robots, and others. She, like all avatars, becomes a networked subject at the same time as she is a medium, writing herself as she is written about. And perhaps, this is all she needs to break out of a literate frame.

We may wonder what the animals in these studies are thinking and what motivates them. Both studies would suggest that non-human animals have sense of place, if not in ways that we might recognize other than in human terms, at least in ways of how they—the sharks, seals, and birds—influence and co-construct us as the observers, as "companion species," to employ Donna Haraway's notion of the concept.

In the work I've conducted on just a few islands I've come to appreciate the intense relationship between human and non-human islanders that, at least to my perception, embody Blair's notion of material rhetoric—that is, that it has real presence and real consequences that may or may not be what the rhetor intends. I would like to extend Blair's notion further, to suggest that material rhetoric is also intertwined with place-based rhetorics and ecologies and discuss the relationships between human-based concepts of domestic, wild, and feral animals in specific bounded places—in particular, the ecologies of small oceanic and continental islands. Among the many islands and island subcategories in the world (see the working definition of islands above), thousands are inhabited by humans with varying levels of permanence and population density—roughly six hundred million people or one-tenth of the world's population. Significantly, "Although islands make up only some 5% of the global land area, their endemic biota are estimated to include about 20% of the world's vascular plant species and 15% of all mammal, bird and amphibian species." (Biodiversity)

Because of such boundaries as climate, resources, and land area and their geographic isolation, islands are ecological niche places for many species. But this also makes them extremely vulnerable to change, both natural and synthetically caused. Isolation, size, and resources also mean that human and animal proximity and interactions are perhaps more pronounced than in mainland and predominantly urban settings. This proximity, reinforced by boundaries, contributes to the sense of "islandness," which recognizes that while individual islands are unique, within and across island communities there is a shared connection based on the commonality of boundedness. Philip Conkling of Maine's Island Institute lists a number of these connections. Among them, he claims that islanders from different archipelagoes share a sense of connection that transcends the particulars of local island culture, that *islandness* is a metaphysical sensation that derives from the heightened experience that accompanies physical isolation, and that *islandness* is reinforced by boundaries of often frightening and occasionally impassable bodies of water that amplify a sense of a place that is closer to the natural world because one is in closer proximity to one's neighbors.

In the literature on *islandness*, the concept is limited almost exclusively to human residents, but these features could just as easily include the non-human residents also. Cultural, social, and national identity with animal species is certainly not limited to islands, but as ecological microcosms, islandness contributes to an amplification not only in reaction and response to such obvious forces as global climate change, global economics, and global communications but also to local non-human animals presence and agency. Reframing global rhetorics must then be considered not only in regard to human perspectives, but also to those of non-human animals and our interspecies relations that are precisely due to materialities of place. Mainland norms for animal behavior do not always apply on islands.

Steve Baker, in his postmodern inquiry on the ambiguity of animal classifications, points to rhetoric even among postmodern scholars that reifies distinctions between the wild and the domesticated. He points to Deleuze and Guattari's categorizing of these two concepts and to an additional category they describe as "State animals . . . those whose symbolic meanings serve exclusively human interests" (168), i.e. primarily livestock. In quoting from Deleuze and Guattari, Baker states that they admire "demonic animals . . . which operate at the greatest distance from humans in 'pack modes,'" and they find contemptible "the individuated animals, family pets, sentimental Oedipal animals each with its own petty history . . . that require us to regress, draw us into a narcissistic contemplation" (168). Embedded in such a distinction, between the wild and domestic, the pack and the individual, are distinctions of place that perpetuate a myth of separation. In actual places, the distinctions are less clear cut and more complex.

For instance, on small oceanic and continental islands, wild animals—and predators in particular—are generally limited to aquatic and avian species. Resources that typically support large packs or herds or even large individual land-based predators are generally not plentiful on oceanic islands, and human inhabitants of small islands would likely have long eradicated any such threats or food sources. Even if mainland pack and herd animals crossed the boundaries of ocean and waterways and immigrated to a small offshore island, it is unlikely that they would be able to continue to function for long in a mainland mode due to limited resources. Additionally, the "island rule" in evolutionary and ecological science supports the phenomenon of the miniaturization of large animals and the gigantism of small animals on islands (Raia and Meiri 1731). Thus: we have extinct examples like the Dodo of Mauritius that was basically a giant pigeon and extant examples such as the giant tortoises of the Galapagos and the tiny red deer of the Florida Keys. The particularities and materialities of place that have constructed the social and evolutionary developments of some island species thus challenge the norms of a mainland lens and further illustrate the value of a reframing of global rhetorics to account for the non-human.

Wild insects and reptiles, especially those that are venomous or disease carrying, tend to be a greater issue for islanders as are so-called "invasive" species, whether self-immigrated or introduced. As you might imagine, such species can wreak havoc on a fragile island ecosystem. For example, the Great Kiskadee (bird) of Bermuda, which was introduced in the 1950s from Trinidad to control the Jamaican Anole (lizard) that was introduced in the early 1900s to control fruit flies, has decimated endemic and native bird populations and eradicated the endemic Bermuda cicada (Government of Bermuda). Unfortunately there are too many stories like this on many islands with species eradication histories also steeped in human conquest, colonialization, slavery, and unbridled development. But islanders in general are very fond of their avian and aquatic wild residents, and many of these species are iconic for small island nations and communities and are frequently represented on local currency (for example, the Bermuda cahow and Faeroe Islands sheep), stamps (the Solomon Islands dolphin, and Isle of Man Manx cat), flags (the Anguilla porpoises and Turks and Caicos conch and spiny lobster), and in island lore and song (the Komodo "dragons" and Caribbean *Yellow Bird*.) The interspecies relationships and place identities that have been forged by humans with non-human animals and are evident in these iconic artifacts further underscore the rich complexities that material presence offers a reframing of rhetorics of globalization.

Deleuze and Guattari's "state animal" or livestock is generally very limited on small islands, again a necessary restriction due to local food and land space resources and the high cost of imported feed and exported animal products. Typically, on the continental mainland, livestock animals are associated almost exclusively with rural and agrarian areas, that is, everywhere that is not urban by default (see US Census Bureau). While this distinction of the non-urban is in itself problematic, as Donehower, Hogg, and Schell have argued, the limitations of what might "normally" be considered agricultural space in island locales brings humans and non-humans into relationships that once again illustrate complexities of materiality and place in rhetorics of global context. In most cases, local livestock on small islands is inadequate for meeting the needs of the human population and are more likely to serve for niche marketing purposes. But, as the following example illustrates, livestock, even for seemingly benevolent purposes can have a presence that is amplified on a small island by the very nature of *islandness*.

In the Isles of Scilly (an archipelago about thirty miles southwest of Land's End, Cornwall, UK and home to about two thousand humans), a controversy has raged for a number of years now over the introduction by the Wildlife Trust (which has management authority granted by the Duchy of Cornwall over most of the land) of a small herd of Red Ruby cattle that were introduced for the purpose of sustainable conservation grazing. A grassroots organization of local residents called Save Our Scilly (SOS) took to the airways and the internet to voice opposition and bring an end to the grazing program. The discourse between the Wildlife Trust and the SOS became polarized as the cattle themselves became the lightning rod for arguments over freedom, safety, environmentalism, rights, science, geography, and a host of other issues, many of which had little to do with conservation grazing or the physical presence and activities of the cows themselves. The debates generated in community meetings, over the broadcast airways, on the internet, and in print media often vilified the cows, with the SOS accusing them of blocking and destroying footpaths, preventing freedom of access and movement, destroying the landscape, driving away tourism, and a host of other ills while, on the other hand, the Wildlife Trust presented academic defenses supporting the cows in terms of best conservation practices and policies. To illustrate, the Wildlife Trust claimed that the muddy hoof prints left by the cows provided habitats for insects, which in turn attracted birds, which in turn would attract more tourists to the Isles of Scilly, a popular bird watching destination. In turn, SOS members claimed that the number of migratory birds was actually decreasing due to the disruptive presence of the cows. This case of the Scilly cows illustrates how various local concerns, in this case those that are particular to a small island community, play out through deliberation in the human realm as it is acted upon by the presence of the cattle. Like Propen's elephant seal cartographers, and Morey's shark avatar, the Scilly cows, while likely not cognizant of the furor their presence generated, were co-participants in the deliberations over conservation grazing in the archipelago and agents of the amplification peculiar to a small island locale. The SOS, the Wildlife Trust, and other stakeholders continue to debate about the cattle's presence in the archipelago and the cows continue to graze.

Through the tripartite lens of place, islands, and animals, the "boundaries" of discursive framing reveal situated complexities that further challenge hegemonic (in this case mainland) global constructs. The more one looks, the more one encounters anomalies that jog us out of a way of seeing through Kenneth Burke's concept of *perspective by incongruity* and highlight the "frictions," those points of encounter in the liminal places and spaces that Tsing exhorts us to pay attention to. This essay concludes with an element within the globally liminal spaces and material places of small islands that represents a liminal area within human constructions of animals themselves. It is an element that Deleuze and Guattari do not address directly. This is the feral.

A feral animal is one that is typically tame—either pet or livestock—and that has left human society (usually escaped or has been abandoned) and is living essentially as a wild animal. Feral animals are not truly wild in the sense that they are generally bred for specific purposes and have been for millennia. Nor are they domestic in that they choose, on some level, to no longer cohabitate with humans, though they may rely on human products such as farms, trash, and structures for sustenance and shelter. Often the feral unintentionally threaten (so we presume) the human societies and environments they disassociate from yet still dwell in. Feral cats are perceived as an environmental problem in many places (though they do have their advocates), but on small islands they can be environmentally catastrophic to native and endemic species. This is also the case for goats (see Anguilla and Saint Helena), pigs (see Santa Cruz and other Pacific islands), and rabbits (see Alderney), among many others that have disrupted Deleuze and Guattari's neat classifications. The final case I point to in this paper is that of feral chickens—the scourge (from a human perspective) of many islands in the Caribbean, the Florida

Keys, and the Pacific. In Bermuda, for instance, controversy rages over what to do, and what not to do, about feral chickens (estimated population thirty thousand and rising). Some people love them. Tourists take pictures of them. Others hate them for the noise they create and the gardens they destroy. A succession of local governments have initiated various costly, and mostly failed, culling programs over the years, and the presence of the chickens on this archipelago has generated much debate as political parties and the public have weighed in on internet forums and in newspaper opinion columns to cast blame and criticize action and inaction concerning the feathery feral residents who generally ignore such deliberations.

Of non-human animals, environmental social theorists, Bob Carter and Nickie Charles note:

> While non-human animals are able to act and to exercise primary agency, they are unable to exercise corporate agency. Animals are therefore agents; they act and their actions have consequences, they also resist conditions which they do not like and, in some circumstances, are able to change the conditions of their agency. (322)

Feral animals, like weeds in a garden, define their place in their own terms, regardless and in spite of human desires and responses to their presence. They not only resist, but they persist. The following case illustrates the point.

In August of 2012, Bermuda Government Minister for Public Works, Michael Weeks, gave a press conference at the Spittle Pond Nature Reserve about the island's feral chicken problem. A ten-minute Bernews.com video clip provides a record of a human/feral chicken encounter. In the video, standing with Minister Weeks at the parking lot entrance to the park, stoically listening, is the Government Conservation Officer Jeremy Madeiros. The minister talks about how feral chickens have become "a serious problem" and that they "destroy crops, create noise and nuisance, and carry parasites and diseases." Minister Weeks goes on to provide historical context that the chicken pestilence is not human caused, but the result of the destruction of chicken coops by Hurricane Emily in 1987 that "seeded the island, and the chickens have flourished on their own ever since." While the minister is talking, feral chickens and roosters begin emerging from the undergrowth behind him. As the press conference continues, the chickens run back and forth across the screen and their numbers increase the longer the minister talks. Both he and the conservation officer appear completely oblivious to the whole video-bombing scenario by the feral flock. Minister Weeks goes on to acknowledge that attempts to reduce the feral chicken population have mostly failed but that he and the government are committed to solve the problem. "Feral chickens are in our yards, our homes, our lawns, our farms, our streets, our parks. Basically," he states while one particularly regal feral rooster struts across the open area behind him, "they are everywhere." The video would appear to support Barad's assertion of agential realism, that in a universe where humans and objects (and I would also add animals here) come into proximity and contact sometimes "the world kicks back" (215) in ways we don't expect—including our encounters with chicken (and cow) agency. In this case, the presence of the feral animals in a discrete island locale defies our human notions of animal categories such as the *Wild*, *State*, and *Oedipal* noted by Deleuze and Guattari. Even the notion of *feral* is itself as fluid and as slippery to pin down as a definition of what constitutes an *island*.

The cases of Bermuda and the Isles of Scilly serve as a synecdoche of the macrocosm of island ecologies and animal species in the world and as tangible examples, along with Morey's shark and Propen's seals, that "unflatten" and "unWalgreen" the discourse of a global terrain where fringe places and species are often rendered invisible and considered (if at all) as inconsequential. Conceptually, the tendency in both local and global contexts is to taxonomize and construct animals and places as bounded things as though discursive and material are independent and fixed. But in local and global contexts, animals (and other life-forms) and islands (and other "fringe" places) refuse to be isolated or ignored. Rather than exceptions, islands, feral chickens, cows, sharks, and elephant seals are more aligned with Haraway's notion of our awareness of proximity. In the world's discursive places and spaces, the multifaceted proximity of animals and islands amplify their material presence and require attention to the making and unmaking of local, global, and rhetorical boundaries.

WORKS CITED

Baker, Steve. *The Postmodern Animal*. London: Reaktion Books, 2000. Print.

Barad, Karen. *Meeting the Universe Halfway: Quantum Physics and the Entanglement of Matter and Meaning*. Durham: Duke UP, 2007. Print.

"Minister Weeks on Feral Chicken Concerns." *Bernews*.com. n.p., 15 Aug. 2012. Web. 20 Oct. 2013.

Biodiversity System Information for Europe. "Islands." *Biodiversity System Information for Europe*. European Environmental Agency, n.d. Web. 15 May, 2014.

Blair, Carole. "Contemporary US Memorial Sites as Exemplars of Rhetoric's Materiality."*Rhetorical Bodies*. Eds. Jack Selzer and Sharon Crowley. Madison, WI: The U of Wisconsin P, 1999. 16–57. Print.

Burke, Kenneth. *Permanence and Change: An Anatomy of Purpose*. 3rd ed. Berkley: U of California P, 1984. Print.

Carter, Bob, and Nickie Charles "Animals, Agency and Resistance." *Journal for the Theory of Social Behaviour*, 43.3 (2013): 322–340. Web. 20 Oct. 2013.

Casey, Edward S. *The Fate of Place: A Philosophical History*. Berkley: U of California P, 1997. Print.

Christopherson, Harry Garretsen, and Ron Martin. "The World is not Flat; Putting Globalisation in its Place." *Cambridge Journal of Regions, Economy and Society* 1.3 (2008): 343–349. Web. 13 July 2012.

Conkling, Philip. "On Islanders and Islandness." *Geographical Review*, 97.2 (2007): 191–201. Web. 15 May 2014.

Deleuze, Giles, and Félix Guattari. *A Thousand Plateaus: Capitalism and Schizophrenia*. Trans. Brian Massumi. Minneapolis: U of Minnesota P, 1987. Print.

Donehower, Kim, Hogg, Charlotte, and Eileen E. Schell. *Rural Literacies*. Carbondale: Southern Illinois UP, 2007. Print.

Goggin, Peter. "Introduction." *Environmental Rhetoric and Ecologies of Place*. Ed. Peter Goggin. New York: Routledge/Taylor Francis, 2013. 1-12. Print.

Bermuda. Ministry of Health, Seniors, and Environment. Department of Conservation Services. "Kiskadee (Pitangus sulphuratus)." N.p., n.d. Web. 16 may 2014

Haraway, Donna J. *When Species Meet*. Minneapolis: U of Minnesota P, 2008. Print.

Morey, Sean. "Fluid Data: Open Loops, Avatars, Sharks." Material Rhetorics. Western States Rhetoric and Literacy Conference, University of Utah, Salt Lake City. 25 Oct. 2013. Address.

Orr, David. *Ecological Literacy: Education and the Transition to a Postmodern World*. Albany, NY: SUNY P, 1992. Print.

Propen, Amy D. "Reading the *Atlas of the Patagonian Sea*: Toward a Visual-Material Rhetorics of Environmental Advocacy." *Environmental Rhetoric and Ecologies of Place*. Ed. Peter Goggin. New York: Routledge/Taylor Francis, 2013. 127–142. Print.

Raia, Pasquale, and Shai Meiri. "The Island Rule in Large Mammals: Paleontology meets Ecology." *Evolution* 60:8 (2006): 1731–1742. Web. 18 May 2014.

Rice, Jenny. "From Architectonic to Tectonics: Introducing Regional Rhetorics." *Rhetoric Society Quarterly* 42.1 (2012): 201–213. Print.

Rickert, Thomas. *Ambient Rhetoric: The Attunements of Rhetorical Being*. Pittsburgh: U of Pittsburgh P, 2013. Print.

Semken, Steven. "Sense of Place and Place-Based Introductory Geoscience Teaching for American Indian and Alaska Native Undergraduates." *Journal of Geoscience Education* 53 (2005): 149–157. Web. 23 July 2012.

Sheller, Mimi. *Consuming the Caribbean: From Arawaks to Zombies*. New York: Routledge, 2003. Print.

Thompson, Krista A. *An Eye for the Tropics: Tourism, Photography, and Framing the Caribbean Picturesque*. Durham: Duke UP, 2006. Print.

Tsing, Anna Lowenhaupt. *Friction: An Ethnography of Global Connection*. Princeton, NJ: Princeton UP, 2005. Print.

United States Census Bureau. "Urban and Rural Classification." N.p., 9 September 2014. Web. 1 December 2014.

Wolfe, Cary. "In the Shadow of Wittgenstein's Lion: Language, Ethics, and the Question of the Animal." Zoontologies: *The Question of the Animal*. Ed. Cary Wolfe. Minneapolis: U of Minnesota P, 2003.

3 Smellscapes, Social Justice, and Olfactory Perception

Lisa L. Phillips

Smells are surer than sights or sounds to make your heartstrings crack.

"Lichtenberg"—Rudyard Kipling

Valentine's Day is a day often imbued with sweet smells of chocolate, roses, and perfume to grown-up romantics. For young children, Valentine's Day is a day for sharing cheesy cards, schoolyard gossip, and saccharine-smelling conversation hearts. Nonetheless, Valentine's Day 2011 in Elizabeth Davies's preschool classroom revealed a different sort of scent. Davies, a twenty-year-veteran, elementary school teacher in the ethnically-mixed, urban Hafod primary school in Swansea, South Wales, claimed that students in her charge "smelled of curry," and she sprayed synthetic air fresher directly on the children (Morris, "Teacher"). Davies routinely applied artificial scent on children of "Asian" origin—children of Indian, Pakistani, and Bangladeshi immigrants—who spoke English as a second language. The youngest of Davies's charges were age three, the oldest six. Davies also forced the children to wash their bare hands in a strong, industrial disinfectant akin to Pinesol (Morris, "Teacher"; "Nursery"). Jan Islam, Davies's "Learning

Support Assistant," reported Davies's behavior to school authorities on several occasions, as did irate parents, but school administrators reacted slowly to the reported abuse ("Nursery").

Davies's abusive behavior begs us to consider what trauma smells like. How we smell, literally and figuratively, and how we describe our sensory perceptions in a hierarchy that privileges vision and hearing shapes our understanding of one another and our environment. Olfactory rhetoric, as I name the conceptual apparatus, is concerned with how we write, think, talk about, and experience smell and scent in different environments, cultural contexts, and disciplinary domains. When we notice the embodied material effects of olfactory rhetoric at work in our lives, scholarship, pedagogy, and environment, we may consider how the rhetorical velocity of olfactory perception and resulting olfactory rhetoric makes us more vulnerable to the rhetorical violence of abled, raced, gendered, generational, nationalized, and classed ideologies surrounding our sense of smell and odors in our entangled environments. Davies's case indicates that the smell of trauma can be a confused, "air-freshened" one, making a commonplace assuming that trauma smells like decaying bodies putrid with the horrors of war, or any number of genocidal pacts instigated by the despotic on the disenfranchised, more complex.

Olfaction—the sense of smell mediated by sensory organs—is, in Davies's case, a complicated imbroglio of politics, prejudicial bias, inner-city immigration, overt racism, child abuse, and more. The children's "curried" odor, so offensive to Davies, likely bore with it the comfort of home for them. When Davies disrupted the children's smellscape, she was in effect taking control of the olfactory rhetoric of the classroom and trying to replace it with a chemical force relevant to dominant culture. If one assumes that Davies was trying to reclaim the olfactory rhetoric of her classroom, one that the students had inadvertently made their own, one might ask how Davies, or her representatives, could possibly justify the abusive actions to a tribunal investigating her actions. If a classroom is meant to be a shared space, the olfactory rhetoric of the space must be shared as well with the acknowledgement that each person adds an individual smellprint—especially important when people are in an unfamiliar and potentially uncomfortable setting. That the children were disrupting the status quo through scent brings with it an unusual shift of power. Davies was asserting her perception of a pedagogical imperative to discipline and control her subjects via an attempt to alter the olfactory atmosphere. She was demanding conformity to dominant culture through the vehicle of artificial scent. The children did not bring the rhetoric of conformity to the classroom; instead, conflict was carried upon their coats into Davies's domain.

I wish to note two gaps in extant rhetoric scholarship related to the persuasive power of our senses. The first gap involves the lack of literature in rhetoric and composition that documents how sensory categories of smell, taste, and touch impact our rhetorical understanding of communication, people, and material embodiment. That is, in addressing how our sense perceptions connect the materiality of language to issues of embodiment is at intersection with Ronald Walter Greene's notion of a "material turn" in rhetoric studies (44). Matter, including odor molecules, is in constant reciprocal relation to languaged, sensed embodiment. Engaging with materiality thus compels us to consider the persuasive force of nondiscursive sensations like olfaction. Moreover, through interrogating a sensory hierarchy devoted to ocularcentric (visually-based) "objectivist" reasoning, the inscription of masculinist scientism that marks some bodies as dispensable or disposable, and the rhetoric of animality as gendered feminine, we may build upon Debra Hawhee's suggestion that "communication is difficult to separate from language's materiality, which is never far from communing, communicative bodies" (124). In so doing, we may answer Thomas Rickert's recent call in *Ambient Rhetoric* to "diffuse outward to include the material environment, things . . . our own embodiment, and a complex understanding of ecological relationality . . . in rhetorical practices and their theorization" (3-5). The literature that discusses any form of sensate knowledge—other than visual and auditory—pertinent to rhetoric and composition appears to come from multimodal research (e.g., Marshall McLuhan and W.J.T. Mitchell) and to a lesser degree from Disability Studies (e.g., Brenda Jo Brueggemann and Georgina Kleege). The second gap is a gap in awareness. Simply stated, there is widespread discussion of visual and aural rhetorics, some about rhetorics of taste, less about touch, and almost nothing regarding smell and olfactory rhetoric. The purpose of this essay is to begin that conversation, providing an entry point for scholars in rhetoric and composition who may opt to direct their attention to how our sense of smell persuades us. We may find the topical opening especially useful as we address contemporary social and environmental justice issues within the "material turn" in rhetoric studies.

Demonstrating the focus of this essay, the Davies case and the Sriracha case (below) provide examples that establish the conceptual significance and argumentative value of olfactory rhetoric while highlighting the worth of olfactory rhetorical analysis to the rhetoric studies community. The Davies case reveals how odor molecules exist in reciprocal relation to olfactory rhetoric—both causing material effects on human and nonhuman life that are entangled with social and environmental justice issues. A 2013 incident in Irwindale, California at the Sriracha (Sree-YAH-cha) sauce factory serves as a second case, illustrating how rhetoric surrounding olfaction plays out in a court of law while demonstrating how olfactory rhetorical analysis can be deployed to understand how smell and odor influence our decisions, language, and placement of industrial waste in historically marginalized communities. Irwindale is a working-class community with ninety-five percent of the population claiming Latino/a heritage. Area residents complained that odor emanating from the Sriracha facility was having a negative impact on their daily lives and health. Judge Robert H. O'Brien of the Los Angeles Superior Court deemed the odor a public nuisance and health hazard. He required the Sriracha sauce factory owner, David Tran, to shut down a portion of the plant and install appropriate air filters (Shyong, "Judge").

In an increasingly crowded, warming, and polluted world an effort to understand how we make sense of it all takes on added importance, and olfactory rhetorical analysis enables us to expand upon that work. Our sense of smell can warn us of danger and persuade us to act, and it provides us another way to consider how we are sensitized toward others across place, space, and matter. Specifically, I propose that we examine a neglected dimension of our sensate life that deals with our experiences of odors and exposes our vulnerability to desensitization—that is, how persistent contact with a sensory experience may dull our capacity to feel or notice the stimulus. How we direct our attention over time shifts our capacity to be persuaded by the rhetorical force of one sense as it comes under the influence of another. Consider how, on the one hand, a normal human olfaction system becomes inured to a persistent scent relatively quickly—something named "extinction"/conditioned stimulus in olfactory research circles (Gilbert 114). On the other hand, as Avery Gilbert argues: "Bad smells are natural candidates for Pavlovian conditioning..." (117). Put these together and we see two common responses to malodorous events: initial exposure exerts a power of persuasion to which we may respond consciously or subconsciously; however, if we are constantly exposed to malodorous events, we become habituated to expect the odor and come to ignore its persuasive power to make us act differently in certain situations (118). Take as an illustration the odor of automobile exhaust, a constant in urban environments and one that we routinely ignore. That we snub the emissions' systematic assault on our sense of smell suggests how many may have been persuaded to dispense with exhausts' larger environmental impact. The issue is important because how we direct our sensory focus and attention suggests how we may fail to notice what is right under our noses, or treat our sense of smell as a joke, which prohibits measured response and ethical responsibility in some instances.

Likewise, insofar as how we select and direct our sensory attention within topical foci, the field of rhetoric and composition has long held deliberations about the role of oral and written literacies in communication strategies. Both literacies rely on visual and aural perception, yet laboratory studies like olfactory cognitive psychologist Rachel Herz's irrefutably demonstrate the impact our sense of smell has upon learning and memory ("Basic" 314). By contrast, the oral and written literacy debates have long-circulated in an agitated confluence wherein hearing and seeing are equated with ideologies, beliefs, and cultural values about learning and knowledge. From this perspective, our eyes and ears have become the privileged sensory sources of persuasion and meaning-making. If we shift our focus to consider how our senses are entwined, then we need to consider the distribution of sensory attention.

According to William J.T. Mitchell (2005), all media are "mixed media" in terms of how our senses interact, and "the very notion of a medium and of mediation already entails some mixture of sensory, perceptual, and semiotic elements" (257). Mitchell builds from Marshall McLuhan's (1994/1964) explanation of sensory ratios devised to explain how different forms of media hail us. Mitchell's own implications expand the sensory ratios to consider synesthesia, nesting, braiding, and parallel tracking of our sensory perceptions. Mitchell explains "synesthesia" as it connotes hearing and vision, and to this I would add smelling, touching, and tasting as synesthesia has multiple manifestations (qtd. Powell 541). Mitchell's nesting vis-à-vis McLuhan explains how different forms of media are inter-nested, or enmeshed. For example, an odor may be nested in a culturally complicated sensory construction, as in Davies's classroom and the Sriracha sauce factory examples. Sensory braiding happens when one "semiotic function" or "sensory channel" becomes entwined with another, and Mitchell considers this in relation to sound and image in film (Mitchell, "No" 262; Powell 542). However, if one moves the sensorium to smell, then one can imagine how the smell of curry and ensuing abuse produce a narrative about classroom air quality and pedagogical ethics for ESL students and their instructors. One may also consider that O'Brien's judicial decision-making process in the Sriracha case included markers of linguistic hedging in his written decision concerning the validity of noxious odors on human health.

Linguistic hedging in O'Brien's language related to olfaction occurs because the sense of smell has been devalued in Western contexts (Classen, Howes, and Synnott; Corbin; Gilbert; Majid and Burenhul). Language about odor and our sense of smell is not as reliable as it is in other cultural contexts according to quantitative evidence from the Max Planck Institute for Psycholinguistics (Majid and Burenhul 266). An international research team conducted empirical research on the "traditional five senses" (taste, touch, smell, hearing, and sight) by creating a sensory stimulus kit that was subsequently tested among "twenty different cultural groups" (266-68). The results upend commonplace assumptions—now reified in western scientific literature—that portray the human ability of odor identification as unreliable while suggesting that our naming capacity of odors is equally defective (266-67). The study indicates that it is English-speaking Americans who are particularly unreliable where odor identification and naming are concerned (267). By contrast, the Jahai community on the Malay Peninsula is quite adept at odor identification and naming, suggesting a different material attunement to matter within their environment.

The recent material turn in rhetoric scholarship affords us the opportunity to examine materially complex sensory studies happening in rhetoric studies, pointing to Barbara Biesecker and John Lucaites's work in *Rhetoric, Materiality, and Politics* (2009) and to Wendy Hesford's work in *Spectacular Rhetorics* (2011). First, Biesecker and Lucaites acknowledge that their project grew from their "interest in the relationship between rhetoric and visual culture" and developed into "a much larger intellectual problem concerning the relationship between rhetoric and materiality" (viiii). The purpose of Biesecker and Lucaites's edited collection is laid out in the introduction, and their chief aim is to "question the conventional assumptions that our capacity to act rhetorically is a function of our status as humans rather than our status as bodies that signify," and to this I would add, as bodies that sense (9). At the same time that I wholeheartedly endorse Biesecker and Lucaites' urging that we take-up as our "primary task a description and account of the effects of the itinerary of the *sensible* inscription or [Derridian-like] trace," I also maintain that primacy of the visual and aural senses in Biesecker and Lucaites' collected essays inadvertently subsume our Othered perceptual modes—olfaction (smell), gustatory (taste), haptic (touch), vestibular (balance and spatial orientation), and proprioceptive sense-making (e.g., a sighted person's ability to find her way in a darkened room) (9). That these Othered modes have received short shrift in rhetoric studies to date offers us abundant opportunities to consider why that may be while we work to remedy the imbalance, for like the vestibular sense such work may cause us to (re) adjust our sense of (ethical) balance and rhetorical orientations as we consider a wider, critical perceptual array available to us and others.

Take as another example, Wendy Hesford's *Spectacular Rhetorics* (2011) wherein she provides an extension to Biesecker and Lucaites' explication of the need for critical visual literacy. Hesford claims to unsettle "an objectivist ocular epistemology" to "address the rhetorical dimensions of recognition . . . and witnessing" of human rights violations and violence (52). The essence of Hesford's argument pertains to our visually witnessing acts of violence that manifest as human rights violations, but may, in affect, reify some forms of voyeurism and subjection of marginalized bodies by so-called moral "American" or "Eurocentric audiences" (ix; 52-56; 60). In Hesford's discussion of ethical (eye) "witnessing," she draws upon Kelly Oliver to resituate vision—correctly in my view—"as a connecting rather than an alienating sense, as part of a system of sensation and perception" (Oliver qtd 49). At stake here is the potential for dissolution of our paternalistic sensory hierarchy and a reformation of political alliances committed to equitable breathing room for more forms of life rather than fostering a "politics of pity" (Hesford 47–8).

Whereas Hesford provides ample evidence of "spectacular" visual and aural rhetorics in filmic displays, human rights visual campaigns, and women's rape testimonials that bear "interdependent" eye and ear witnessing; Jim Drobnick (2006), Constance Classen, David Howes and Anthony Synnott (1994), and Rachel Herz's (2007) works on semi-subjective olfactory epistemologies convince me that *scent*sational olfactory rhetorics add complexity and knowledge to our "system of sensation and perception" as we ponder ways to "recognize" and redress human and nonhuman rights violations no matter where the violations occur. In other words, we do not always have to see something happening to know when something is awry: we can smell it. As illustration, one reason that Nazi death camps and crematoria were exposed was attributed to the smells that wafted to nearby communities (Friedlander 93, 107, 108, 112). Headlines from recent massacres in war-torn Syria also suggest a correlation between the agency of odor and witnessing of human rights violations (Solomon, "Smell"; Associated Press, "Overpowering").

Because rhetors have long-claimed that "knowing as seeing" or "seeing as believing" correlates with efficacy in evidentiary hearings wherein ideological belief must be substantiated with extrinsic proof to maintain an ethical stance, a growing body of interdisciplinary research in fields ranging from evolutionary biology, cognitive psychology, and artificial intelligence shows that "knowing as smelling" as opposed to "knowing as seeing" warrants serious study as a topic for analysis (e.g., "seeing" Biesecker and Lucaites ix; Hesford 45–8, 98–100). If I am correct, and empirical research suggests that I am, then major consequences follow for rhetoricians interested in the persuasive power of olfactory rhetoric.

When it comes to the topic of smell, many American English-speakers will readily agree that describing the nuance of a scent or odor is difficult to do convincingly. Where this agreement ends, however, evokes questions of (1) why discussion about odors and the affective associations with odors themselves can make us laugh with embarrassment, blush with shame, react with pleasure, recollect a moment, or recoil with abject disgust, and (2) how reactions to odor or scent may be culturally constructed, or may exist as a byproduct of sensory extinction inferring an inattention due to our focus on visual and verbal "evidence" in rhetorical studies and elsewhere. Building upon the richness of our field's demand for social justice and complex understanding of embodiment, I suggested an opening by describing Davies's classroom behavior, which serves as an example of olfactory rhetoric whose function "adjusts [our] sights" productively, as Biesecker and Lucaites invite, so as to redress harmful rhetorical and pedagogical practices (ix). That is, Davies's disgust at the smell of the Other bears with it an ethical imperative to consider how our discourse dedicated to olfaction might underrepresent the way in which cultural constructions of our shared smellscape have undergone an aroma shadow because we exclude the sense of smell from rhetorical analysis. That we do so reflects a hierarchy of sensation in which "sight and hearing" have greater "prestige" (Corbin 8).

Rhetoricians are interested in how human attention is distributed, directed, persuaded, and maintained. Why is it that no one in rhetoric appears to be talking about our sense of smell, how odors direct our attention, or what scent does to persuade us to move in for a deep whiff or back off in disgust? As we draw upon the scientific research from other fields to fathom the rhetorical velocity of the "chemical" sense known as olfaction, rhetoricians have an ethical obligation to analyze how language works in these fields and others that try to persuade us to do things we might not ordinarily do like sniffing our computer screens or scenting our air with artificial odorants.

In sum, research pertinent to olfaction suggests an opportune challenge for rhetoric and composition scholars—that is, we may consider the materially complex ways in which people make decisions about what to consume, what to say, what to smell, and "know," not on a "rational" basis but on a basis of affect, cultural and social construction, embodied needs and desires, psychological conditioning, and evolutionary inheritances, all of which are systemically entangled within our sensory perceptual systems and matter in our environments. These perceptual systems are materially braided and go far beyond the visual and auditory realms. I suggest a hitherto neglected area for rhetoric and composition pedagogues and scholars interested in the material turn as it intersects with social and environmental justice issues—olfactory rhetorics. Once we begin to engage in sensory rhetoric discourse, and olfactory rhetoric discourse most specifically, it is possible to imagine how persuasive our senses are in word and deed, thus facilitating explanation and remediation of some forms of ecological damage and social injustices and improving our understanding of how and why some kinds of destruction travels to certain bodies more than others while enabling ethical remediation. Put simply, we can examine our (de)odorized environments and interpret rhetorical reactions and beliefs surrounding our sense of smell with greater efficacy.

WORKS CITED

Associated Newspapers. "Nursery Teacher 'Sprayed her Asian Pupils with Air Freshener for Smelling of Curry.'" *Daily Mail*. Daily Mail Mag., 15 Feb. 2011. Web. 10 Jul. 2014.

Associated Press. "Overpowering Smell of Death Greets UN Monitors in Syrian Town of Haffa." *New York Daily News*. New York Daily News, 14 June 2012. Web. 6 Feb. 2014.

Biesecker, Barbara A., and John L. Lucaites. *Rhetoric Materiality, and Politics*. New York: Peter Lang Pub, 2009. Print.

Brueggeman, Brenda Jo. *Lend Me Your Ear: Rhetorical Constructions of Deafness*. Washington, DC: Gallaudet UP, 1999. Print.

Classen, Constance, David Howes, and Anthony Synnott. *Aroma: The Cultural History of Smell*. London: Routledge, 1994. Print.

Corbin, Alain. *The Foul and the Fragrant: Odor and the French Social Imagination*. Trans. Miriam Kochan. Cambridge: Harvard UP and Berg, 1986. Print.

Drobnick, Jim, ed. *The Smell Culture Reader*. New York: Berg, 2006. Print.

Friedlander, Henry. *The Origins of Nazi Genocide: From Euthanasia to the Final Solution*. Chapel Hill, NC: U of North Carolina P, 1995. Print.

Gilbert, Avery. *What the Nose Knows: The Science of Scent in Everyday Life*. New York: Crown, 2008. Print.

Greene, Ronald W. "Rhetorical Materialism: The Rhetorical Subject and the General Intellect." Biesecker and Lucaites 43–66. Print.

Hawhee, Debra. *Moving Bodies: Kenneth Burke at the Edges of Language*. Columbia: U of South Carolina P, 2009. Print.

Herz, Rachel S. *The Scent of Desire: Discovering Our Enigmatic Sense of Smell*. New York: Harper Collins, 2007. Print.

—. "Basic Processes in Human Olfactory Cognition: Current Findings and Future Directions." *International Symposium on Olfaction and Taste Program Papers*. New York: New York Academy of Sciences, 2009. 313–317. Print.

Hesford, Wendy. *Spectacular Rhetorics: Human Rights Visions, Recognitions, Feminisms*. Durham and London: Duke UP, 2011. Print.

Kleege, Georgiana. "Blindness and Visual Culture: An Eyewitness Account." *Journal of Visual Culture* 4.2 (2005): 179–90. Print.

Majid A., and N. Burenhult. "Odors Are Expressible in Language, As Long as You Speak the Right Language." *Cognition* 130.2 (2014): 266–270. Print.

McLuhan, Marshall. *Understanding Media: The Extensions of Man*. 1964. Boston: MIT Press, 1994. Print.

Mitchell, W.J.T. "Showing Seeing: A Critique of Visual Culture." *Journal of Visual Culture* 1.2 (2002): 165–181. Print.

—. "There Are No Visual Media." *Journal of Visual Culture* 4.2 (2005): 257–266. Print.

Morris, Steven. "Teacher Banned for Spraying Asian Primary Children with Air freshener." *The Guardian*. 15 Feb. 2011. Web. 15 Jun. 2014.

Powell, Kimberly. "Making Sense of Place: Mapping as a Multisensory Research Method." *Qualitative Inquiry* 16.7 (2010): 539–55. Print.

Rickert, Thomas. *Ambient Rhetoric: The Attunements of Rhetorical Being.* Pittsburgh: U of Pittsburgh P, 2013. Print.

Shyong, Frank. "Judge Orders Sriracha Hot Sauce Plant Partly Closed over Odors." *Los Angeles Times.* Los Angeles Times, 27 Nov. 2013. Web. 27 Nov. 2013.

Solomon, Erica. "Smell of Death Lingers at Syrian Massacre Village." *Reuters US Edition.* Reuters News, 8 June 2012. Web. 6 Feb. 2014.

The Telegraph Media Group. "Teacher 'Sprayed Asian Pupils Who Smelt of Curry.'" *The Telegraph.* The Telegraph Online News, 15 Feb. 2011. Web. 25 Jun. 2014.

4 Blurring the Boundaries: Projective Embodiment in Videogames

Jeffrey B. Holmes

This chapter argues that gaming is an embodied phenomenon that is distributed across multiple conceptual domains. Videogames, as James Paul Gee argues, are "'action-and-goal-directed preparations for, and simulations of, embodied experience'" (23) and playing the game is about making meaningful interactions with the complex systems of the game world. Embodiment, in this sense, is a metaphor for a *way of thinking*, of processing information through our experience with the world we inhabit. The body (and mind) stands as a symbol for the self, a persistent perceptive system that exists and is enmeshed in a world around it. It is through that persistent perceptive system—the "mind-body"—that thinking occurs and how we make the world meaningful. Further, Art Glenberg claims that "the meaning of an object, event, or sentence is what that person can do with the object, event, or sentence" ("Memory" 3). We make meaning by how we can act upon the world (and how the world acts upon us), and it is through the body that this action occurs. Since videogames are "action spaces," there is a natural fit with this way of understanding gameplay as embodied meaning-making.

However, gaming is more than just what happens on screen. It is a highly mediated experience in which the player straddles two worlds. They simultaneously exist in the "virtual" world as their character on the screen as well as in the "real" (non-virtual) world as they press buttons and manipulate the interface of the game. Indeed, Jesper Juul argues that playing a game is a "dual structure" in which "the actions we perform have the duality of being real events and being assigned another meaning within the fictional world" (141). When I click the mouse, for example, I perform a real world action (moving my finger to press the button) as well as a symbolic action in-game (moving a character). Whereas Gee was primarily interested in what happens between the player's mind and the screen, I intend to examine embodiment across this dual structure of virtual—non-virtual experience—that is, not just in the game but in the *gameplay* through things like the material interface—as the more appropriate site for meaning making.

Indeed, the material nature of videogames has always been an essential part of understanding gameplay and a key part of the gaming experience, from the colorful arcade cabinets of games like *Space Invaders* and *Centipede* or the complex joystick movements in fighting games like *Soul Caliber* and *Mortal Kombat*. More recently, gaming systems like Nintendo's Wii and Microsoft's Kinect have integrated the body and the interface in interesting and unique ways. Indeed, as Thomas Apperley and Darshana Jayemane note, "materiality has become a key thread in game studies and also a bridge to other disciplines" (7). In part, this chapter looks at the ways the material elements of gaming—the controller, the screen, and so on—inform and influence play, how players conceive of the possibilities of their participation through these elements, and how these elements often determine the limits of interaction.

There is another important way of thinking about materiality in videogames beyond just the physical artifacts. Videogames are performative; while the "game" exists as a set of rules symbolically executed by computer code through hardware, the game doesn't really exist until it is performed. Ontological oddities notwithstanding, in the same way that a symphony or a dance are material practices, a videogame becomes a type of material thing when it is enacted by a player. It is a shared material relationship between the actor and the abstract design of the game (or symphony or dance). This shared performative relationship is the other essential material that forms the basis for the argument I will make here and a key way of understanding how a game is an embodied phenomenon across several structures.

This conceptualization of embodiment relies on a particular understanding of the way we make meaning by extending the mind into other tools, the world, and even other minds. The mind-body is part of a network of things.

Some of these can be incorporated ad-hoc into the processes of thinking (using objects to count); some are designed to be incorporated into thinking (paper and pencil); others are simply sensory information (the color of a car passing in the street). The mind-body unit, together with these objects as part of the extended network that constitutes the world, makes up the *embodied system* through which we create meaning.

This chapter extends Gee's notion of the "projective stance" to describe the embodied system that makes the gameplay experience meaningful, particularly the simultaneous virtual and non-virtual nature of gaming. For Gee, the projective stance describes the relationship between the goals of the player and the goals of the in-game character (and the game design more broadly), and the way gameplay arises from how these align (or don't). The player's goals influence how the character behaves (they perform some action, say, attacking and enemy, that the player wishes), and "projects" these goals into the game. The in-game character has goals that also influence how the player behaves (the character is an assassin and "wants" to remain undetected, so the player uses stealth to silently kill the enemy rather than using a loud gun). In other words, the player "projects" some goal, and the character "projects" a different goal, and they must align in order to enact game play. The projective stance is, ultimately, a *combination* of the player's goals and the game's goals.

I wish to adopt this concept of *combination* to include not only these various goals but also the relationship between the player and the tools of the game (including the virtual gameplay system and the material interface) and the way they must work together to make gameplay meaningful. A player has their goals as well as some knowledge and takes some action in playing the game. But the game also has some designed goals (perhaps different than the player's) as well as some knowledge (almost certainly different from the player's) and allows or disallows some actions as part of gameplay. Further, since the dual virtual—non-virtual nature of the game is about what happens on screen as well as what the player does with the control interface in their hands, the game allows and disallows several different "kinds" of things.

In the virtual domain (what happens on screen), this might include things like the types of possible actions and usable objects or the kinds of people the player gets to inhabit and so on. These features are the content of the game, and "project" certain types of knowledge and possible actions. These "projections" influence what the player does and help to frame their experience with the world and their play. The game is also made up of several interface elements, including physical interfaces like the controller, and gameplay must flow through these interfaces. In particular, the physical interface allows certain types of action (pressing buttons or moving a joystick) and certain limitations (only a few buttons or movements are possible at any given time, for example). These material realities also influence how a player acts and how they interpret the world, projecting some kinds of knowledge and some affordances that the player must account for. What makes videogames especially illuminating, as Juul suggests, is this dual structure, where the tools (virtual and real), goals (virtual and real), and possible actions (virtual and real) of the game combine with the player to collectively enact gameplay.

PROJECTIVE EMBODIMENT

To make this complex network of interactions meaningful, then, I want to develop the concept of *projective embodiment,* where the embodied (that is, meaning-making) system is a combination of the player and the various virtual and non-virtual features of the game itself. Projective embodiment suggests that players are one node in a network of actors and that other nodes can "push back" to influence *how* meaning-making occurs. In other words, meaning doesn't arise solely in the player's head, but is the result of the way the player extends their mind into other tools (and even other minds) and how those other tools and minds become *part* of the embodied system. I will begin with a brief outline of three key concepts: embodiment, networks of knowledge, and mediation. Then, I will explore the concept of projective embodiment in a particular game, *Brothers: A Tale of Two Sons,* in order to describe how the player, through the extended network of mind-body-tool, makes their gameplay meaningful.

Embodiment

What is important about the body that shapes our thinking? In the most literal sense, the body is ever present in our experience. As Glenberg notes, "Bodies are there during all of our development, they are there during all social interaction, they are there when we think, and they are there when psychological processes run awry" ("Embodiment" 3). We might also say that a person "embodies" certain values or beliefs and, in so doing, we privilege the body as a container, a boundary that separates it from the world around it. Here, the body is a metaphor for being that is tied to its physicality.

However, embodiment is more than just the presence of a physical body. It is a way of thinking and knowing the world and is a part of the mind, too. For Paul Dourish, embodiment is a "sense of 'phenomenological presence,' the way that a variety of interactive phenomena arise from a direct and engaged participation in the world" (115). Embodiment involves a vehicle to engage with the world (the body) but also the ability to act within it to create meaning. That is, we are *beings* capable of *doing*. Dourish argues that we "inhabit our bodies and they in turn inhabit the world, with seamless connections back and forth" (102). The mind and body are inseparable; the body is an extension of the mind, the mind a part of the body, both part of the larger system that is the world. Furthermore, making the world and our experiences within it meaningful is a critical component of Dourish's argument. He claims that "[e]mbodiment is the property of our engagement with the world that allows us to make it meaningful" (126). Dourish suggests that thinking is inseparably derived from being—that existing is a prerequisite for thinking, and therefore thinking is just a *way of being*. We think through the "mind-body" and our continuous engagement with the world.

In videogames, where the mind-body is spread across several different "kinds" of worlds (the virtual and non-virtual), our engagement takes on several meanings; using the controller means something specific to the non-virtual world (pressing a button, for example) and the in-game action means something specific to the virtual world (swinging a sword). However, these dual actions (virtual + non-virtual) are primarily meaningful in relation to each other; pressing a button on a controller when the computer is off still involves the same basic set of actions in the physical world, but carries with it a different meaning since there is no virtual action that accompanies it. The videogame adds another dimension of the world (the virtual) to our mind-body engagement and another way of making our embodied actions meaningful.

Networked Knowledge

Since we are enmeshed within the world, and we interact with other objects in the system, it's important to further clarify the relationship of the mind-body unit with other nodes in this network of things. As I've already hinted at above, the mind-body unit is actually a somewhat arbitrary distinction since we are constantly engaged with other parts of the world. Indeed, Andy Clark contends that thinking extends to the environment in which that thinking occurs, and is distributed across multiple domains:

> What the brain is best at is learning to be a team player in a problem-solving field populated by an incredible variety of non-biological props, scaffoldings, instruments, and resources [. . . .] a complex matrix of brain, body, and technology can actually constitute the problem-solving machine that we should properly identify as *ourselves*. (26-27, emphasis in original).

In this view, the tools I use become a *part* of the mind. When I write, the piece of paper and pencil are incorporated into my cognitive processing which enables me to think. I have off-loaded an internal process (memory) onto the outside world; I have effectively extended the mind onto a technological tool. If I want to move or perform some action in a videogame, I need to do it through the controller, so in order to think about moving or acting in the game I need to use that technological tool (the controller) as part of my processing-action system.

These tools and objects (and other minds, too) themselves have certain capacities and limitations. Incorporating them into the cognitive process requires using them in the right kind of way by capturing their *affordances*. Gee describes an affordance as a "feature of the world (real or virtual) that will allow for a certain action to be taken, but only if it is matched by an ability in an actor who has the wherewithal to carry out such an action" (25). For example, in *World of Warcraft* players can assign "professions" to their characters such as mining, skinning, or alchemy. Certain enemies are skinnable, but only to those players who learned the skinning profession. To these players, there is an affordance for performing some action (skinning), but not to other players without the skinning profession. Other enemies are not skinnable to any player, so there is no affordance even if the player has the skinning profession. There needs to be a fit between the action at hand (skinning), the tool (the right kind of enemy), and the actor (who knows the skinning profession) in order to function properly.

These tools/objects can extend the mind (both thinking and acting) in ways not possible to the bounded mind-body unit alone. Writing, of course, is a prime example: it can record and store vast amounts of information beyond the practical limits of human memory. This is especially true in videogames; players can pause or reverse time (like in *Braid* or *Super Hot*), manipulate the terrain of the world (like in *Black and White* or *From Dust*), or control and manipulate multiple "agents" simultaneously (like in *Starcraft II* or *Child of Light*). These actions and ways of perceiving the world work differently than the "native" processing of the mind but can supplement (and even alter) the way we make meaning and act in the world.

Indeed, in this sense it is even possible to consider that these tools and objects "know" things themselves, and our engagement with them creates a distributed network of knowledge which we activate for some purpose. Affordances are one kind of knowledge. For example, I leverage the potential for action possible in a hammer (that it can be used to hit a nail), but it does some work in the system (it actually hits the nail); the hammer "knows" how to do this work in a kind of way possible because of its shape and the laws of gravity and so on. But it also requires me—and my mind-body unit, which now includes the hammer (as well as the nail, the wood, gravity and so on)—to activate this affordance.

In this case, most of the knowledge is stored in my bounded mind-body unit and the tool is a low-knowledge node in the network. Other tools may store greater knowledge; clicking a mouse to open a program on the computer activates a great deal of knowledge on the part of the mouse (the physical object) as well as the computer's operating system, the software of the program, the screen on which it displays, the electrical system of the computer, and a host of other nodes. Here, a simple action by my bounded mind-body (clicking a button) triggers a host of other actions (knowledge) to accomplish the action at hand (opening the program). My mind-body unit is low-knowledge in this case (I know very little about computer code or electricity), while the tools/objects know a great deal that I leverage accordingly.

Since embodiment is a metaphor for thinking (and acting), even these networked and distributed systems are a function of the body across space. I "project" my mind into other nodes in the network that become a part of how I think and act. These nodes also "project" back onto me and influence, extend, and change how I think and act as well. I adopt a *projective embodiment* that incorporates these extra-body affordances, limitations, and knowledge.

Mediation

These tools/objects are both conceptual and concrete links between the mind-body and the world; they mediate my experience. For example, when gaming, the screen sits between me and the virtual spaces it displays; the keyboard sits between my input (pressing the keys) and the input into the program (electronic signals). Seen in this way, mediators are things that stand between; they separate, symbolically and literally, object and subject, thought and thinker.

There is another view, however, that suggests that mediators act as extensions of those things that they mediate rather than obstacles or objects in their own right. As Marshall McLuhan argues, "[a]ll media are extensions of some human faculty—psychic or physical" (26). In other words, I am not looking at the screen itself, but "through" the screen at whatever it is I am doing within the virtual space. The screen is not "that which lets me see" but *is seeing* as part of the networked and distributed mind-body-tool system. Certainly, the computer monitor does not disappear—it remains firmly on my desk. It *functionally* disappears, however, as I configure my projectively embodied mind-body to play the game. I remain aware of it as a physical object but incorporate this concession into my actions and do not focus on the tool as an object but rather as a means of acting. Dourish summarizes Heidegger's explanation of this phenomenon by describing the state that tools exist to us conceptually; they can be *zuhanden* ("ready-to-hand") or *vorhanden* ("present-at-hand"):

> [C]onsider the mouse connected to my computer. Much of the time, I act through the mouse; the mouse is an extension of my hand as I select objects, operate menus, and so forth. The mouse is, in Heidegger's terms, *ready-to-hand*. Sometimes, however, such as when I reach the edge of the mousepad and cannot move the mouse further, my orientation toward the mouse changes. Now, I become conscious of the mouse mediating my action, precisely because of the fact that it has been interrupted. The mouse becomes the object of my attention as I pick it up and move it back to the center of the mousepad. When I act on the mouse in this way, being mindful of it as an object of my activity, the mouse is *present-at-hand*. (109, emphasis in original)

It is important to stress here that it is not the tool that changes, but our perception of the tool. When it is apparent in its function, it becomes an obstacle, and the mediating effects of the technology become evident. The tool, the mediator, can be both transparent and opaque, depending on how I perceive it.

Projective embodiment further suggests that the tools effectively become an extension of myself; what they mean to me is what I can do with them and how I relate to them in terms of my enmeshed existence and experience in the world, networked with other objects/tools, but that these objects/tools also drive how I act and think based on their affordances within the world. This is important in regards to videogames; while projective embodiment is applicable beyond games and other digital media, I am especially interested in the ways games mediate the relationship between different conceptual domains (virtual and non-virtual) by using tools such as the graphical and physical interfaces as extensions of the player's embodied experience.

BROTHERS: A TALE OF TWO SONS AND PROJECTIVE EMBODIMENT

Brothers is designed to be played with a modern controller (with two joysticks and several buttons) on a computer or console. The player navigates a two-and-a-half dimensional world in search of a cure for the main characters' sick father. The player must solve different puzzles (such as crossing a river with no bridge) using the characters they control in order to beat the game. Part of what makes *Brothers* so interesting—and so demonstrative of projective embodiment in games—is the unique way the player interacts with the game. In most games, players inhabit an avatar (a representation of the player such as a character or other tool like a race car) to navigate the world. In *Brothers*, the player actually controls *two* avatars simultaneously. Each character is controlled by a joystick so that the player is moving, manipulating, and interacting with the game world in double.

This relationship between user input and game output is typically referred to as *interactivity*. This term is highly debatable, certainly, but for the purpose of this analysis I define interactivity as a process where human input and output and tool input and output meet to produce some change in the system. There are times when there is a (nearly) direct correlation between my actions and the outcome in the game—I press a button, the game responds; there are other times when the game provides some input for me (narrative, say, or instructions on how to move) that I must process in order to act. Further, as these processes are spread across both the real world (I see the screen, I press buttons) and the virtual (my input is translated, the simulation runs), my actions are mediated by the videogame between these two conceptual domains.

The avatars are the most direct representation of the player's mind-body in the game. They are the primary tool through which the player acts, and they serve as the object that most directly affects the player's behavior on screen. There are other objects in the game (other characters as well as the world itself), but the player is bound to the avatars. They are the player's agent-by-proxy. These avatars mediate the player's interactions with the game world and act as a surrogate and extension of the player's mind-body unit into the virtual domain. They also have certain affordances and limitations and are a core part of the projectively embodied experience by both constraining and expanding the ways the player can interact with the world.

Each of these characters has different features and capacities; the older brother is bigger and stronger while the younger brother is smaller and faster. The player uses them in different ways, and the puzzles are designed to capitalize on these differences. For example, early in the game the brothers must cross a bridge by pulling a large lever. The lever is too heavy for the younger brother, so the player *must* use the older brother to complete the puzzle. The player needs to utilize the affordances of each avatar in order to complete the puzzles. In other words, the player must leverage the knowledge (affordance) of each avatar (tool) in certain ways and connect features of the network (the problem, the affordances, the knowledge and capacity) appropriately in order to succeed.

The player must also combine the affordances of both avatars, not just use each individually. At several points, the player must get past a cliff which is too tall for either character alone to climb. The older brother must kneel down so that the younger brother can climb over him to reach the top and then let down a rope so the older brother can join him. The game is designed in such a way as to force the player to incorporate both avatars (their networked knowledge) into their problem solving strategies.

Since each avatar has particular affordances and limitations, they "know" different ways of acting within the system. The player activates these affordances at the right time to complete the puzzle. The avatars also know *how* to act contextually; pushing the "action" button on the controller does different things at different times. For example, pushing the "action" button near a wall makes the avatar jump and grab the ledge, while pushing the same "action" button near a ball causes the avatar to pick it up. This contextual knowledge highlights a key feature of projective identity. The same action for the player (pressing the "action" button) creates different changes in the system through the "knowledge" of the avatar. In one way, the player is a low-knowledge node (they don't need to know how to climb a wall or pick up a ball) while the avatar has high-knowledge (they know how to climb and grab). Activating this contextual knowledge requires the player to choose it *at the right time*, since without the player the avatar can do nothing. It is only together (the player + the avatar) that the system changes, and it is through the networked, projective mind-body that the player activates these affordances.

Knowledge is not limited to just the avatars, however. There are many different objects in the game that also "know" things within the system. For example, early in the game the player encounters a troll who helps the avatars cross several large chasms. The troll throws the avatars across, or stretches his arms across them so the player can climb over him. The player has no "direct" control over the tool (the troll), but the game "knows" how to act in order to provide the player with the opportunity to complete the puzzle. Here again, the player's problem-solving process is networked across the extended mind-body unit that incorporates the nodes under the players control (the avatars) and the game world (the troll).

There is one other core feature of *Brothers* (and other videogames): the controller itself. The controller is a kind of boundary object that serves as the most visible mediative tool in gameplay. It is through the controller that the player instructs the avatars on how to act, and it is the primary site where the player "connects" with the avatars. Certainly the screen (which "shows" the avatar) is another important site of mediation, but it is the controller that serves as the primary instrument through which the player projects their embodied cognitive processes.

Brothers brings this boundary object to the forefront in an important and illuminating way. The unique control scheme itself is an interesting feature, one that challenges some conventions of gameplay; this is most obvious for experienced gamers, who normally use the two joysticks to control features of one avatar at a time. By adding a separate avatar to each joystick, *Brothers* emphasizes the controller and the way it mediates the interaction with the game world.

At a crucial moment in the game, the player loses control of one of the avatars. They are then forced to solve a puzzle that seems possible only with both characters; they must swim across the river, but one character is afraid of the water. In previous encounters with water, the brother who is afraid clung to the other brother, who swam across. Now, the brother who is afraid must cross the water alone, without the aid of the brother who "knows" how to swim. Initially it is a moment of frustration. It also highlights the nature of the controller itself and the controller's relation to the avatars. Without one node in the problem solving network (the brother who knows how to swim), the player is forced to reconsider their controller. It forces the player's relationship with the controller to shift (in Heideggerian terms) from ready-at-hand to present-at-hand. Ultimately, the solution is that the brother who is afraid of the water *can* swim by using the joystick "vacated" by the other brother. This moment—changing the control scheme—is not only a powerful narrative moment, it emphasizes the relationship between the player, the controller (mediative tool), and the game as a network for problem-solving (thinking).

What the game mediates, then, is the player who inhabits a physical space and the conceptual space of the game world simultaneously. The division between the gamer and the game is a productive space with multiple meaning-making possibilities; it is a multimodal state, where the player acts in overlapping spheres of reality and virtuality. That is, the division of subject and object—the projective embodiment of the player's mind-body networked with the tools and knowledge of the game—*is* the game. Playing the game is about shifting across these networked nodes and conceptual domains.

IMPLICATIONS

This conceptualization of projective embodiment has several important implications, both in gaming and beyond. For game designers, creating experiences which capitalize on the relationship between the player's mind and the designed tools is not just a crucial challenge but one that is at the very heart of gameplay. Understanding how to capture (and challenge) these relationships (such as the way *Brothers* highlights the mediative tool of the controller) is a core design principle. For players, much of the same holds: understanding how they relate to and utilize tools and objects is central to making their gameplay meaningful while also providing an important point for critique.

Beyond games, projective embodiment plays an important role in our interaction with all kinds of tools and other media. As we increasingly incorporate the virtual into everyday life—from digital representations of our social selves through things like Facebook and Twitter to fictional role-playing in massively multi-user virtual worlds like *World of Warcraft* and *Second Life*—it becomes especially important to understand just *where* the mind is in relation to the world, and how we interact with it.

Finally, more broadly, the notion of projective embodiment highlights an important critical and methodological stance: analysis of any phenomena, gaming or otherwise, increasingly requires understanding the *system* in which that phenomena occurs. Our world is becoming more complex, and these complex systems create new and greater challenges. Exploring these systems is more necessary than ever, and projective embodiment is one key way of understanding just where in the world we fit in.

Works Cited

Apperley, Thomas H. and Darshana Jayemane. "Game Studies' Material Turn." *Westminster Papers*9.1 (2012): 5–25. Print.

Clark, Andy. *Natural Born Cyborgs*. New York: Oxford UP, 2003. Print.

Dourish, Paul. *Where the Action Is: The Foundations of Embodied Interaction*. Boston: MIT Press, 2004. Print.

Gee, James Paul. *Good Video Games and Good Learning: Collected Essays on Video Games, Learning, and Literacy*. New York: Lang, 2007. Print.

Glenberg, Art. "What Memory Is For." *Behavioral & Brain Sciences* 20.1 (1997): 1–19.

—. "Embodiment as a Unifying Perspective for Psychology." Unpublished.

Juul, Jesper. *Half-real*. Cambridge: MIT Press, 2005. Print.

McLuhan, Marshall. *The Medium Is the Massage*. New York: Bantam Books, 1967. Print.

Crossing Cultures: Refiguring Audience, Author, Text and Borders

5 Toward a New Understanding of Audience in the Medieval Arabic Translation Movement: The Case of Al-Kindi's "Statement on the Soul"

Maha Baddar

Audience is among the slipperiest of rhetoric notions, and it will and should probably remain that way. It belongs to that special class of terms (like "writer" and "text"), the foundational terms defining the field, which in any discipline, are the ones most likely to resist efforts to fix their meaning or function.

—James Porter

As scholars of rhetoric and composition, we often place the author in a more central position than the audience when analyzing a given rhetorical situation. The general understanding is that the author has a purpose to fulfill and it is the audience's role to fulfill that purpose;

this is accomplished through persuasion. Depending on the time period or school of thought, this audience is either a passive recipient of the rhetor's discourse or an equal in a dialectic exchange mostly initiated by the speaker. In available theories, the audience is a real person or group of people, an imagined or invoked entity in the text, or a combination of both (Park, Ede and Lunsford). The author herself could become her own audience through identification or by being a member of a discourse community whose culture shapes the author's way of thinking and hence the text produced (Burke, Bloomfield, Bizzell, Faigley, Fish, Chase, Herzberg). While indeed there is substantial theoretical work available to help us unravel the evasive and ever-evolving notion of *audience*, none of these accounts provides a sufficient framework for understanding the concept of *audience* in the Medieval Arabic Translation Movement that took place in Baghdad between the eighth and tenth centuries. During the Translation Movement, a massive amount of scholarship was translated from Greek, Persian, Sanskrit, and Syriac in what was referred to as translation circles. These were led by masters who managed groups of translators whom in many cases were themselves experts in the fields of knowledge they translated. Abu Yusuf Ya'qub Ibn Ishaq al-Kindi, whose treatise, "A Statement on the Soul," is the focus of this article was a master of one of Baghdad's most respected translation circles and is considered the first Arabic philosopher (Adamson *Al-Kindi* 4).

The Translation Movement constitutes a unique rhetorical situation where the audience was the initiator of communication. In this context, the *audience* was an ambiguous term that may have referred to one or more of the following groups: the sponsors of the translations; the translators themselves; the commentators; the intellectuals who read these works; the scholars who questioned the validity of the translated knowledge; and/or a particular group (ethnic, social, professional, or religious) whom a sponsor sought to influence using the translated knowledge. It was not uncommon for one facet of an audience, such as a sponsor, to use translated knowledge to move another audience to action, creating a hierarchy within an audience that includes several groups (a sponsor, a translator, a commentator, and an individual or group whom the sponsor seeks to influence).

The fact that an audience of sponsors and translators was in charge of initiating communication in the Translation Movement inverts the rhetorical triangle and shifts the dynamics of the rhetorical situation as well as our notion of how communication takes place. The audience that comprised the Translation Movement not only decided which authors and texts would be translated to produce new knowledge but also which texts would be deemed heretical, dangerous, or simply irrelevant to their cultural context and hence banned from rebirth in what is referred to as the First Renaissance. The

Translation Movement was not a rhetorical situation where an author imagines, invokes, or identifies with an audience. Instead, based on a sponsor's social, political, or religious agenda, an audience of translators selected particular authors and texts. These texts were refigured through commentary, additions, omissions, and/or refutation.

This paper will attempt to expand rhetoricians' understanding of *audience* by examining the blurred boundaries between audience and author in the Medieval Arabic Translation Movement. My analysis focuses on "A Statement on the Soul" and explores how this blurred boundary informs two prominent translation genres from the period: commentary and summary. Although available theories on audience are helpful, none of them provides an adequate framework for understanding the exceptional role of audiences in orchestrating the production of knowledge during the Translation Movement, one of history's most significant epochs of collaborative knowledge-making.

In the classical tradition, an audience was viewed as an individual or group moved to action by the speech of the rhetor, on whose shoulders fell the task of invention, organization, and delivery. Michelle Ballif argues, "The rhetorical tradition has historically posited a rhetorical situation involving a speaking subject and a receiving audience, just as it more recently theorizes composition as a writer writing to an audience" (51). Audience members are passive recipients of (inaccurate) information and are easily manipulated by the sophists in the Platonic oeuvre. Aristotle explains that persuasion is effected "through the hearers when they are led to feel emotion [pathos] by the speech; for we do not give the same judgment when grieved or rejoicing or when being friendly or hostile" (38). Even though Aristotle elaborately covers means of persuasion as well as classifies the types of character and emotion, he does not explain how the two work together to influence how the rhetor makes decisions about the content and organization of the speech (Porter "Audience" 44). When the classical tradition considers audience, they are either passive recipients of information, individuals or groups who are expected to be moved to action by the rhetor's discourse. Other classical rhetorical treatises, such as *Rhetorica ad Herennium* and *De Inventione* ignore audience character analysis (Porter "Audience" 44). The classical understanding of audience is not helpful in understanding the complexities of the rhetorical situation of the Translation Movement; sponsors and scholars, in an audience role, decided which authors and topics written in a source language would be translated into Arabic, hence shifting the dynamics of the rhetorical situation by putting the audience in the active role of initiator of communication. In the Translation Movement the discourse of an author who wrote at a previous date and in a different cultural context (such as Aristotle or Galen) was used by active, highly selective groups of audience to accomplish goals relevant to their own context.

The classical model, nevertheless, is helpful in its distinction between the audience of rhetoric (a passive, mass audience) and an audience of peers in dialectic (Porter *Audience and Rhetoric* 17). The latter characterizes the Translation Movement where the audience is composed of specialists who not only worked on translation but also had produced original scholarship that was in direct dialogue with the source texts. When rhetoric's audience comes into the picture in the Translation Movement, it is oftentimes after the audience of dialectic, audience as peer, has studied and appropriated translated texts and used them, from the standpoint of author, to effect change through persuading another audience group. It is a murky rhetorical situation when sometimes this latter audience, assumed to be a passive recipient, is not always as passive as presumed by the traditional model. Examples include fellow philosophers, theologians, and politicians who are not easily moved by a sponsor's use of translated knowledge to change their stance on a given issue.

A more appropriate theoretical framework for understanding the complex role Arabic scholars played as audience-author can be found in Mikhail Bakhtin's work on dialogism. Bakhtin gives the audience an equally active and powerful role as the writer/speaker. Dialogism is the creation of meaning out of a past utterance and the constant need for utterances to position themselves in relation to one another (Vice 45). In "Discourse in the Novel," Bakhtin states, "every word is directed toward an answer and cannot escape the profound influence of the answering that it anticipates. . . . Responsive understanding is a fundamental force, one that participates in the formulation of discourse (qtd. in Vice 52). In accordance with this theory of discourse, Arabic scholars responded to and reshaped earlier knowledge, and new knowledge was produced in the process. The end result was an audience-author position occupied by scholars involved in the Translation Movement. In dialogism, knowledgemaking is part of a communication system where every utterance is a response to a previous one. In "A Statement on the Soul," al-Kindi responds to classical and Neo-Platonic ideas through adapting and challenging them; his audience-author position challenges the classical audience model of audience as passive recipient.

Translator as Audience-Author: The Case of al-Kindi's "A Statement on the Soul"

Arab thinkers had access, through translation, to the philosophical knowledge of Presocratic, Greek, and Alexandrian/Neo-Platonic thinking. This included the work of Thales, Pythagoras, Plato, Aristotle, Plotinus, and

Porphyry (Ibn an-Nadim 507-11). The availability of this knowledge resulted in two groups of audience: an audience sympathetic to imported philosophical knowledge and an audience resistant to the integration of "pagan"
thinking into an Islamic setting. The former group saw philosophy as a helpful tool in addressing religio-ideological problems, while the latter viewed
Islam as a self-sufficient religion that did not require the assistance of foreign
thinking for its maintenance.

In "A Statement on the Soul," al-Kindi claims that his epistle is a summary of ancient philosophers' views on the soul. The summary subgenre of
translation could falsely indicate a lack of contribution on al-Kindi's part.
However, a close examination of the text shows enough original ideas and
stylistic elements to position al-Kindi as both audience and author. Al-Kindi,
as audience-author, was addressing what Perelman and Olberts-Tyteca describe as composite audience, "embracing people different in character, loyalties, and function" (qtd. in Jasinski 69). This position challenges current
theories that do not account for an audience-author who addresses multiple
audiences via a hybrid text.

Arabic philosophers such as al-Kindi, al-Farabi, and Ibn Sina tried to
legitimize Aristotelian and Neo-Platonic philosophical thinking through
translation subgenres such as summaries and commentaries. These philosophers occupied the ambiguous position of audience-author: they were an
audience to Greek and Neo-Platonic thinking but author when hybridizing
the content and style of these texts with Arabic and Islamic elements. These
Arabic philosophers' audience was a composite audience that included sympathetic fellow philosophers and politicians as well as antagonistic traditional
theologians. Arabic philosophers' awareness of their audience's ideological
diversity can be explained using the notion of the moral field presented by
Richard Eastman. Russell Long summarizes Eastman's scholarship on the
moral field as follows:

> [The] "mapping" of the moral field takes place on a matrix where
> the horizontal planes are made up of, in turn, what would be hoped
> for by the audience, what would be feared by the audience, what vir-
> tues would be needed on part of the audience to accept change, and
> what vices might enter into the audience's decision to think or act as
> they do. The vertical columns in the matrix are simply divided into
> those supporting and opposing the issue. (Long 75)

In order to accommodate opposing ideologies, Arabic philosophers used
summary and commentary as subgenres of translation and interjected these
genres with their own original contributions. They showed shrewd awareness and sophisticated analysis of the moral fields shaping the different audi-

ences whom they needed to persuade of the compatibility of philosophy and religion.

Al-Kindi's "A Statement on the Soul" is an example of what Bakhtin describes as dialogism or Vincent Leitch characterizes as "text as intertext or Text." Al-Kindi's treatise does not meet the traditional, simple definition of text as an utterance produced by one author for a specific audience. Leitch calls these "fictions for domesticating discourse" (qtd. in Porter 68). Instead, it is a work which generically claims to be one thing (a summary) but includes the translator's own interpretations and contributions. Specifically, "A Statement on the Soul" claims to be intended for one audience, the caliph's son addressed at the beginning, but is intended for a composite audience. In this treatise, al-Kindi engages in conversation with fellow philosophers, attempts to persuade resistant traditional theologians of the compatibility of religion and philosophy, and shows allegiance to the caliphate.

Al-Kindi's awareness, as audience-author, of traditional Islamic thinkers' antagonistic stance toward philosophy as a pagan field of knowledge led him to exclude pagan Greek and Neo-Platonic references that appear throughout the source texts, and to include Qur'anic ones. One such adaptation to Plato's and Pythagoras's views on the soul is the use of an Islamic name of God, *al-Barei*, and its qualification using Islamic descriptions such as *the Great* and *Almighty* throughout the treatise. These Islamic references replace Greek and Neo-Platonic references such as Demiurge, First Cause, and First Intellect that his primary sources used. He says:

> The soul, according to Plato and the majority of the philosophers, survives after death. Its essence is similar to the essence of *al-Barei*, the Great and Exalted. When the soul is in an abstract state, it is able to know everything in the same way that *al-Barei* does, or in a manner that is a slight degree below His, because it has been filled up with the light of *al-Barei*, the Great and Almighty. (Baddar 82)

These references are present throughout the treatise and represent al-Kindi's critical attitude to the new knowledge he was introducing as audience-author to one of his audience groups, traditional Islamic theologians who were resistant to pagan philosophy.

Al-Kindi, as audience-author, adapts and adds to the foreign heritage he claims to be only summarizing, an inventional decision that suggests his cognizance of the "moral field" of his Arab-Muslim audience (Eastman). One such addition is the reference to angels, entities that constitute a part of the monotheistic belief system but are not present in the traditions he is reporting on in this treatise. In his account of what he claims to be Aristotle's views on the soul (either through an inaccurate reference or extant treatise), al-Kindi writes of a king who, after awaking from a coma, "informed people about the arts of the unknown and told them about what he saw including souls, forms, and angels" (Baddar 85). Another reference to angels is when al-Kindi claims that "Plato compared the sensual faculty in man to the pig, the anger faculty to the dog, and the rational faculty to the angel" (Baddar 81). The latter comparison is based on Plato's *Republic* where Plato compares the three parts of the soul to three creatures: desire is compared to a chimera; spirit is compared to a lion; and intellect is compared to man (Adamson *Al-Kindi* 228 12n). Al-Kindi replaces Plato's man with an angel, a creature closer to perfection according to al-Kindi's monotheistic environment and perhaps as a reference to the Islamic interpretation of the Neo-Platonic ninth intellect as Gibril, the angel of revelation.

The additions illustrate the evolution that the field of metaphysics underwent at the hand of the medieval Muslim scholars who, in the role of audience-author, wrote under different circumstances than the Greek and Neo-Platonic philosophers. As rhetors, they created, not just transmitted knowledge. Al-Kindi's treatise is a clear example of the diminishing boundaries between author and audience:

> the traditional distinction between composer and audience breaks down eventually. . . . Rather, discourse is developed through interaction—it is developed dialogically, through the process of the "person" moving from speaker role to audience role and back-and-forth. In fact the roles of rhetor/author and audience blur. The boundaries between the two roles disappear. (Porter *Audience and Rhetoric* 81)

Al-Kindi's audience-author position is further complicated by his subject position as a member of a Muslim discourse community. Angels are not present in the Platonic and Aristotelian traditions but were an integral part of al-Kindi's Muslim context as well as the Christian Alexandrian and Syriac commentaries he utilized. The reference to angels positions al-Kindi as a member of a discourse community whose beliefs and values inserted themselves in a text that he claims to be conveying as merely a receptacle-audience, further complicating the notion of audience in this text and providing it with authorial, creative qualities.

The organization and tone in "A Statement on the Soul" are indicators of the authorial role al-Kindi adopted. The tone of al-Kindi's treatise follows an Arabic and Islamic rhetorical tradition reminiscent of *khutbas* (sermons) and religious circles at mosques, which are present even today in both written and oral Arabic discourse. He starts by praying for his audience: "May Allah guide you toward the truth and assist you in overcoming the difficulties involved in striving for it" (Baddar 79) and ends with a general prayer: "Praise be to Allah, the Lord of the two worlds, and blessings be upon Muhammad and all his household" (Baddar 86). Moreover, al-Kindi inserts didactic passages to comment on the Greek and Neo-Platonic philosophers' views, such as when he says:

> O you ignorant person: do you not know that your dwelling in this world is like the blink of an eye, and then you will reach the real world, where you will stay forever?! You are just a passer-by. God's will, which the great philosophers have known and that we have summarized from their statements, is that the soul is a simple essence. (Baddar 86)

In the above passage, he hybridizes religious advice while paying homage to philosophical thinking. In another part of the treatise he adds: "If you understand and follow what I wrote to you, you will be happy with it. May Allah, Glory be to Him, make you happy in this life and the afterlife" (Baddar 86). These gestures show that the purpose of the treatise was to advocate an Islamic philosophy rooted in a (Neo)Platonic version of virtue; virtue purified the human soul, qualifying the person to acquire knowledge, which in its turn lead to happiness.

Al-Kindi practices more mapping of the moral field of his audience in "A Statement on the Soul" by addressing a controversial issue of his time and declaring his stance on it in an attempt to gain the favor of the Abbasid caliphate. Al-Kindi's scholarship took place in the wake of the Inquisition, a theological controversy revolving around the question of whether the Qur'an was eternal or created that took place in Baghdad during the reign of Abbasid caliphs al-Ma'mun, al-Mu'tasim, and al-Wathiq, whose patronage and approval al-Kindi sought. Notably, the Caliphate adopted the latter stance, and traditional Islamic scholars who adopted the former viewpoint fell out of favor with the Caliphate. This problem is addressed by al-Kindi who took the opportunity to gain the favor of the Caliphate, one group of his "composite audience" (Perelman and Olbrechts-Tyteca), when he asks: "what if our souls have become abstract, have been comparable to the world of eternity, and have started to see with the light of *al-Barei*" (Baddar 81). The reference to eternity here seems casual. However, a close examination of al-Kindi's immediate context and some of his other treatises such as "Epistle on the Oneness of God and Finiteness of the Body of the Universe" show that any mention of eternity during this time period is neither causal nor a coincidence. It is a reference to the Inquisition and the division that took place religiously and intellectually in the Abbasid Empire. Here al-Kindi, by associating the world of eternity with *al-Barei* and by saying that the soul is only "comparable" (i.e. not identical) to it, is claiming that eternity is something that is *only* attributed to God. This exclusiveness could be interpreted as a denial of the eternality of the Qur'an and the promotion of an ideological perspective al-Kindi likely believed would be regarded favorably by his sponsors, the Abbasid caliphs. Keeping in mind that the treatise was addressed to Ahmad, al-Mu'tasim's son whom al-Kindi tutored, it could be believed that al-Kindi would take the opportunity to show his support for his sponsors as a gesture of allegiance at a time of religious and political turmoil.

Al-Kindi cautiously lists the qualities of God present in the texts of Aristotle, Plato and Pythagoras. As a member of a monotheistic discourse community, he selects qualities compatible with his monotheistic context while eliminating qualities that would be offensive to all members of his audience. Al-Kindi's cautious composition of this section of his treatise could be described as *evaluative* and positions him more as an author of the treatise than a passive audience who is merely summarizing a few texts. Al-Kindi claims to be summarizing, via reported speech, the views of others on a topic. However, the act of reporting is not always a simple act of faithful conveyance because evaluation of the reported utterance takes place on the part of the reporter and makes the text his/her own property, not only the original authors'. Theoretical work on reported speech is part of the larger body of work on dialogism done by Bakhtin, Medvedev, and Voloshinov; Voloshinov mentions that "between the reported speech and the reporting context, dynamic relations of high complexity and tension are in force" (Morris 64). Indeed, complexity and tension characterize the encounter between a pagan culture and a monotheistic one in the scholarship of al-Kindi, whose ultimate goal was to use the former as a foundation for social and political development of the latter. Al-Kindi's evaluative approach to Greek and Neo-Platonic material can be seen in his selectivity regarding the qualities of God and his distinction between divine and human qualities. In the section where he summarizes Plato's views on the soul, he says: "the things which we find in *al-Barei*, praise be to Him, are wisdom, power, justice, benevolence, beauty, and truth" (Baddar 81). Al-Kindi only mentions qualities attributed to God by Plato that are compatible with Qur'anic attributes of God. In accordance with Islamic teachings that stipulate that perfection can only be attributed to God, al-Kindi emphasizes that acquiring noble qualities such as wisdom, generosity, and benevolence resemble God's qualities but are always of an inferior caliber. In the same section, al-Kindi refers to unruly horses, a reference based on Plato's *Phaedrus*:

> The faculty of anger may occasionally be stirred within a person, moving him to commit terrible deeds. The soul opposes this anger and stops the person from committing these deeds. It stops rage

from committing its [unfair] actions and controls it in a way similar
to that of a horseman regulating or pulling his horse if it attempts to
run away. (Baddar 80)

While presenting the charioteer metaphor, al-Kindi compares only the human soul to a horseman trying to control two horses, one obedient and the
other unruly, omitting fully half of Plato's account in which the gods are
described as also having two horses each, but theirs are both good. In Plato's
dialogue, the gods in their chariots follow in a procession led by Zeus, another reference omitted by al-Kindi. This illustrates that the Arabic Translation
Movement and the scholarship based on it were selective toward the material
that was borrowed from other civilizations. In his account of Plato's views
on the soul, as previously noted, al-Kindi only includes divine qualities that
are compatible with Islamic teachings. He not only omits any pagan or poly-
theistic references but also omits qualities below God's utter perfection in
the Islamic tradition. His treatise excludes Platonic references to the four
kinds of madness that Plato attributes to Apollo, Dionysius, the Muses, and
Aphrodite. Unlike Greek deities who engage in human acts and even follies
at times, God's sovereignty is highly preserved and distinguished from human qualities. A faithful account of Plato would have repulsed al-Kindi's
sympathetic and resistant audience equally and rendered his project of incorporating philosophy into Muslim life impossible. It would have also had dire
ideological consequences by widening the divide between the philosophers
and the traditional theologians that was already existent in the Abbasid society by giving strength to the trend among traditionalist scholars to dismiss
philosophy as heretical. The inclusion of such material would have compromised al-Kindi's larger philosophical goal and illustrates that such evaluative
gestures were quite common and strategically considered in light of the larger
ideological atmosphere in Baghdad.

I have used al-Kindi's "A Statement on the Soul" to illustrate the ambiguous position Arabic philosophers who produced scholarship as part of
the Translation Movement occupied as both audience of foreign scholarship as well as authors of hybrid and authentic texts. As audience, al-Kindi
had access to numerous texts, out of which he selected what he thought was
compatible with his beliefs as a Muslim philosopher. He made substantial
changes and contributions to the works he accessed as a head of a translation
circle, which qualifies him as author of the text that he claims to be summarizing. In this capacity as author, al-Kindi was addressing different audience
groups and had different purposes. By substituting Greek concepts and terms
with Islamic equivalents, interspersing the paragraphs reporting the older
Greek philosophers' views with didactic passages of an Islamic nature, add-

ing monotheistic elements, and writing in a style reminiscent of an Islamic sermon, al-Kindi makes his context—ninth century Islamic Baghdad—the locale in which Hellenistic and Neo-Platonic views could be positively received by his different audience groups.

WORKS CITED

Aristotle. *On Rhetoric: A Theory of Civic Discourse.* Trans. G. Kennedy. New York: Oxford UP, 1991. Print

Adamson, Peter. *Al Kindi.* Oxford: Oxford UP, 2007. Print.

Adamson, Peter, and Richard C. Taylor, eds. *The Cambridge Companion to Arabic Philosophy.* New York: Cambridge U P, 2005. Print.

Al-Kindi, Ya'qub ibn Ishaq. *Rasa'il al-Kindi al-Falsafiyah.* Ed. Muhammad A. Abu Rida. Cairo: Dar al-Fikr al-Arabi, 1950. Print.

Baddar, Maha. "Translation of al-Kindi's Treatise on the Soul." *From Athens (Via Alexandria) to Baghdad: Hybridity as Epistemology in the Work of al-Kindi, al-Farabi, and in the Rhetorical legacy of the Medieval Arabic Translation Movement.* Diss. U of Arizona, 2010. Ann Arbor: ProQuest/UMI, 2010. 79–86. Print.

Bakhtin, Mikhail. *The Dialogic Imagination: Four Essays by M.M. Bakhtin.* Ed. Michael Holquist. Austin: U of Texas P, 1981. 259–422.

Ballif, Michelle. "What is it That the Audience Wants?" *JAC* 19.1 (1999): 51–70. *JSTOR.* Web. 12 Feb. 2015.

Bitzer, Lloyd. "The Rhetorical Situation." *Philosophy and Rhetoric.* 1.1(1968): 1–14. Print.

Ede, Lisa and Andrea Lunsford. "Audience Addressed/Audience Invoked." *College Composition and Communication* 35.2 (1984): 155–71. *JSTOR.* Web. 11 April 2014.

Endress, Gerhard. "The Circle of al-Kindi: Early Arabic Translations from the Greek and the Rise of Islamic Philosophy." *The Ancient Traditions in Christian and Islamic Hellenism.* Eds. G. Endress and R. Kruk. Leiden: CNWS, 1997. 43–76. Print.

Fakhry, Majid. *A Short Introduction to Islamic Philosophy, Theology, and Mysticism.* Oxford: Oneworld, 1997. Print.

Gutas, Dimitri. *A Short Introduction to Islamic Philosophy, Theology, and Mysticism.* Oxford: Oneworld, 1997. Print.

Ibn an-Nadim, Mohamed Ibn Ishaq. *Al-Fihrist.* Ed. Nahid Uthman. Doha: Dar Qatary Ibn al-Foujaa, 2004. Print.

Ivry, Alfred L., ed. and trans. *Al-Kindi's Metaphysics: A Translation of Ya"qub ibn Ishaq al-Kindi"s Treatise "On First Philosophy."* Albany: State U of New York P, 1974. Print.

Jasinski, James L. "Audience." *Sourcebook on Rhetoric.* London: Sage Publications Inc., 2001. 68–73. Print.

Kirsch, Gesa, and Duane H. Roen, eds. *A Sense of Audience in Written Communication.* London: Sage, 1990. Print.

Long, Russell C. "The Writer's Audience: Fact of Fiction?" *A Sense of Audience in Written Communication*. Eds. Gesa Kirsch and Duane H. Roen. London: Sage, 1990. 73–84. Print.

Morris, Pam, ed. *The Bakhtin Reader: Selected Writings of Bakhtin, Medvedev, and Voloshinov*. London: E. Arnold, 1994. Print.

Park, Douglas P. "The Meaning of 'Audience.'" *College English* 44.3 (1982): 247–57. *JSTOR*. Web. 11 April 2014.

Plato. *Phaedrus. The Rhetorical Tradition: Readings from the Classical Times to the Present*. 2nd ed. Eds. Patricia Bizzell and Bruce Herzberg. Boston: Bedford/St. Martin's, 2001. 138–65. Print.

—. *The Republic*. 2nd ed. Trans. Desmond Lee. London: Penguin Books, 1987. Print.

Porter, James. "Audience." *Encyclopedia of Rhetoric and Composition: Communication from Ancient Times to the Information Age*. Ed. Theresa Jarnagin Enos. New York: Routledge, 1996. 42–49. Print.

—. *Audience and Rhetoric*. London: Prentice-Hall, 1992. Print.

Salem, Sema'an I., and Alok Kumar, eds. and trans. *Science in the Medieval World: Book of the Categories of Nations*. By Ibn Sa'id al-Andalusi. Austin: U of Texas P, 1991. Print.

Vice, Sue. *Introducing Bakhtin*. Manchester: Manchester UP, 1998. Print.

Walther, Joseph B. "Audience." *Encyclopedia of Rhetoric*. Ed. Thomas O. Sloane. New York: Oxford UP, 2001. 59–75. Print.

6 All Nations, One Blood, Three Hundred Years: Martin Luther King, Jr., Fannie Lou Hamer, and Civil Rights Rhetoric as Transatlantic Abolitionism

Keith D. Miller

In his germinal *The Black Atlantic*, Paul Gilroy critiques long-entrenched paradigms that insulate the study of British history, culture, and rhetoric from the study of American history, culture, and rhetoric. He proposes to replace these paradigms with a Transatlantic framework capable of encompassing the hybrid culture and politics of the many black people who crisscrossed the Atlantic. In this essay, I claim that Gilroy's Transatlantic framework proves helpful in understanding an important strand of rhetoric that leading British abolitionists and American abolitionists developed and that Martin Luther King, Jr., Fannie Lou Hamer, and others extended throughout the civil rights era. Gilroy's framework proves useful when enlarged to include a diachronic dimension that can account for a continuous fabric of discourse that, over a period of literally three hundred years, radicals used to dispute white supremacy.

Civil rights orators repeated a number of elements of anti-slavery rhetoric. For example, as scholars note, American slaves, abolitionist orators, King, and Hamer alike produced songs and oratory that equated African Americans with Biblical Hebrews toiling under the lash of the Egyptian Pharaoh.[1] Researchers, however, ignore radical orators' strong reliance on a very different portion of the Bible—a single sentence contained in *Acts* 17:26 ("God hath made of one blood all the nations for to dwell on all the face of the earth").[2]

To investigate the many Transatlantic iterations of this appeal-by-citation between 1676 and 1976 is to notice a significant pattern of interargumentation that would escape any scholar attempting to analyze any single rhetor in isolation from her predecessors and descendants or even any scholar attempting to analyze an entire century of rhetors in isolation from those who came before and later. Here I use the term *interargumentation* to designate a specific system of argument developed by a group of anti-slavery rhetors that operated diachronically when later generations of anti-slavery and civil rights orators addressed later generations of audiences. Below I, first, sketch the history of this *interargumentation* and, second, analyze reasons for its attraction to those who relayed it to one generation, then another, then another.

Rhetors apparently began tying *Acts* 17:26 to race relations when they offered distinctly religious (and more-or-less apolitical) appeals for recognizing the humanity of diverse people. In 1676 George Fox, the British Quaker, quoted *Acts* 17:26 while urging Christians to recognize Africans as human beings. In 1700, again in England, Bishop Morgan Godwyn quoted *Acts* 17:26 as a means of asserting the humanity of Native Americans (18). By the beginning of the eighteenth century, *Acts* 17:26 was leaping back and forth across the Atlantic. In 1700 Samuel Sewell, an American Puritan, cited *Acts* 17:26 while appealing for the humanity of American slaves (7).

During the second half of the eighteenth century, as the horrors of slavery became more and more apparent, abolitionism gained momentum, particularly in Britain, but also in the US. On both sides of the Atlantic, passionate opponents of slavery seized *Acts* 17:26, treating it as the revelation of an authoritative Biblical principle that self-evidently militated against slavery. In 1754 John Woolman, a Quaker from Philadelphia, quoted *Acts* 17:26 as he criticized slavery (274). In 1762, Anthony Benezet, another American Quaker, argued for abolition by quoting the same Biblical verse on the title page of his book about Africa. In his popular autobiography of 1789, former slave Olaudah Equiano, who was living in England, copied Benezet by quoting *Acts* 17:26 in order to assail slavery and assert racial equality (31).[3] In 1786, Thomas Clarkson, an eminent anti-slavery crusader in Britain, cited the same verse while making the same argument (132-33).

After Britain emancipated its slaves, anti-slavery American orators continued to brandish *Acts* 17:26 as they assaulted bondage. In 1836, Sarah Grimke, a well-known American abolitionist, repudiated slavery while quoting *Acts* 17:26 (105). In 1853, Wendell Phillips, another renowned American abolitionist, urged the repeal of slavery while citing the same passage even as he treated this argument-by-citation as a commonplace of anti-slavery discourse (346). One can readily surmise that he did so because, among the many thousands of American anti-slavery speeches and sermons that were never published, a large number featured the same argument-by-citation from *Acts* 17:26.

While generating their rhetorical and political struggle against slavery, African American leaders joined white abolitionists in gravitating to *Acts* 17:26. Absalom Jones inserted that verse into an 1808 sermon that celebrated a new national law designed to outlaw the further importation of slaves (74). In 1852 Frederick Douglass wielded the same quotation in his most luminous oration—"What to the Slave Is the Fourth of July?" (126). Like Benezet, Clarkson, Equiano, Sewell, Woolman, Sarah Grimke, and Jones, Douglass spotlighted the claim of *Acts* 17:26—"God hath made of one blood all the nations. . ."—as he lambasted slavery. Douglass's ability to locate that Biblical passage helped prompt him to tell a Scottish audience, "The slaveholders hate the gospel of the Lord Jesus Christ" ("Speech" 173).

Long after emancipation, white racist oppression still blighted millions of lives. For that reason, well into the early and middle twentieth century, rhetors continued to harness the same verse from *Acts* as a Biblical proof-text against resurgent white supremacy. In 1925 the brilliant Vernon Johns, who preceded Martin Luther King, Jr., as pastor of Dexter Avenue Baptist Church of Montgomery, Alabama, affirmed racial equality by quoting *Acts* 17:26 (410). During the 1960s, William Holmes Borders, a prominent African American preacher in Atlanta, paraphrased the same verse while making the same argument ("The Way Out" 106). In another sermon titled "'All Blood Is Red,'" Borders emphasized interdependence and racial equality.[4] In 1954, speaking at a gathering of the World Council of Churches, Benjamin Mays, president of Morehouse College and mentor to the undergraduate King, denounced racial segregation by plucking *Acts* 17:26 ("The Church" 217).[5]

In 1956, delivering a sermon titled "Paul's Letter to American Christians," King himself followed Johns, Borders, and Mays by quoting *Acts* 17:26 as he scorned racism (343). King did so again in two homilies from 1957 ("For All" 124; "Look" 274). He also included "Paul's Letter to American Christians"—and the same sentence from *Acts*—in his homiletic collection, *Strength to Love*, which appeared in 1963 (142). Further, while responding to a letter from someone who wondered what the Bible said about segregation, King replied that *Acts* 17:26 militated against segregation ("To Wilbert").

As Maegan Parker Brooks cogently explains, Hamer, a school dropout and sharecropper, championed racial equality in stellar speeches composed in her own version of the African American Vernacular English that flourished among the small towns and cotton plantations of the Mississippi Delta (*A Voice*). In many ways, the oratory of Hamer—a rural, impoverished, oppressed, and relatively unlettered woman—contrasts with that of King, an urban, middle-class, relatively privileged male who received a PhD at Boston University. Yet, between 1963 and 1976, Hamer, like King, repeatedly embraced *Acts* 17:26 as a Biblical proof-text against white supremacy.[6] Hamer's daughter, Vergie Faulkner, explains the religious roots of Hamer's passionate rhetoric by discussing her reliance on the Bible. Although Hamer quoted different Biblical passages, Faulkner only mentions Hamer's use of a single Biblical text—*Acts* 17:26—thereby emphasizing its importance in Hamer's addresses (Brooks, "Interview" 202). One can easily imagine that many other African American orators from the civil rights era joined Johns, Borders, Mays, King, and Hamer in citing the same Biblical text while delivering addresses that were neither recorded nor published.

What advantages did rhetors gain by avidly replaying this specific Biblical appeal that ties centuries of Transatlantic oratory into a large fabric of interargumentation? Of course, many speakers routinely referred to the Bible while arguing for abolition and, later, for African American equality. Angelina Grimke, an important American abolitionist, noted: ". . . our [antislavery] books and papers are mostly commentaries on the Bible, and the Declaration [of Independence]" (55). But why did rhetors favor this particular passage?

Investigating the appeal of *Acts* 17:26—"God hath made of one blood all the nations. . . "—for those who read *Acts* as a sacralized Biblical text is helpful to understanding the advantages that the passage supplied to radical orators.

The author of *Acts* presents the assertion as a line from a speech that Paul delivered on Mars Hill in Greece. Failing to supply reasons or evidence for this assertion, both Paul and the author of the *Acts* treat the assertion as apodictic. And it does appear to validate itself. To the naked eye, skin colors differ but all blood looks identical, all blood looks to be one. Further, for readers of *Acts*, the phrase "one blood" serves as a vivid and powerful synecdoche that presents a concrete image of a portion of the body that is common to all humanity while also suggesting other portions of a body—for example, one brain, one nose, two legs, two arms, two eyes, and ten fingers—that are shared by either all or most people of all races. The assertion serves as a lively synecdoche not only for physical congruence, but also for a broadly shared, underlying commonality.

In addition, *Acts* 17:26 touched and reinforced the religious sensibilities of many readers. The line refers directly to God, who, this passage asserts, "made of one blood all the nations." Obviously, devoted readers regard God as the highest possible authority and the Bible as a divinely inspired text. Credited as the author of no fewer than thirteen Biblical books, Paul also appears as a major character in *Acts* and is known as the evangelist who initially spread Christianity around the Mediterranean Rim. His sermon on Mars Hill is certainly well-known. Believers would, therefore, incline to accept the sentiment of *Acts* 17:26 as authoritative not only because it is biblical but also because Paul utters it in a noteworthy address.[7]

Further, for many believers, these words from Paul recall the well-remembered story in *Genesis* about Adam and Eve. A clear implication of the *Genesis* narrative is that Adam and Eve serve as common ancestors for all humanity and that, therefore, all people share blood relayed to them by Adam and Eve. Because many who read Paul's sermon in *Acts* were already acquainted with the story of Adam and Eve in *Genesis*, *Acts* 17:26 served as a forceful reminder of a conclusion that they already understood.[8]

For rhetors wielding *Acts* 17:26 as a biblical witness against slavery centuries after *Acts* was written, the passage still functioned as a clear, self-validating affirmation of humanity that God authorized and conveyed through a striking synecdoche spoken by a great Christian evangelist and recorded in a sacralized text.

Over several long centuries, several types of pro-slavery and anti-slavery rhetoric circulated widely, sometimes mixed together: fervent appeals to the Bible, fierce disputes about constitutional government, heated disagreements about the principles of the Enlightenment, and elaborate debates about biological evidence pertaining to racial origins. To investigate these arguments religious, constitutional, rationalist, and scientific is to uncover a rhetorical web almost unimaginably vast and intricate.

In part, radical orators plucked *Acts* 17:26 because it could be readily accepted as an aphorism whose simplicity flattens entire mountain ranges of pro-slavery and anti-slavery appeals that arose from the time of the Renaissance until the end of the American Civil War. With a single stroke, *Acts* 17:26 seemed to slice through massive debates with a biblical principle that overruled all other considerations. To reiterate this verse was to articulate what Charles Sellers calls "the uncompromisingly egalitarian credo that abolitionists regularly laid down . . . as their fundamental premise" (xi).

Because *Acts* 17:26 seems to directly affirm the precept of racial equality, abolitionists' reliance on it challenged attempts to moderate slavery through gradual emancipation, a process that the British implemented in the Caribbean. The repetition of *Acts* 17:26 also undermined the proposal to define American slaves as undesirables and to ship them overseas—a notion seriously advocated, at one point or another, by such prominent figures as Thomas Jefferson, James Monroe, James Madison, John Marshall, Henry Clay, and Abraham Lincoln. As Sellers explains, "The African-American community found its united voice in denouncing the inherent racism of the movement to colonize American blacks in Africa" (xi). The frequent repetition of *Acts* 17:26 aided and amplified that united African American voice.

In order to grasp the clarity afforded by *Acts* 17:26, consider one of the many thousands of pro-slavery and anti-slavery sermons, speeches, newspaper editorials, and treatises—Angelina Grimke's "Appeal to the Christian Women of the South" from 1836. While avoiding *Acts* 17:26, the abolitionist Grimke displays an impressive and thorough grasp of many portions of the Bible. She explicitly refers to twenty Biblical characters: Adam, Moses, Solomon, Shadrach, Meshach, Abednego, Daniel, Moses, Miriam, Aaron, Deborah, Esther, Huldah, Mordecai, John the Baptist, Jesus, Mary, Martha, Lazarus, and Paul. While doing so, she quotes twenty-two biblical books: *Genesis, Exodus, Leviticus, Deuteronomy, Judges, II Chronicles, I Kings, II Kings, Psalms, Proverbs, Isaiah, Esther, Daniel, Matthew, Luke, John, Acts, Ephesians, Colossians, Galatians, Philemon*, and *I Timothy*. Included in her learned analysis is a very detailed contention that slaves during the Biblical era received unimaginably better treatment than did slaves in the American South.

Like Theodore Weld and numerous other abolitionists, Angelina Grimke rejects slaveowners' exceedingly illogical and self-serving claim, based on lines in *Genesis*, that, in response to a very vague offense committed by Noah's son Ham, God cursed Noah's grandson Canaan and, thereby, cursed every subsequent generation of African people. As David Goldenberg explains, the argument about this curse spread widely among slaveowners and grew deeply entrenched in slaveholding culture. Trying to refute this argument proved very difficult for two reasons. First, as David Brion Davis observes, the salient passage in *Genesis* is so inscrutable that no one anywhere can unravel its meaning. Second, as Davis contends, slaveowners' argument about the passage is exceedingly tortured and convoluted (64-66). To dive into this argument—even to rebut it—is to leap into a complicated maze.

For that reason, abolitionists and later radicals who embraced *Acts* 17:26 often ignored slaveowners' complex arguments about Noah, Ham, and Canaan. While sometimes supplying additional biblical references, many of these radicals eschewed the kind of intricately detailed biblical analysis that Grimke forwards in her tract and instead embraced beautiful simplicity merely by opening their Bibles to *Acts* 17:26. For many, to cite this passage was to refute slavery while obviating the need to jump into other complicated religious, constitutional, political, philosophical, anthropological, and scientific arguments about bondage.

Segregationists did not usually repeat slaveowners' common interpretation of Noah, Ham, and Canaan. But, as Brooks explains, Hamer reached for *Acts* 17:26 in order to counter what Brooks calls "such widely circulating [white] supremacist claims as 'God was a segregationist'" (*A Voice* 32). Other civil rights orators harnessed *Acts* 17:26, in part, for the same reason.

King was able to fold the now-traditional argument of *Acts* 17:26 into his appeal, in part, because he argued that, while slavery had assumed a different form, it had never ended. Delivering his most heralded address, "I Have a Dream" in 1963, King contended that although Lincoln's Emancipation Proclamation appeared as a "joyous daybreak" in 1863, blacks "one hundred years later" were still gripped by the "manacles of segregation" and the "chains of discrimination." In King's rhetorical universe, the argument of *Acts* 17:26 remained salient in 1963 because abolitionists' struggle against slavery had not ended.

Both anti-slavery and civil rights rhetors maintained that segregationists—like their slaveowning predecessors—suffered from what Kenneth Burke calls "trained incapacity" or "occupational psychosis" (*Permanence* 7-9, 40-43). In this argument, large numbers of whites also manifested what Burke terms "bureaucratization of the imaginative," which occurs whenever an institutional procedure becomes so routinized that, as Burke explains, it serves as a "'cow-path'" that is followed "in pious obedience to its secret grounding in the authority of custom" (*Attitudes* 225-29). For many Southern whites, the system of slavery and racism had become so normalized and so institutionalized that it bureaucratized their imaginations and anesthetized their minds. By citing *Acts* 17:26, radical orators supplied what Burke calls a "perspective by incongruity" designed to upset customary patterns of thought (*Attitudes* 308-14). By crashing a biblical principle against the institutions of slavery and segregation, social crusaders, over a period of three centuries, repeatedly offered a perspective by incongruity that assaulted and re-assaulted white racists' enormous psychological resistance to racial equality while also militating against any tendency toward African American self-effacement.

The sheer, unabated repetition of this citation generated an additional effect for later rhetors. By invoking the passage, speakers could reassure black audiences aligning themselves with the rhetorical tradition of predecessors like Equiano, Jones, Sarah Grimke, and Douglass.. During the civil rights era, Johns, Borders, and Mays demonstrated their worthiness in part by composing texts through a process of diachronic collaboration with their exemplars while passing the same rhetorical baton to their successors. Civil rights orators validated themselves as astute interpreters of the Bible and able opponents of segregation by reaffirming and extending the well-entrenched practice of asserting racial equality through a single, already prized sentence from their shared, sacralized text. They created themselves and their listeners by enlisting audiences into a sturdy—and seemingly irrefutable—tradition of religious protest. For that reason, even as the language of this specific argument-by-citation remained largely unchanged, the argument itself gained the additional impact of ratifying a speaker or writer as a capable biblical interpreter and an able torchbearer of a treasured rhetorical tradition that stoutly resisted white supremacy. Grasping the formidable intertext created by this argument-by-citation means defying not only nationalist categories of analysis but also the longstanding and largely unquestioned practice of dividing British and American culture and history into distinct conceptual and chronological units, such as the Scientific Revolution, the Enlightenment, British Romanticism, the American Revolutionary Period, Jacksonian America, Transcendentalism, the Civil War, Reconstruction, and post-World War I Modernity. Such an intertext prompts startling questions: Why does this argument keep replicating itself without regard to these familiar conceptual and chronological categories? How do the Scientific Revolution, the Enlightenment, Romanticism, and Reconstruction actually differ from post-World War I Modernity? Or do they? Does the unspeakable tragedy and catastrophe of weed-choked centuries of slavery and segregation problematize such designations and categories? Were Lincoln and the Civil War useless? Is it even possible to understand the texts of Fox in England in 1676 and Hamer in Mississippi in 1976 as separate from each other? Perhaps they were living in the same place and in the same time period attacking the same problem—white supremacy. Do such categories as the Scientific Revolution, the Enlightenment, Romanticism, Transcendentalism, and post-World War I Modernity only matter to those who ignore black people?

In order to comprehend the discourse of these allegedly distinct periods, scholars need to confront and to conceptualize an often-repeated biblical argument-by-citation that formed a huge rhetorical intertext that stretched across the Atlantic and persisted literally three hundred years. Only by adding a diachronic dimension to a Transatlantic paradigm similar to Gilroy's can researchers be able to understand so many rhetors' continual reliance on *Acts* 17:26 and its effect of dissolving familiar conceptual and chronological categories. Just as *Acts* 17:26 straddled the Atlantic, so must scholars, who need to grasp the seamless fabric of interargumentation created by British and American abolitionists and reaffirmed and extended by King, Hamer, and other civil rights orators.

NOTES

1. See, for example, Levine; Genovese; Glaude; Miller, *Voice*; Miller, *Martin*; Brooks, *A Voice*; and Selby. Selby devotes his entire book to analyzing King's reconfiguration of African Americans' traditional equation of their struggle to that of the biblical Hebrews enslaved in Pharaoh's Egypt.

2. In the first translation of the Bible into English—completed in 1395—John Wyclif rendered *Acts* 17:26 as follows: "And [God] made of one all the kind of men to inhabit all the face of the earth . . . ." Translating the Bible into English in 1525, William Tyndale presented *Acts* 17:26 as follows: "God made of one blood all nations. . . ." Note that, by introducing the word "blood" into his translation of this passage, Tyndale diverged from Wyclif. Later translators copied Tyndale's wording into the Coverdale Bible (1539), the Geneva Bible (1560), the Bishop's Bible (1568), and the exceedingly popular King James Bible (1611). Like the Wyclif Bible, the Douay-Rheims Bible (1582) omits the word "blood" from this verse. So do several recent translations. For the purposes of radicals who favored this passage, Tyndale's choice of the word "blood" for his translation proved pivotal. Without the word "blood," *Acts* 17:26 sounds bland and less-than-quotable. As far as I can tell, no radical ever cited the Wyclif or Douay-Rheims translations or more recent translations that also lack the word "blood." Borders, however, paraphrased the passage while managing to omit the word "blood."

3. For Equiano's reliance on Benezet, see Carretta 319 and Jackson 194.

4. Copies of Border's two locally published, now rare books are in the author's collection.

5. Inasmuch as Mays had earlier written about Equiano's autobiography, Mays may have known that Equiano cited *Acts* 17:26 as a bulwark against slavery. See Mays, *The Negro's God* 109–110.

6. See Hamer, "I Don't Mind" 4; Hamer, "To Tell" 88; Hamer, "What" 82–83; and Hamer, "We're" 49. Hamer also cited *Acts* 17:26 in her unpublished "It's Later Than You Think." See Brooks, *A Voice* 219, 292.

7. In both versions of "Paul's Letter to American Christians," King announces that Paul delivered the words of *Acts* 17:26 on Mars Hill ("Paul's Letter," *Papers* 343; "Paul'ss Letter," *Strength* 142). On another occasion, King proudly relates that, on a trip to Greece, he visited Mars Hill, which he identifies as the location of Paul's sermon ("Palm Sunday" 147). Certainly he regarded Mars Hill as a significant Christian site. Although most of the radicals whom I discuss in this essay do not directly mention either Paul or Mars Hill, many of the biblically literate members of their audiences had read *Acts* and realized that this verse came from Paul on Mars Hill. Speakers and writers usually did not feel obliged to remind them.

8. This point is so obvious that most radicals who quote *Acts* 17:26 leave it implicit. Sewell (7) and Woolman (274), however, explicitly relate Paul's statement to the story of Adam and Eve in *Genesis*.

Works Cited

Benezet, Anthony. *A Short Account of That Part of Africa*. 1762. Evans Early Imprint Collection. 6 June 2015.

Borders, William Holmes. "'All Blood Is Red.'" *Seven Minutes at the 'Mike' in the Deep South: "I Am Somebody."* 1943. Atlanta: Arnold's, 1980. 16-18. Print.

—. "The Way Out." *Television Sermons on M.S.B.* Atlanta: n.p., n.d. 102–19. Print.

Brooks, Meagan Parker. *A Voice that Could Stir an Army: Fannie Lou Hamer and the Rhetoric of the Black Freedom Movement*. Jackson: UP of Mississippi, 2014. Print.

—. "An Interview with Vergie Hamer Faulkner." In Brooks and Houck, 194–209.

Brooks, Meagan Parker, and Davis Houck, eds. *The Speeches of Fannie Lou Hamer: To Tell It Like It Is*. Jackson: UP of Mississippi, 2011. Print.

Burke, Kenneth. *Attitudes toward History*. 1937. Berkeley: U of California P, 1984. Print.

—. *Permanence and Change*. 1935. Berkeley: U of California P, 1984. Print.

Carretta, Vincent. *Equiano, the African: Biography of a Self-Made Man*. New York: Penguin, 2007. Print.

Ceplair, Larry, ed. *The Public Years of Sarah and Angelina Grimke: Selected Writings, 1835-1839*. New York: Columbia UP, 1989. Print.

Clarkson, Thomas. *An Essay on the Slavery and Commerce of the Human Species, Particularly the African*. 1788. Arizona State University. Hayden Library. Eighteenth Century Collections. Web. 6 June 2015.

Davis, David Brion. *Inhuman Bondage: The Rise and Fall of Slavery in the New World*. New York: Oxford UP, 2006. Print.

Douglass, Frederick. "Speech at Glasgow, Scotland." 1846. *Negro Orators and Their Orations*. Ed. Carter Woodson. Washington, DC: Associated Publishers, 1925. 170–78. Print.

—. "What to the Slave is the Fourth of July?" 1852. *The Oxford Frederick Douglass Reader*. Ed. William Andrews. New York: Oxford UP, 1996. 108–130. Rpt. in Foner and Branham.246–28.Print.

Equiano, Oladauh. *The Interesting Narrative of the Life of Olaudah Equiano, or Gustavus Vassa, the African, Written by Himself*. 1789. Ed. Werner Sollors. New York: Norton, 2001. Print.

Foner, Philip and Robert Branham, eds. *Lift Every Voice: African American Oratory, 1787-1900*.Tuscaloosa: U of Alabama P, 1998. Print.

Fox, George. *Gospel, Family-Order: Being a Short Discourse Concerning the Ordering of Families, both of Whites, Blacks, and Indians*. 1676. Arizona State U. Hayden Library. Hayden Microforms. Film 3754. Web. 15 June 2015.

Genovese, Eugene. *Roll, Jordan, Roll: The World the Slaves Made*. New York: Vintage, 1976. Print.

Gilroy, Paul. *The Black Atlantic: Modernity and Double Consciousness*. Cambridge, MA: Harvard UP, 1993. Print.

Glaude, Eddie. *Exodus!: Religion, Race, and Nation in Early Nineteenth-Century Black America*.Chicago: U of Chicago P, 2000. Print.

Godwyn, Morgan. *The Negro's & Indians Advocate, Suing for Their Admission to the Church*. Arizona State U. Hayden Library. Hayden Microforms. Film 3754. Web. 15 June 2015.

Goldenberg, David, *The Curse of Ham: Race and Slavery in Early Judaism, Christianity and Islam.*Princeton, NJ: Princeton UP, 2003. Print.

Grimke, Angelina. "Appeal to the Christian Women of the South." 1836. Ceplair 36–79.

Grimke, Sarah. "An Epistle to the Clergy of the Southern States." 1836.Ceplair 90–115.

Hamer, Fannie Lou. "I Don't Mind My Light Shining." 1963. Brooks and Houck. 3–6.

—. "To Tell It Like It Is." 1969. Brooks and Houck 86–93.

—. "What Have We to Hail?" 1968. Brooks and Houck 74–83.

—. "We're on Our Way!" 1964. Brooks and Houck 46–56.

Jackson, Maurice. *Let This Voice Be Heard: Anthony Benezet, Father of Atlantic Abolitionism*. Philadelphia: U of Penn P, 2009. Print.

Johns, Vernon. "Transfigured Moments." 1925. Simmons and Thomas 401–11.

Jones, Absalom. "A Thanksgiving Sermon." 1808. Foner and Branham 73–79. Rpt. in Simmons and Thomas. 69-76.

King, Martin Luther, Jr. "For All . . . A Non-Segregated Society: A Message for Race Relations Sunday." 1957. *The Papers of Martin Luther King, Jr.* Vol. 4. Eds. Clayborne Carson, et al. Berkeley: U of California P, 2000. 123–31. Print.

—. "I Have a Dream." 1963. *American Rhetoric*. N.p., n.d. Web. 15 June 2015.

—. "A Look to the Future." 1957. *The Papers of Martin Luther King, Jr.* Vol. 4. Ed. Clayborne Carson, et al. Berkeley: U of California P, 2000. 269–276. Print.

—. "Palm Sunday Sermon on Mohandas K. Gandhi." 1959. *The Papers of Martin Luther King, Jr.* Vol. 5. Ed. Clayborne Carson, et al. Berkeley: U of California P, 2005. 145–57. Print.

—. "Paul's Letter to American Christians." 1956. *The Papers of Martin Luther King, Jr.* Ed. Clayborne Carson, et al. Vol. 6. Berkeley: U of California P, 2007. 338–46. Print.

—. "Paul's Letter to American Christians." *Strength to Love*. New York: Harper, 1963. 138–46. Print.

—. "To Wilbert J. Johnson." *The Papers of Martin Luther King, Jr: Birth of a New Age*. Vol. 3. Ed. Clayborne Carson, et al. Berkeley: U of California, 1997. 378–79. Print.

Levine, Lawrence. *Black Culture and Black Consciousness*. New York: Oxford UP, 1977. Print.

Mays, Benjamin. "The Church Amidst Ethnic and Racial Tensions." 1954. *Dr. Benjamin E. Mays Speaks: Representative Speeches of a Great American Orator*. Ed. Freddie Colston. Lanham, MD: UP of America, 2002. 213–223. Print. Rpt. in *Rhetoric, Religion, and the Civil Rights Movement*. Ed. Davis Houck and David Dixon. Waco, TX: Baylor UP, 2006. 56–64. Print.

—. *The Negro's God as Reflected in His Literature*. 1938. New York: Russell, 1968. Print.

Miller, Keith D. *Martin Luther King's Biblical Epic: His Final, Great Speech.* Jackson: UP of Mississippi, 2012. Print.

—. *Voice of Deliverance: The Language of Martin Luther King, Jr, and Its Sources.* Second edition. Athens: U of Georgia P, 1996. Print.

Phillips, Wendell. "The Philosophy of the Abolition Movement." 1853. *Critical Situations: A Rhetoric for Writing in Communities.* Ed. Sharon Crowley and Michael Stancliff. New York: Pearson, 2008. 341–71. Print.

Selby, Gary. *Martin Luther King and the Rhetoric of Freedom: The Exodus Narrative in America's Struggle for Civil Rights.* Waco, TX: Baylor UP, 2008. Print.

Sellers, Charles. "Foreword." *Of One Blood: Abolitionism and the Origins of Racial Equality.* By Paul Goodman. Berkeley: U of California P, 1998. Print.

Sewell, Samuel. *The Selling of Joseph: A Memorial.* 1700. Amherst, MA: U of Massachusetts P, 1969. Print.

Simmons, Martha and Frank Thomas, eds. *Preaching with Sacred Fire: An Anthology of African American Sermons, 1750 to the Present.* New York: Norton, 2010. Print.

Weld, Theodore. *The Bible against Slavery.* 1837. Detroit: Negro History P, 1970. Print.

Woolman, John. *Some Considerations on the Keeping of Negroes.* 1754. New York: Arno P, 1969. Print.

7 "Carry Your Green Book With You": The Green Book as Representative Anecdote

Elizabethada A. Wright

In *Rhetorical Landscapes in America*, Gregory Clark uses the work of Kenneth Burke to illustrate the rhetorical functions of American landscape and tourism of that landscape. Clark describes Burke's trip across the United States by stating, "it always is for an American, a public experience that constitutes anew one's understanding of self and one's place within the imagined community that is the home nation" (126). According to Clark, Burke—like all Americans—experienced "a shared sense of national identity . . . through the individual experience of touring a common national landscape" (18). Clark argues that Burke's touring, like that of all Americans, functioned as a kind of epideictic rhetoric, prompting "individuals to make themselves over in the image of the collective identity that they find symbolized in their national landscape" (25). Within his argument, Clark illustrates how the American landscape acts as a representative anecdote, or a public rhetorical project "of constituting in diverse and divergent individuals a shared sense of national identity" (147). Clark's work is outstanding as it explicates how the landscape works as a representative anecdote of a nation, a symbol that captures the essence of America, and how this rhetorical process "enable[s] Americans to use the symbolic landscapes of their nation to teach each other who . . . they collectively are" (26). However, Clark does not quite succeed in explaining how *all* of America could experience the representative anecdotes of America's symbolic landscapes.

While pre-Civil Rights African Americans certainly could vicariously tour the landscape, they would almost certainly not have had the same experience Burke had when they became actual tourists. Jim Crow laws, self-appointed vigilantes, and hostile cities made the African American experience of tourism completely different from that of White Americans.[1] Still, Clark's understanding of how tourism of American scenery constitutes a collective identity for Americans is not moot for this population of America. What this essay demonstrates is how a travel guide, colloquially called the *Green Book* and created by Victor H. Green for an African American audience, constituted for its readers a socially conservative middle class identity. Agreeing with Meagan Monahan who, in her thesis on the *Green Book*, argues that the book "supported a particular image of the black traveler, which ultimately reflected the black middle class way of life" (42), I argue the *Book* did more than support and reflect this middle-class black America: it gave African Americans the "imagined community that is the home nation" that much of white America tried to deny blacks. Acting as a representative anecdote, the *Green Book* worked to be capable of "constituting in diverse and divergent individuals a shared sense of national identity" (Clark 147)

In this essay, I will briefly describe the Jim Crow America that prohibited traveling African Americans from sharing a national identity that Caucasian Americans created via their tourism. I then provide a brief history of the *Green Book*, a text that was published from 1936 to 1963 under various similar titles and in many ways defies generic categorization. Finally, I detail how this text instructed its readers to create for themselves a socially conservative, but idealized, America that they were very much a part of. Recognizing that black Americans did and desired to cross cultures in order to interact with other communities, the *Green Book* advocated a conservative approach to ending racism, working to make (and waiting for) the white population to desire to also cross cultures and accept otherness.

I

In outlining the purpose of his book's chapters, Clark states American landscapes do "important rhetorical work by enabling many individual Americans to encounter landscapes that symbolized the national community" (25–26). When this experience was vicarious, African Americans of the first half of the twentieth century could encounter the landscape, experience the symbols, and be part of the nation. However, when African Americans got on the Lincoln Highway or hopped on a train to visit Yellowstone to physically experience the landscape, they could not "feel at home together in the same imagined America" that White America could (26).

In his autobiography, current Alabama Congressional Representative John Lewis describes his first long trip as a child and the preparations that excluded African Americans from the rhetorical touring Clark describes:

> There would be no restaurants for us to stop at . . . so we carried our restaurant right in the car with us . . . Stopping for gas and to use the bathroom took careful planning. Uncle Otis had made this trip before, and he knew which places along the way offered "colored" bathrooms and which were better to just pass on by. Our map was marked and our route planned that way, by the distances between service stations where it would be safe for us to stop. (38)

When Lewis states that his uncle knew where "it would be safe" to stop, he uses no hyperbole. Stopping their cars in the wrong place could mean torture and death to African Americans.

A white collective anxiety over African American leisure was yet another factor that hindered African Americans from the same kinds of experiences of the American landscape that white Americans had. Despite the fact that African Americans had done significant amounts of difficult labor on Southern plantations, in Northern industrial locations, and within homes all across the country, white popular culture in America portrayed African Americans as lazy and carefree.

For example, the printers Currier and Ives, well-known through-out the East Coast for their bucolic scenes of America and cited by Clark as creators of picturesque scenes of landscape (57), rarely portray African Americans. However, when they do, as in the "Darktown Series," the printers present African Americans as "completely incapable of advancing beyond their previous condition of servitude" (LeBeau 71). Illustrations of firefighting brigades, horse races, lawn parties, and church services all portray African Americans aping Caucasian customs—and failing comically and miserably. One in this series is particularly relevant. A two-part illustration, entitled "Darktown Tourists," presents threadbare African Americans heading out on a trip and returning contemptuously to dismiss the other African Americans (LeBeau 76). This illustration thus appears to argue that black tourists "didn't know their place" and would not reintegrate well if they engage in rhetorical touring.

II

Yet many African Americans, like Rep. Lewis' uncle, did not let all these hindrances stop their tourism. Victor H. Green was one such person. As an employee for the US Postal Service, Green was among the African American elite with time, money, and means.[2] According to an article published on the twentieth anniversary of the *Green Book*'s debut, Green conceived his idea to publish a travel guide for an African American audience in 1932 "when, not only himself but several friends and acquaintances complained of the difficulties encountered; often times painful embarrassments suffered which ruined a vacation or business trip" (Dashiell 5). Using his surname for the book's title (a title that also happened to be the name of a popular guide for whites during the early decades of the twentieth century (Liedholm)), Green then partnered with a friend to publish a small, local pamphlet. The purpose of the pamphlet was to tell its African American readers where they would be welcome during their travels. According to this narrative, modestly describing the threats to traveling African Americans as "painful embarrassments," the demand for the pamphlet was so widespread "that by the following year [the *Green Book*] became a national institution" (Dashiell 5). The demand for the *Green Book* was also matched by its reputation: in "Correspondence to the Publisher" from the 1940 *Green Book*, the reader William Smith wrote, "Many of my friends have joined me in admitting that 'The Negro Motorist Green Book' is a credit to the Negro Race. It is a book badly needed among our Race since the advance of the motor age . . . . We earnestly believe 'The Negro Motorist Green Book' will mean as much if not more to us as the A.A.A. means to the white race" (2).

Figure 1. From the 1940 *Green Book*, this advertisement encourages its readers to think of themselves as people who are a part of the "talk of the town" with their well-pressed suits serviced by other people with "a smile."

It meant so much to its readers because the *Green Book* provided listings of businesses in all fifty states—as well as in Bermuda, Mexico, and Canada—businesses who were happy to receive black travelers, and it became increasingly indispensable to African Americans, though few whites had (or have) ever heard of it. However, the *Green Book* also acted as a representative anecdote with its editorial comments, selection of photographs and illustrations, advertisements that asked its readers to identify themselves as and to work toward being a genteel middle class community (fig. 8.1). In the narrative created by Green's periodical, African Americans could feel good about themselves as they appreciated the past, and looked to a promising future. This audience could teach white America a thing or two as it modeled for all (especially white) Americans, tolerance of difference.

From her or his first interaction with the text, the *Green Book* audience member knew s/he was above the lower class. The *Green Book* was not simply a periodical, since it made much of the fact that it was "not sold in newsstands but in bookstores" (EXPLANATION 4), it could be purchased via agents, or it could be obtained at "schools, colleges, Y.M.C.A.'s, Y.W.C.A.'s, Beauty Parlors and Barber Shops" (4). It was a "Guide," a "book." With this initial interaction of purchasing his *Book*, Green made his publication different. Instead of a newspaper or other kind of periodical, something picked up on the street corner to be discarded at the end of the day, the *Green Book* was something to be treasured, something that was part of an educational and cultural experience.[3] If people were unfamiliar with books, stores, or institutions like the YMCA, they could become familiar with them via the *Green Book*. Additionally, Green provided the means for social climbing to any potential audience members who thought they could not join this elite, literary audience. Green even suggests these potential audience members work as agents promoting the *Book*:

> You'll earn money—Yes, even if you've never tried before. Because people want to buy our guides. Never has there been a greater demand than now.—People don't know where to purchase them—We make it possible for you to make the sale. Join our agents staff [sic] now. Write for information on how to get started, so that you can make some easy money with little or no effort. ("EASY" inside front cover)

When readers purchased and opened their *Green Book*, bound with a cover and filled with illustrations of travel, the readers found the *Book*'s interior full of listings by state, city, and (eventually) country of locales that would welcome traveling African Americans. Initially, the *Green Book* presented its readers with places of lodging only: however, it eventually printed names of restaurants, barber shops, garages, funeral homes and the like. In addition to cataloguing businesses, the *Green Book* included numerous advertisements, some paid for by commercial industries and many promoting the *Green Book* itself. Most significantly, each *Green Book* offered significant editorial commentary on the value of the *Book*, advice for traveling, and various highlighted tourist locations.[4]

One such editorial commentary discusses New Jersey's seashore, "within easy reach of New York City" ("New Jersey"). As the commentary describes the boardwalk and entertainment, it adds "You've earned your vacation, now enjoy it!" With this encouragement, the *Green Book* commentary counters images such as that offered by Currier and Ives in the Darktown series. The *Green Book* emphasizes that its readers have earned their vacation and invites them to see themselves as members of the middle class, well deserving of leisure. Another article in a 1956 *Green Book* builds on this message: "TWO WEEKS WITH PAY." The article tells the *Book's* readers that they not only deserve a vacation, they deserve to be paid for their leisure. And they will get what they deserve via the *Green Book*. The *Book* both helps its readers' planning and enables them to envision what they deserve.

Like the narratives discussed by Clark, the *Green Book* provided its readers with instructions on "social interaction and community life" that Green believed his readers should follow. Repeatedly, the *Green Book* subtly tells readers how to behave as it creates an ideal for the readers to identify with. For example, the editorial commentary advises readers what to wear for autumn travel, suggesting "perhaps a lightweight coat or wrap for chilly evenings" (54). The text then becomes more specific: "Casual but conservative sportswear is in order. Keep the 'city' look. Abroad it is the American tourists' trademark" (54). The quote, thus, not only gives instructions on behavior, but also tells the reader that s/he is the typical "American tourist," and s/he must learn to play the part.

In its discussion of New Orleans, the *Green Book* celebrates the exclusiveness of certain African American social clubs: "To get in to one of the Mardi Gras Balls, they must know your grandparents and what they stood for. It is much easier to get into Buckingham Palace than it is to be invited to the Young Men's Illonios [sic] and the Old Men's Illonois [sic], they are out of the question" ("New Orleans" 27). Thus, the *Green Book* invites its audience to not only recognize that the Mardi Gras celebration is on par with those of the British royalty but that this African American community is better than any of the prosperous white communities. After all, people can go to Buckingham Palace more easily than they can go to the New Orleans' African-American social clubs.

Another way the *Green Book* promotes certain types of genteel social action is by subtly denigrating social action framed as being outside the *Green Book's* norms. For example, its 1954 discussion of San Francisco acknowledges some of the less respectful forms of entertainment but then tells the reader, "[f]rom the bawdy examples of San Francisco's hospitality, one may turn to more elegance and sophistication within a few short steps" ("Golden"17). Though these words are not explicit, their tone and content suggest that the "bawdy examples of San Francisco's hospitality" are not worthy the *Green Book* reader. The same commentary acknowledges that Chinatown had "brothels, gambling houses, opium dens and slums." However, the *Green Book* notes these brothels, gambling houses, opium dens, and slums were "destroyed in the great fire of 1906. Today exotic pagoda roof tops and iron grilled balconies appear side by side with American tin roof and straight fronts" (17-18). With its observation that the San Francisco of 1954's present was "tidy, serene and cordial" (13), the *Green Book* not so subtly makes its preference for pagoda over brothels known.

While the *Green Book* celebrates the move from past to present in this Chinatown narrative, other articles encourage their readers to envision themselves in an idealized past, a past somewhat rewritten. For example, the 1949 *Green Book* praises Pennsylvania's "nearly 300 covered bridges which have been preserved from the earlier times" (12) whereas the 1953 *Green Book* praises Louisville as a "colorful Bluegrass State ... with a rare blend of history, progress and tradition" (24), not mentioning this rare blend's reliance on slavery. Similarly, this article discusses Louisville's Churchill Downs and the mix of people watching the horse race as a celebration of democracy:

> Time has not dimmed the ardent desire of the Kentucky Derby's originator nor has it reduced the thrills, the fire, and the hospitality which it creates, but rather has contributed to the splendor and glory of one of America's great traditions . . . Democracy! (29)

The celebration overlooks, however, the traditional exploitation and then exclusion of African Americans in the "great traditions" of both the Kentucky Derby and American Democracy.[5]

This apparent amnesia, however, is a means that the *Green Book* uses to (using Clark's words) "constitute anew [its readers'] understanding and [their] place within the imagined community that is the home nation" (Clark 126). Mostly overlooking the legacy of slavery in its discussions of history, the *Book* encourages its readers to look forward confidently by presenting examples of a hopeful future. Repeatedly, the *Book* celebrates accomplishments of forward-thinking African American innovators. For example, embedded within this list of Chicago sites, the *Book* has an article about a town

near Chicago—Robbins, Illinois: "OWNED AND OPERATED BY NE-
GROES" (Sheppard 26, emphasis in original). Noting that the "opportunities for the Negro are unlimited" in this town because "of the absence of prejudice and restrictions" (26), the author strongly advises the readers to visit:
"IT IS WORTH THE TROUBLE TO GO OUT AND TAKE A LOOK
AT AN EXPERIMENT OF AN EXHIBITION OF WHAT NEGROES
WORKING TOGETHER CAN DO," especially when the town is run by
"straight thinking citizens who will refuse to get lost in a maze of politics and
internal strife" (27).

The amnesia appears to be part of the *Green Book*'s strategy to move its
audience to become "absent of prejudice and restrictions" despite the prejudice and restrictions that the readers continually face. Thus, the *Green Book*
creates and promotes very conservative images of community life, ones that
don't challenge the status quo—except in regard to race. One of the best
examples of Green's socially conservative agenda can be found in the *Green
Book* examples of what "negroes working together can do" as the *Green Book*
encourages African Americans to embrace a consumer culture. With advertisements from major companies such as Esso Standard Oil and Ford, articles written by representatives of these companies, photographs of ideal businesses, and suggestions for the audience to advertise (e.g., "What don't you
Advertize? Everbody reads the *Green Book*" on page 79 of the 1949 edition),
Green's *Book* mixes celebration of its own success with concern that all African Americans don't recognize their own consumer power.

Despite its middle-class conservative consumerism, the *Green Book* clearly aims to end Jim Crow. Continually, the text suggests middle-class conservative consumerism can end Jim Crow by arguing that African Americans
must make Caucasians recognize the potency of traveling blacks' business.
For example, a self-congratulatory article praising the *Green Book* observes:
"Through this guide a number of white business places have come to value
and desire your patronage" (Dashiell 7). Repeatedly the *Green Book* promotes the idea that by traveling and showing white people what respectable
consumers they are, African Americans can remedy the world. Thus, the
Green Book encourages its readers to live out a quote of Mark Twain's published on its 1949 cover: "Travel is Fatal to Prejudice."

Another goal of the *Green Book*'s conservative philosophy was tolerance
of difference. Over and over, the editorial commentary notes differing peoples and the appreciation the audience should have of these peoples. For example, a *Green Book* article states that New Orleans is "a melting pot for
peoples of several nationalities; being Spaniards, Frenchmen, Italians and
British" (1952 25). Including Europeans in this melting pot, the *Green Book*
also encourages its readers' tolerance of light-skinned others—despite the

light-skinned others' lack of tolerance for African Americans. Similarly, the 1953 issue inclusively presents a photograph of a racially integrated group—various black and white, well-dressed businessmen.

IV

Yet, the *Green Book* may not have been blind to the history of slavery. Instead, the *Green Book* may have united its African American audience in a shared community that recognized the "second sight," the "double consciousness," the "twoness" of African Americans, as described by W.E.B. du Bois. African Americans could only survive in racist America if they understood how white America saw them. Then, as now, the result of this "second-sight" is a kind of "double-consciousness" (45). African Americans can see what White America sees; additionally, African Americans have their own perspective of the world. Caucasian Americans do not have this ability, this "second-sight." The *Green Book* continually identified such a double-consciousness of the African American in oblique terms such as citing the "painful embarrassment of travel" or the frequent saying on the *Book*'s cover "Carry Your Green Book With You, You Might Need It" (e.g., 1952). Using these terms white readers would not understand, the *Green Book* created a representative anecdote that united its African American audience, helping them envision themselves as middle-class Americans, and teaching them to create this conservative community. Though this vision excluded white Americans, it only did so because white Americans were not people tolerant of difference, as the *Green Book* readers were. The *Green Book* then looked forward to a day when white people would also envision themselves as part of this middle-class community tolerant of difference, when the "difficulties" and "anxieties" that the *Green Book* obliquely references would not exist, when black people would see what the white people see and vice versa, when the *Green Book* would no longer need to exist.[6]

This ideal goal was part of the *Green Book*'s representational anecdote. Like Timothy Dwight's *Travels in New England and New York*, the public experience of the Lincoln Highway, and the children's books like *New York Scenes* discussed by Clark—the *Green Book* provided its audience with a narrative that became a symbol of a collective experience that individuals enact for themselves to "constitute" a public identity (Clark 107-08). *The Green Book* provided a "presentation of an experience of itinerary" (Clark 23) in the form of commentary and illustrations. Additionally, specifically like Dwight's narrative as described by Clark, Green offered his audience (to use Clark's words, slightly revised) inviting images of the sort of social interaction and community life he believed would follow if his...principles were enacted....[Green] invites [his] readers to make themselves over in the image of this America that it so vividly describes, and seems to assume that once they have so identified themselves, they will eventually work to realize the community that together they have been prompted to imagine. (Clark 23)

The *Green Book* invited readers—with its editorial comments, selection of photographs and illustrations, and advertisements—to identify themselves as middle-class consumers and then to continually work together to be this middle class community. His *Book* helped its audience reenvision itself as hardworking, genteel Americans. In the narrative created by Green's periodical, African Americans were anything but low-class laborers; they could feel good about themselves as they appreciated the past but looked to a promising future. This audience could teach white America a thing or two as it modeled for all (especially white) Americans tolerance of difference. Like the representational anecdotes described by Clark, the *Green Book*s are not totally inclusionary. The less-well-heeled are not included in the world created by this unique text. Nevertheless, the *Green Book* looks toward a world that is not racially defined, toward an ideal and unified America, when all Americans with the means to travel can do so "without embarrassment."

NOTES

1. This paper focuses on the discrimination facing African American travelers prior to the Civil Rights era, when the world drastically changed for African Americans. Outside the scope of this article are the conditions of African Americans in the post-civil rights period, though it is clear that discrimination did not end. The twenty-first century still presents challenges to African American travelers, and unfortunately phenomena such as "driving while black" still exist.

2. See Earl Hutchinson re: the Postal Service having some of the highest paying jobs for African American employees.

3. This paper does not explore the significance of equating "Beauty Parlors and Barber Shops" with "schools, colleges, Y.M.C.A.'s, Y.W.C.A.'s," although there is some excellent research on the role of these beauty institutions within the African American community (e.g., Boutte and Hill as well as Alexander).

4. For additional accounts of why African Americans could not share white Kenneth Burke's experience, see also Boutte; Foster; Kahrl; Johnson; C. and R. Lewis; Loewen; Seiler; Smith, Ellis and Aslanian, and Wilkerson.

5. See Lisa K. Winkler for more information.

6. Thanks to Suzanne Bordelon, Martha Cheng, and Sharron Rowlett for their support and comments. Also, thanks to the University of Minnesota Grant-in-Aid of Research, Artistry & Scholarship Program for its financial support.

WORKS CITED

Alexander, Bryant Keith. "Fading, Twisting, and Weaving: An Interpretive Ethnography of the Black Barbershop as Cultural Space." *Qualitative Inquiry* 9.1 (2003): 105–129. Web. 11 June 2015.

Boutte, Gloria Swindler and Edward L. Hill. "African American Communities: Implications for Culturally Relevant Teaching." *The New Educator* 2(2006): 311–329. *Taylor & Francis Online*. Web. 11 June 2015.

Clark, Gregory. *Rhetorical Landscapes in America: Variations on a Theme from Kenneth Burke*. Columbia: U of South Carolina P, 2004. Print.

Dashiell, Novera C. "Many Happy Returns." *The Negro Travelers' Green Book*. Ed. and Pub. Victor H. Green. New York, 1956: 5–7. Print. Schomburg Center for Research in Black Culture. 27 July 2013.

Du Bois, W.E. Burghardt. *The Souls of Black Folk*. New York: Signet, 1995. Print.

"EASY MONEY FOR YOU!" *The Negro Travelers' Green Book: The Guide to Travel and Vacations*. Ed. and Pub. Victor H. Green. New York,1954: inside front cover. Print. Schomburg Center for Research in Black Culture. 27 July 2013.

"EXPLANATION." *The Negro Travelers' Green Book: The Guide to Travel and Vacations*. Ed. and Pub. Victor H. Green. New York,1954.

Foster, Mark S. "In the Face of 'Jim Crow': Prosperous Blacks and Vacations, Travel and Outdoor Leisure, 1890-1945." *The Journal of Negro History* 84.2 (Spring 1999): 130–149. Print.

"The Golden Gate: San Francisco, Calif." *The Negro Travelers' Green Book: The Guide to Travel and Vacations*. Ed. and Pub. Victor H. Green. New York, 1954: 11–18. Print. Schomburg Center for Research in Black Culture. 27 July 2013.

Hutchinson, Earl, Sr. *A Colored Man's Journey Through 20th Century Segregated America*. Chicago: Middle Passage Press, 2000. Print.

Johnson, Charles S. *Patterns of Negro Segregation*. New York: Harper, 1943. Print.

Kahrl, Andrew W. "'The Slightest Semblance of Unruliness': Steamboat Excursions, Pleasure Resorts, and the Emergence of Segregation Culture on the Potomac River." *Journal of Negro History* (March 2008): 1108–1136. Web 15 June 2013.

LeBeau, Bryan F. "African Americans in Currier and Ives's America: The Darktown Series." *Journal of American and Comparative Cultures* 23.1 (Spring 2000): 71–83. Print.

Lewis, Catherine M and J. Richard Lewis, eds. *Jim Crow America: A Documentary History*. Fayetteville: University of Arkansas, 2009. Print.

Lewis, John with Michael D'Orso. *Walking with the Wind: A Memoir of the Movement*. New York: Harcourt Brace, 1998. Print.

Liedholm, Carl. "Clason's Green Guides." *The Legend* 50 (2011): 1, 9–11. Web. Road Maps Collector's Association. 14 November 2014.

Loewen, James W. *Sundown Towns: A Hidden Dimension of American Racism*. New York: New Press, 2005. Print.

"Louisville, Kentucky." *The Negro Travelers Green Book*. Ed. and Pub. Victor H. Green. New York, 1953: 24–29. Print. Schomburg Center for Research in Black Culture. 27 July 2013.

Monahan, Meagan. *"The Negro Motorist Green Book: An International Travel Guide": Following in the 21ˢᵗ Century the Travel Guide of the Jim Crow Years*. Upperclass Monroe Scholars Summer Research Project. 21 May 2013._

"New Jersey." *The Green Book Vacation Guide*. Ed. and Pub. Victor H. Green. New York, 1949: 10. Print. Schomburg Center for Research in Black Culture. 27 July 2013.

"New Orleans." *The Negro Travelers Green Book*. Ed. and Pub. Victor H. Green. New York, 1952:23–29. Print. Schomburg Center for Research in Black Culture. 27 July 2013.

"Pennsylvania." *The Green Book Vacation Guide*. Ed. and Pub. Victor H. Green. New York, 1949: 12. Print. Schomburg Center for Research in Black Culture. 27 July 2013.

Rugh, Susan Sessions. *Are We There Yet? The Golden Age of American Family Vacations*. Lawrence: University of Kansas, 2008. Print

Seiler, Cotton. "So That We as a Race Might Have Something Authentic to Travel By": African American Automobility and Cold-War Liberalism. *American Quarterly* 58.4 (December 2006): 1091–117. *Project Muse*. Web. 15 June 2013.

Sheppard, George W. "Robbins, Illinois Steps Out In Front." *The Negro Motorist Green Book*. Ed. and Pub. Victor H. Green. New York, 1949: 26–27. Print. Schomburg Center for Research in Black Culture. 27 July 2013.

Smith, Alfred Edgar. "Through the Windshield." *Opportunity: Journal of Negro Life* 11.5(1933): 142–144. Print.

Smith, Stephen, Kate Ellis, and Sasha Aslanian. *Remembering Jim Crow*. American Public Media, 2013. Web. 6 November 2013.

Smith, Wm. "Correspondence to the Publisher." *The Negro Motorist Green-Book*. Ed. and Pub. Victor H. Green. New York, 1940: 2. Print. Special Collections, Robert James Terry Library, Texas Southern University. 22 July 2014.

Terrell, Mary Church. "Society Among the Colored People of Washington." *The Voice of the Negro* June (1904): 150–156. Print.

"...TWO WEEKS WITH PAY." *The Negro Travelers' Green Book*. Ed. and Pub. Victor H. Green. New York, 1956: 54-56. Print. Schomburg Center for Research in Black Culture. 27 July 2013.

Wilkerson, Isabel. *The Warmth of Other Suns: The Epic Story of America's Great Migration*. New York: Random House, 2010. Print.

Winkler, Lisa K. "The Kentucky Derby's Forgotten Jockeys." Smithsonian.com. Smithsonian Institution 24 April 2009. Web. 6 November 2013.

8 GERTRUDE STEIN ON THE BORDERS OF IDENTITY

Patrick Shaw

At any moment when you are you you are without the memory of yourself because if you remember yourself while you are you you are not for the purposes of creating you.

—Gertrude Stein

While in many ways controversial, Gertrude Stein's place in American literary modernism is secure. Even though her own work was largely underappreciated for much of her career—until the extraordinary success of *The Autobiography of Alice B. Toklas* in 1933— she nonetheless was something of an oracle, the destination of a pilgrimage, for many (mostly male) American literary modernists in the decade after World War I. Her cultural reach also was significant in the art world, including a number of (mostly male) artists, most famously Pablo Picasso, with whom she maintained a long and complicated relationship until her death in 1946. Even though *The Autobiography* brought her to the attention of a more general reading public, before its publication she already had produced a significant portfolio of work in a wide range of genres, including fiction, drama, poetry, opera, as well as several *sui generis* texts, such as her portraits of friends and historical figures.

As controversial as her work was to many of the literary aesthetes of the era, her work in rhetoric was, and remains, largely overlooked. The number of critical texts that address any sort of rhetorical presence in Stein's work is small indeed. A search of the MLA bibliography using the terms "Gertrude Stein" and "rhetoric" produces only sixteen entries, four of which are dissertations, and two of which are articles in French. The earliest of all of those entries is from 1972. Only Sharon J. Kirsch has managed to develop a more sustained focus on Stein's contributions to rhetoric, publishing two articles on the subject in the last six years and most recently a book, *Gertrude Stein and the Reinvention of Rhetoric*. The reasons for this oversight are manifold, but two of the more prominent ones regard rhetoric's declining reputation in the early twentieth century and its contentious relationship to aesthetics. It would be a mistake to suggest that Stein sought the kind of recognition in the realm of rhetoric that she eventually gained in the world of aesthetics, but it also would be a mistake to suggest that Stein was wholly unaware of the rhetorical implications of her work, especially the implications readily apparent in her lectures and the *sui generis Geographical History of America or the Relation of Human Nature to the Human Mind*. Despite this oversight, as Kirsch argues, "Placing Gertrude Stein's writing practices in the rhetorical traditions of the nineteenth century reveals a Gertrude Stein who is not necessarily or not only a literary figure, but rather, a twentieth-century rhetorician who refigures past traditions to teach a new century how to write" ("Delivers" 285). Moreover, Stein's contributions to rhetoric are not limited to the belletristic and to the reconceptualization of classical principles. They also include an epistemological strain that anticipates the deconstructive turn. Still, Stein's rhetoric exists on the borders of rhetoric, or perhaps more precisely, is a liminal rhetoric, one that exists in the moments when rhetorical elements are related to one another.

Stein's epistemological rhetoric is constituted by a dialectic of identity that constructs the relations among writer, reader, and text, and constructs a negative dialectic between written text and spoken text and between the writer and her verbal image. These two dialectics enact a more general dialectic between identity and nonidentity. Despite the highly abstract qualities of this dialectic, it nonetheless has anthropological implications, for its philosophical tenets have their cognates in Stein's statuses as a Jew and a lesbian in modern Western culture. Simply put, her dialectic explores the boundaries of what human being is. Both of these statuses contribute in varying degrees and at various moments in a number of ways to her aesthetic and rhetorical canon. Complete explorations of their contributions to her dialectic would call for separate and extensive essays in and of themselves. Consequently, my inquiry here occurs on a more general and abstract level, focusing on Stein's place in twentieth-century rhetoric and her outlines of the basic rhetorical relations among writer, reader, and text. I will also briefly indicate some of the relations between the abstract, philosophical notions of identity and non-identity and Stein's anthropological realities. This dialectic situates Stein's work in a liminal moment, one that is not between one ethnic identity and another, one sexual identity and another, or one verbal art and another but between ethnicity and non-ethnicity, sexuality and non-sexuality, and rhetoric and non-rhetoric.

The dialectic between identity and nonidentity resonates in a number of ways throughout her work. The epigraph to this essay constitutes a particular instance of its enactment. The sentence is constructed via a technique that is not uncommon in Stein's work: its terms emphasize one form of signification while its unfolding meaning undermines that very signification. The sentence uses the pronouns "you" and "yourself" ten times, as though pointing emphatically at the reader, underscoring the reader not only as Other to Stein but as Other to the reader herself, while the sentence itself undermines this very identity, or any identity for that matter, of anyone in the process of writing. You are you while you are writing, but you are not aware that you are you while you are writing. If you try to remember who you are while you are writing, you will not be who you think you are; you will be—you are—Other to yourself. This Other is more you than the you by which you are identified. It is a creating and a created you, a constructed you. Stein thus locates the place of the Other, not in some external reality but in an internality, an inside of us—in the form of memory—that both helps to constitute the horizons of who we are while also announcing who we are not. So on the one hand, Stein clearly eschews identity; on the other, she clearly acknowledges its necessity to human being: identity enables us to define ourselves as Other to how we are perceived by Others and Other to ourselves as memories.

The dialectic between identity and nonidentity has both linguistic and anthropological implications. Linguistically, Stein sets writing against speaking. "What Are Master-pieces" begins:

> I was almost going to talk this lecture and not write and read it because all the lectures that I have written and read in America have been printed and although possibly for you they might even being read be as if they had not been printed still there is something about what has been written having been printed which makes it no longer the property of the one who wrote it and therefore there is no more

reason why the writer should say it out loud than anybody else and therefore one does not. (83-84)

In effect, she adds two more dimensions to the identity/nonidentity dialectic. One defines talking as Other to the writing self; the second defines the written as Other to the writing self. Or perhaps more accurately, the writing self is Other to the talker and to the written, for the writing self exists outside of identity, or at least has no awareness of identity. Identity functions as an inauthentic self that points to but does not circumscribe the writing self.

Anthropologically, Stein reconfigures the relation between self and Other. This reconfiguration points to the potential for a wholly new definition of what human being is. Stein's move here does not merely reverse the relation between self and Other so that Other is "self" and self is "Other": it turns that relation inside out, and it reverses the function of the dialectic. It is reversed to the extent that identity functions as Other to nonidentity. Conventionally, we assume that our being may be defined by an identity while our Other remains an ambiguous enigma, necessary to define ourselves but not wholly defined in itself, or, if it is defined, we can assume that that definition is inauthentic. Stein's statement asserts that the ambiguous Other is our "true identity" while the defined self is an inauthentic image of ourselves. The act of writing characterizes this ambiguous Other—the self in what she elsewhere calls the "continuous present"—while the self in memory—the image of the self in a past now— characterizes identity. Conventional identity is Other to Stein's identity, to Otherness; what distinguishes the two is their respective temporal locations. They are turned inside out with respect to consciousness. Again, conventionally, our self, our identity, is the locus of consciousness. We are who we are because we are aware of our own awareness. This is our self-consciousness, and this self-consciousness defines one side of the horizon circumscribing who we are. The Other is that which is outside of our consciousness. More precisely, it is the appresent other side of the horizon of our consciousness. It is appresent because we know it is there inferentially, just as we know the reverse side of a coin exists even though we can see only the obverse side. It is the Other precisely to the extent that it escapes our awareness of what it is exactly. For Stein, we are who we are precisely to the extent that we are unaware of our consciousness, to the extent that we are not self-conscious. It is not that we now see the reverse side of the coin instead of the obverse, but that we have no awareness of the coin's presence even though we face the reverse side of the coin. The moment we become aware of the coin, of the horizon, we return to identity and the obverse side of the coin. Who we are is not this identity constructed in self-awareness, but we can know who we are only to the extent that we acknowledge this self-aware identity. We can be who we are only to the extent that we remain unaware of who we are. Stein's dialectic is a negative dialectic: it does not merely pull apart the elements of a transcendental dialectic, identifying the elements that had been assimilated into a One; instead, it acknowledges that unity even as it undoes that unity.

Stein's rhetoric of identity contrasts with one of the more dominant notions of rhetoric in the modern era, namely, Kenneth Burke's rhetoric of identification. In fact, Burke distinguishes his notion of *rhetoric-as-identification* from his notion of *symbolic-as-identity*. The symbolic, as Burke briefly describes it, has a number of affinities with formalist poetics. Burke contrasts symbolic and rhetoric in *A Rhetoric of Motives*. The key term for rhetoric is *identification*, he asserts, "[b]ecause, to begin with 'identification' is, by the same token though roundabout, to confront the implications of *division.* . . . Identification is affirmed with earnestness precisely because there is division. If men were not apart from one another, there would be no need for the rhetorician to proclaim their unity" (22). By contrast—or perhaps as a complement—the key term for Burke's symbolic is *identity*:

> The thing's *identity* would here be its uniqueness as an entity in itself and by itself, a demarcated unit having its own particular structure. . . . The *Symbolic* [Burke's planned but unfinished companion volume to *A Rhetoric of Motives* and *A Grammar of Motives*] should deal with unique individuals, each its own peculiarly constructed act, or form. These unique 'constitutions' being capable of treatment in isolation, the *Symbolic* would consider them primarily in their capacity as singulars, each a separate universe of discourse" (21–2).

Burke then contrasts the two realms: "The individual should be at peace, in that the individual substances, or entities, or constituted acts are there considered in their uniqueness, hence outside the realm of conflict. For individual universes, as such, do not compete. . . . But insofar as the individual is involved in conflict with other individuals or groups, the study of this same individual would fall under the head of *Rhetoric*" (22-3). In effect, Burke places identity and identification in dialectical opposition to each other, figuring *identity* as a unity, a oneness that ironically divides a one from an other, and *identification* as a division, a partition that—ironically—unifies a one to others. Burke's rhetoric ultimately reconciles self to Other, emphasizing similarities and downplaying differences. Burke's broader dialectic assigns difference to the Symbolic, to poetics, and difference is expressed in the form of identity. By contrast, Stein situates difference as the predominant trope in her rhetoric. *Difference* refers to not only the relationship between self and

Other, but also to self and image of self, that is, the relationship between self and identity.

Despite their contrasting approaches to self and identity, Burke and Stein both effect theories of invention that are based in grammar. Kirsch argues that Stein "professes a theory of rhetorical grammar that correlates the study of grammar with rhetoric's first canon, invention" ("Suppose" 285). Because it associates the study of grammar with the canon of invention, Stein's rhetoric is structurally commensurate with Burke's, whose framework for the grammatical study of terms for substance, presented in *A Grammar of Motives*, likewise situates the study of grammar in the rhetorical canon of invention. Stein's rhetorical grammar is situated firmly within twentieth-century rhetorical traditions, even though her rhetorical grammar is not as easily reduced to a single heuristic, as powerful as that heuristic—Burke's pentad—may be.

The relation between grammar and invention is not the only quality that Stein's rhetoric shares with other twentieth-century rhetorical traditions. Richard McKeon argues that rhetoric in the twentieth century serves as the connecting link between poetry and philosophy, as it did during the twelfth century. McKeon holds that the problems facing Western civilization during the twentieth century are similar to those of the twelfth century, and the poets, philosophers, and rhetoricians of the twentieth century have coincidentally—or perhaps consequently—adopted similar themes as those of their twelfth-century counterparts. Poetry, and with it, philosophy and rhetoric, has "returned to themes similar to those of medieval poetry and to echoes of philosophical and theological discussion which recall that [human beings are] in a grave predicament, that words are ambiguous" (193). McKeon takes a rather pessimistic view of this twentieth-century reinvention of medieval arts and themes, concluding that "poets in the twentieth century convey a sense of treating philosophic problems, but their philosophy has become little more than a play with the color of language which medieval poets employed to express a philosophy" (193). Like McKeon, Stein's work situates rhetoric as the connecting link, the common method, between poetry and philosophy. She furthermore agrees that language is ambiguous and that humans are in a grave predicament, but her work poetically, philosophically, and rhetorically celebrates the playfulness of ambiguity and maintains an optimism regarding how this grave predicament will eventually turn out. Even in some of the darker moments of World War II, when she and Alice Toklas were living precariously in Vichy France, Stein maintained her optimism that Nazism would be defeated; that Paris would be saved; and, implicitly, that she and Toklas would be able to resume their lives as American expatriates in a free France. Such faith is expressed, however, not through a desire for clarity and identity, but in the attraction to ambiguity and the desire for nonidentity. For it is one thing to assert oneself in a crowd of many; but it is quite another thing to be singled out—that is, identified—by others for one's race, sexual orientation, or nationality, especially when such identities can cause death.

The attraction to ambiguity and the desire for nonidentity also reflect the place(s) of rhetoric, especially in the twentieth century. Rhetoric exists on the borders, between the edges of other arts and academic disciplines. "Rhetoric must always be read in the structural interplay with its neighbors (Grammar, Logic, Poetics, Philosophy)," Roland Barthes asserts. "[I]t is the play of the system, not each of its parts in itself, which is historically significant" ("The Old Rhetoric" 46). Stein too locates her rhetoric in this structural interplay, most broadly, between the presence of identity and its total absence—between which is the place of nonidentity—and in the tropic play between what she calls human nature and human mind.

Explaining what these terms may signify and how Stein may have arrived at them requires a little background on Stein's history—on what she might call her life in human nature. After the publication of *The Autobiography of Alice B. Toklas*, Stein embarked on a lecture tour of America. Kirsch documents Stein's careful efforts to manage her image during the tour and argues that "Stein's handling of the lecture tour itself [was] a theoretical performance of her art of inventive delivery" (256), thus further situating Stein in the rhetorical tradition. In some respects, her efforts were successful: she was met with much interest wherever she went, she spoke to packed rooms, and the tour resulted in even greater sales of *The Autobiography*.

In other respects, her efforts were a failure. After the publication and the tour, Stein felt her identity was compromised. While the image she presented was a carefully crafted one, Stein realized that the interpretations of that image were beyond her control. To return to the coin analogy I used earlier, it was not that she inferred the presence of the reverse side of the coin even though she could see only the obverse. Instead, the audiences' responses to her made her aware of the coin itself, of the horizon between her self and her Other. She thus manifested an identity—or one was manifested for her by the audiences—and her nonidentity—her writerly "self"—disappeared. She became conscious of her consciousness, and it had serious consequences for her.

One consequence, Catherine N. Parke notes, was that, for the first time in her life, she suffered a serious case of writer's block (554). Identity had usurped nonidentity. She could not forget who she was as she wrote. Moreover, Richard Bridgeman states that the success of *The Autobiography of Alice B. Toklas* led her to suspect the book was a sentimental one, and she knew "that she now possessed a commercial value" (276). Whatever she attempted to put to paper was not what she would define as writing. A second, more tangible consequence was that her relationship with Toklas suddenly possessed a public identity in ways that it apparently had not before. In 1937, after their book tour of America and an extended stay in the South of France, Stein and Toklas were evicted from 27 Rue de Fleurus. James R. Mellow argues that the circumstances surrounding their eviction are open to question. The landlord claimed he wanted his son, who was soon to be married, to move in to the apartment (Mellow 433). However, some speculate that Stein's newfound fame had brought too much attention to the Rue de Fleurus for her landlord's comfort—and too much attention to the all-too-obvious fact that the famous people who inhabited it were a Jewish lesbian couple. Once again, identity had usurped nonidentity. In the context of Stein's dialectic between identity and nonidentity, I want to address Stein and Toklas' eviction and its two aspects first, even though it occurred after Stein's bout of writer's block.

In terms of her Jewishness, the consequence to Stein comes not from *being* a Jew. Except perhaps during World War II, when she and Toklas lived in Vichy France, Stein did not deliberately hide her Jewishness. The consequence comes from *naming*—from giving an identity to—certain aspects of her character. As I have argued elsewhere, "Identifying herself as a Jew would, ironically, be a gesture towards assimilation, an assimilation that clearly has its limits, for while Stein, or any modernist Jew, could adopt many of the characteristics of Western culture, she could not, ultimately shed her Jewishness" (22). In fact, her Jewishness is evident in the construction of the Other in the passage with which I began this essay: "*When* you are you." This is the Other of time, not of space. "We are so accustomed to thinking of time and space as contrasting axes," Jonathan Boyarin argues, "that [the] emphasis on spatiality tends to marginalize discourses of temporal Othering. We speak of distant times, but not of places long ago. Different places exist simultaneously, but different times do not exist in the same place—except in the minds and writings of extraordinary individuals such as Walter Benjamin" (81-2) and, I would add, Gertrude Stein. "No one is ahead of his time," Stein writes in "Composition as Explanation," "it is only that the particular variety of creating his time is the one that his contemporaries refuse to accept" (*Masterpieces* 27). The Other here is not a location but a time, and the differences in time can characterize the distinction in the Western modern world between the (Christian) present and the present (Jewish) Other. While Stein's texts may not openly proclaim themselves as parts of a Jewish tradition, they nonetheless possess qualities that can easily situate them within such a tradition. The degree to which Stein's efforts to manage that aspect of her image are successful can be measured by the degree of ambiguity surrounding questions concerning her Jewishness: the greater the ambiguity, the more successful she can claim to be. Moreover, her position on the ambiguity of the Other further situates her in the modernist tradition of rhetoric. It is a disposition on language most notable in Burke's grammar of invention, which seeks terms "that clearly reveal the strategic spots at which ambiguities necessarily arise" (*Grammar* xvii). Stein's ambiguity of the Other is likewise strategic, but it is a liminal time, rather than a space, a time between this identity and that identity.

Much the same can be said of her sexual identity. There is a famous "family portrait" photograph of Stein and Toklas in 27 Rue de Fleurus by Man Ray. Toklas sits on the left, near the fireplace, in a small chair. Stein sits on the right in a stuffed, upholstered chair. Janet Malcolm describes the photograph as

> a kind of parody of the conventional society portrait of a husband and wife at home – it shimmers with the genre's sense of appearances being kept up and things not being said. The word "lesbian" was never publicly uttered by either of them about their relationship— as it was the custom of the day not to utter it. But the intensity of their love is documented by Stein's erotic poems (published after her death) [and] by the memoirs of contemporaries. (45-7)

The photograph is one instance of the stereotypical representation of lesbian relations common to images and impressions of Stein and Toklas, images and impressions that Stein (and perhaps Toklas) appears to have encouraged. Stein entertained the male geniuses in the salon while Toklas entertained their wives in the kitchen. Stein drove the car. Toklas did all of the household work. Stein did none of it, with the exception of trimming the hedges at their summer home. Their adherence to the stereotypical modernist "heterosexual" relationship is undermined, however, by Ulla Dydo's discovery of the reasons for all the awkward "cans" in the first published version of *Stanzas in Mediation*. As Malcolm recounts the story, Dydo discovered in the manuscript "that almost everywhere the auxiliary verb 'may' appeared Stein had crossed it out and put in the word 'can.' . . . The revisions make no sense and are clear disimprovements" (59). But May is the name of Stein's first lover, and apparently her typist, Toklas, read each "may" in the text as a reference to May Bookstaver. Dydo imagines the scene that ensued as "punitive," one in which Toklas sends Stein to her room and forces her to cross out all of the "mays" and replace them with "cans." Some of the slashes go through the page (Malcolm 63). Such a scene would not be common in the stereotypical "heterosexual" relationship between the dominant "husband" and the submissive "wife" Stein and Toklas appear to present. Like Stein's statement on the relation between the writer and her text, the images of Stein and Toklas's relationship assert a particular kind of unity even as they undo that particular unity. To return once more to the coin analogy, the stereotypical representations of Stein and Toklas' relationship function precisely to the extent that those representations are read as the reverse side of the heterosexual coin. They appear, that is, to signify a lesbian relationship structured heterosexually. To be completely the reverse and consistent with the stereotype, however, Toklas would need to be in the overstuffed chair and Stein in the small chair. The revision scene that Dydo imagines suggests that neither image, neither identity, adequately represents their relationship; their relationship exists somewhere on the borders of the two identities, or somewhere beyond the borders of each one. It thus enacts the dialectic between identity and nonidentity, a liminal moment when Stein and Toklas' relationship is both and neither of the two identities the heterosexual coin proffers.

The liminal time that writer-as-identity represents disappears for Stein in the moment she perceives herself to have written a sentimental book, that is, a book with a particular kind of identity. Its disappearance is the first consequence brought about by the success of *The Autobiography of Alice B. Toklas*, namely, Stein's writer's block. While the cure to her writer's block remains a mystery—it is hard to say how Stein rediscovered the moment in which the writer functions without an identity—*The Geographical History of America or the Relation of Human Nature to the Human Mind*, which appeared two years after Stein's tour of America, at the very least serves as evidence that her writer's block has been cured. Far from a sentimental book, this *sui generis* text, arguably more than any other of Stein's texts, demonstrates the structural interplay among rhetoric, poetics, grammar, and philosophy. It is here that she develops her notions of *human nature* and the *human mind*, which form the basis for her articulation of the relations between identity and nonidentity. Just as she adopts themes that are consistent with twentieth-century modernist literature and rhetoric but turns those themes to her own ends, so Stein adopts what appears to be a rather conventional pair of dialectical opposites—human nature and the human mind—and turns them to her own ends as well.

Human nature often signifies the fundamental traits of human beings, those things that today we may account for through DNA. For Stein, human nature signifies those qualities that we may call habits. They thus are cultural phenomena and are the results of an enculturating process. So while they may appear absolute and rigid, they are phenomena ultimately arrived at through the traditional process of persuasion, of rhetoric in its classical sense. This is the realm of identity, and it is arrived at through memories—ours and those of others—of who we are in the context of others. This is the realm in which Stein may be understood as a Jew, as a lesbian, as a husband.

These are not identities, for identities are neither true nor false; each merely is constructed within a particular context, one that we may say is constituted ultimately by the liminal relations among reader, text, and writer. Identities are useful. They enable us to function in the world of other human beings, in the world of human nature, by marking the limits of the liminal moments in which we live.

Identities are not, however, precisely who we are. At least, we are not they alone, no matter how many we may be able to enumerate for ourselves. For we exist not only in human nature but are also human mind. We might say human mind is a consciousness, the decision-making area of our brains, or something like that. For Stein, human mind is writing: the act of writing. And the act of writing is meditation, a conscious non-consciousness. For although, just before we write, we may consider who our audience is, and we may consider what our subject matter is, and we may consider what image of ourselves we may wish to project to our audience and through our texts, these concerns are of no concern in the liminal moments when writing instrument touches paper or when fingers touch keys. This is the realm of human mind.

Is there a rhetoric to the human mind? Yes and no. No, in that all those conventional concerns of rhetoric—writer, audience, text, and their relationships to one another—are of no concern to the human mind, but yes in that human mind—that place of nonidentity—needs such concerns to define precisely where the habits of human nature end and the meditations of human mind begin.

Works Cited

Barthes, Roland. *The Semiotic Challenge*. Trans. Richard Howard. Berkeley: U of California P, 1994. Print.

Boyarin, Jonathan. *Storm from Paradise: The Politics of Jewish Memory*. Minneapolis: U of Minnesota P, 1992. Print.

Bridgman, Richard. *Gertrude Stein in Pieces*. New York: Oxford UP, 1970. Print.

Burke, Kenneth. *A Grammar of Motives*. Berkeley: U of California P, 1969. Print.

—. *A Rhetoric of Motives*. Berkeley: U of California P, 1969. Print.

Kirsch, Sharon J. "Gertrude Stein Delivers." *Rhetoric Review* 31.3 (2012): 254–270. Print.

—. "'Suppose a grammar uses invention': Gertrude Stein's Theory of Rhetorical Grammar." *Rhetoric Society Quarterly* 38.3 (2008): 283–310. Print.

Malcolm, Janet. *Two Lives: Gertrude and Alice*. New Haven: Yale UP, 2007. Print.

McKeon, Richard. *Rhetoric: Essays in Invention and Discovery*. Ed. Mark Backman. Woodbridge: Ox Bow P, 1987. Print.

Mellow, James R. *Charmed Circle: Gertrude Stein and Company*. New York: Henry Holt and Company, 1974. Print.

Parke, Catherine N. "'Simple Through Complication': Gertrude Stein Thinking." *American Literature: A Journal of Literary History, Criticism, and Bibliography* 60.4 (1988): 554–74. Print.

Shaw, Patrick. "The Surrender to Ethos: Gertrude Stein's 'Introduction to the Speeches of Marechal Petain.'" *Chasing Esther: Jewish Expressions of Cultural Difference*. Eds. David Metzger and Peter Schulman. Santa Monica: Kol Katan P, 2005. 9–31. Print.

Stein, Gertrude. *The Geographical History of America or the Relation of Human Nature to the Human Mind*. Baltimore: Johns Hopkins UP, 1995. Print.

—. *What Are Mastepieces?* New York: Pitman, 1970. Print.

9 (Re)Bordering the Scholarly Imaginary: The State and Future of Rhetorical Border Studies

*Antonio Tomas De La Garza, D. Robert DeChaine, &
Kent A. Ono*

Increasingly, the political and material exigencies heralded by the immigration policies of the United States have contributed to an intensification of surveillance on the US-Mexico border. This surveillance takes many forms, including night vision, motion detection, and yes, scholarship. As the apparatuses of knowledge production begin to grind the artifact known as the US-Mexico Borderlands into ever-finer fragments of truth, rhetorical scholars interested in the border should begin by considering how, if at all, a scholarly genre of "rhetorical border studies" ought to be defined. Should the theorization of borders be extended to include *metaphorical* borders, such as the borders between humans and animals? How does one attempt to describe the limits of a discipline that critiques, denaturalizes, and attempts to intervene against the violence associated with contemporary borders? Is the border simply a tired metaphor for discussing any limit, boundary, or threshold? Can or should border studies focus only on the US-Mexico border, hence foreclosing opportunities for discussing bordering phenomena more broadly? While asking such questions can be far more productive than searching for definitive answers, this essay is a provocation to rhetoricians to engage in a more intentional and rigorous discussion of what borders are, why they matter, and what the field of rhetoric can contribute to understanding them.

This essay provides us an opportunity to show that it is possible, and indeed beneficial, to study border rhetoric beyond a strict focus on the US-Mexico border, while simultaneously recognizing the intimate role that the US-Mexico border plays in shaping US American culture. Broadening the rhetorical study of borders involves a shift in focus from borders to *bordering*. Bordering is fundamentally an act of power, one that refigures not only physical but also intellectual and social space. To invoke bordering as a verb is to recognize that borders are rhetorically *enacted*; they are "produced, defined, managed, contested, and altered through human symbolic practices" (DeChaine, "Introduction" 2). As such, border rhetorics can assume many forms. If that is true, it is important to carefully define "rhetorical border studies" and indicate what it should be.

Our argument unfolds in three sections. First, we survey contemporary rhetorical theories of the border, which ultimately reveals that defining border rhetorics as a scholarly genre is, itself, a political matter. Second, we address the question of the US-Mexico border as a contextual problematic that is both formative of modern border studies and over-limiting of its focus. This section demonstrates that the materiality and discursivity of borders require researchers to engage with the historical and political conditions that give meaning and power to the study of *any* border. Last, we attempt to find a path forward, one that simultaneously addresses the anxieties and tensions surrounding the borderlands and develops topographies for future research. To that end, we articulate four organizing principles, each of which entails a valuative commitment on the part of the researcher:

1. Rhetorical border studies are a critical enterprise that should extend beyond mere explanation or description. One of its principal goals is to challenge, resist, or destabilize discourses and their formations responsible for the creation and maintenance of borders.

2. Borders are brought into being in order to demarcate self from other, inside from outside, and emic from etic.[1] Because borders define the terms of such demarcations and because bordering practices constrain human action, rhetorical border scholars pay special attention to issues of power and agency.

3. Borders are made real, given form and power, through performance and affect. Absent the actions of the state and citizenry, a border is nothing more than a discursive fiction. Actions animate borders;

they may include public and local discourse events, but without agency they no longer function. Thus rhetorical border scholars attend to the affective and performative dimensions of bordering practices.

4. Rhetorical border scholars combine research with public pedagogy. Border scholarship engages in a critique of structures, institutions, and practices that affect people's lives, prompting an obligation to render our work accessible to non-scholarly publics.

SURVEYING THE BORDERLANDS

The present controversies surrounding "illegals," *sans papier*, Roma, and other border transgressors help to explain what may appear to many as the relatively sudden surge of interest in rhetorical border studies. Gloria Anzaldúa's foundational text, *Borderlands*, conceptualizes how borders shape cultural, social, and psychic landscapes. Citations of her work appear across disciplines, such as in History (Gutiérrez; Hanisch), Chicano/a Studies (Santa Ana; Saldívar), and Gender Studies (Moraga; Saldívar-Hull). *Borderlands* is a starting point for theorizing the processes and performances constituting the borderlands and expands the study of a physical locale (the US.-Mexico border) to include the co-constitutive relationships between spaces and identities.

In 2002, Kent Ono and John Sloop were arguably the first to make explicit the ties between rhetoric and borders. In their book, *Shifting Borders*, they write that "rhetoric at times even determines where, and what the border is" (5). Despite their materiality, borders come into being and meaning through discourse. This insight is further developed by Lisa Flores, who argues "the deportation drive and the repatriation campaign of the 1930s served to create rhetorically a border between Mexico and the U.S., between 'Americans' and Mexican/Americans" (364). As scholarship began to focus increasingly on the rhetoricity of the border, scholars like Anne Demo began to highlight how "border imagery . . . functions metonymically as both a symbol and index of U.S. sovereignty" (293). Borders, then, are key figures that help to reproduce and shore up the "civic imaginary" (DeChaine, "Bordering" 45; Cisneros, "Looking Illegal" 27) by demarcating space and identity both figuratively (Ono 20) and literally.

Moreover, against the traditional view of borders as static and given, such rhetorical scholarship signals a shift in focus from borders to *bordering*— that is, a recognition of border making as a discursive, sociocultural production. Moving from borders to bordering makes it possible to understand how communication can shape, produce, or even intervene against the alienizing power of border rhetoric. Scholarship by rhetoricians such as Karma R. Chávez makes clear that scholars can and should challenge discourses that mask or (hetero)normativize unjust immigration practices (145). Singularly, each of these works (and a vast array of work we cannot mention here because of space constraints) represents an important contribution to the field and our understanding of borders. Collectively, these writings serve as waypoints, pointing toward the intellectual and political commitments that have and will continue to shape the topography of rhetorical border studies. However, despite the importance of borders to the study of rhetoric and of rhetoric to the construction of borders, there has as yet been no attempt to develop a heuristic for the burgeoning field of rhetorical border studies.

The Ghosts of Aztlán

In the 1990s, border theory was at its peak, with works like those of Anzaldúa and Americo Paredes having already inspired a generation of Chicano, Queer, and Critical Race scholars. However, in disparate fields ranging from cultural studies to literary theory, scholars seemed to lose interest in such research, and quickly. In part, this was a result of theorists taking border theory to logical extremes. Scholars found borders everywhere, and borders could apply to just about anything. With the rush to theorize any and all borders, the material, historical border itself—which was what inspired Anzaldúa's original work—was no longer the center and focus of border studies but an almost cliché historical curiosity, one without sufficient theoretical traction on which to base further work. Once one demonstrates that borders are everywhere and are relevant to everything, the metaphor loses its ability to describe. Like the clay letters on a printing press, through repeated printing they get worn to the point that they cease to make a clear impression.

Border studies may now appear anachronistic within disciplines like communication, geography, literature, and cultural Studies. However, if we dust that tired old metaphor off and read the literature with fresh eyes, and do so with the specific field of rhetorical studies in mind, new theoretical possibilities emerge, ones that pertain to the here and now. After all, rhetoricians are guided by exigencies and contingencies, and it would be nearly impossible not to recognize the social significance of immigration and border policy in 2014. During the last presidential election, candidates and the press paid significant attention to undocumented migrants, the DREAM Act, and Latina/o voters. The next presidential election promises more (possibly much more) of the same. Undocumented migrants are establishing themselves as unapologetic and unafraid, and willing to engage in discursive, legal, and political struggle to change the terms of the immigration debate. Globally, transnational capitalism and its amazing thirst for deregulation, increasingly flexible (and disposable) labor supplies, and greater and more profound and deeper consumption of resources continues unabated. New markets, new resources, new branding, and new creative materials go hand in hand with the importation and exploitation of creative, inventive, hard-working immigrants, from the highly skilled to the unskilled. Immigrants; transnational laborers; and virtual laborers, e.g., from gold miners on World of Warcraft (Nakamura) to remote call center workers (Carrillo Rowe, Malhotra, and Pérez) and human trafficking (Soderlund) render the discussion of borders imperative, not obsolete, as some strains of critical theory might have pronounced the field moribund, if not dead, as early as the mid-1990s.

Stepped-up efforts to militarize the nearly two-thousand-mile dividing line between Mexico and the United States have contributed to yet another shift of the border in our time, a shift directly linking state power with multiple forms of violence. Despite forceful "prevention through deterrence" strategies, including policies like Operation Gatekeeper, Operation Hold the Line, and Arizona Senate Bill 1070 have not ended migration. For those who remember that huge swaths of what is now the United States were once northwest Mexico, it is hard not to be reminded of the impermanence of the borders erected to demarcate national boundaries. For those who recognize that the United States came into being through conquest, it is imperative to be reminded that "All locality building has a moment of colonization, a moment both historical and chronotopic, when there is a formal recognition that the production of a neighborhood requires deliberate, risky, even violent action in respect to the soil, forest, animals, and other human beings" (Appadurai 183).

Borders are artificially erected dividing lines, which slice the land into pieces and parts. They are products of ideology and are performed through violence, and that violence leaves scars in the land and on its people. As keepers and producers of knowledge about the borderlands, it falls to us to remember and bear witness. Too little focus has been on the role rhetoricians, not merely the rhetoric they study, play in *memoria*. The mutilation of the land and its people through colonization haunts the continent. Theorizing borders that linger, historicizing rhetoric and border projects, and reminding people of that persisting and lived history is constitutive of rhetorical border studies, give it substance and power and makes this research a political project.

Indeed, rhetoric has much to say about memory. Are borders and their history things remembered? Do they continue to have meaning? Can we remember all that was once Mexico without obfuscating the violence that was so foundational to the nation-state? Can we be merely reminded of these old facts, or does this space, this location, *become* something, somewhere else in that moment of memorializing? Borders haunt, they intervene, and they wait for the right time before they seize the moment, reterritorializing occupied territories and remaking the discursivity and materiality of locations. Rhetoric has much to say about borders, but the material is absolutely crucial to what rhetoricians can and do say. And knowing history, thus being reminded of it, can change how and what things are.

Cartographies of Resistance

As we have suggested, rhetorical border studies provides researchers with a critically engaged, potentially impactful means of addressing contemporary exigencies. Yet, one possible future for rhetorical border studies—a future about which we are particularly concerned—is a movement toward abstraction, dehistoricization, and depoliticization that would neutralize what we argue to be its heuristic value for political and social critique. Central to our future vision is a conviction that the production of knowledge about borders impels researchers to bear significant responsibilities. To lend clarity and urgency to our vision, we propose four mutually reinforcing organizing principles. Each principle entails a valuative commitment that emphasizes the rhetorical border scholar's obligation to a project invested in critique, agency, affect and performativity, and public pedagogy. Such principles and commitments, we submit, may provide those of us who study borders with some productive strategies for moving forward.

Far from neutral or ineffectual, bordering practices involve discursive ascriptions that produce affects and effects upon places, bodies, subjectivities, and social imaginaries. As a stratagem for shoring up knowledge about people, places, and social statuses, border-making is always interested; its purveyors, as well as its bordered subjects, are mutually implicated in its truth regimes. Put succinctly, bordering practices are violent, ethico-political acts with consequential, material entailments. If a project grounded in a critique of structures, practices, and institutions of power—as we argue rhetorical border studies ought to be—is to live up to the charge of its own ethico-political *telos, rhetorical border studies is and must remain a critical enterprise.* Because discursive ascriptions of difference always presuppose relations of power, *and* because border rhetorics inevitably produce material effects on those bordered, there is an imperative to critique, not simply describe or explain, sociocultural bordering structures, institutions, and practices. We underscore this point because we worry that the figure of the border, as heuristically valuable as it is, can just as easily be deployed to analyze, aestheticize, or rationalize nearly anything, and as such, is susceptible to serving any number of hegemonic projects.

As a site for the application of power and the production of knowledge, borders become a terrain for critically interrogating bordering processes and practices. Those marked physically by national boundaries or gated communities are perhaps only the most obvious. There are, in fact, numerous other borders whose delineations reflect complex geopolitical and sociocultural configurations. Take, for example, the recent debate over Pennsylvania House Bill 1077, the so-called "Women's Right to Know Act," which if passed would have required women to undergo mandatory trans-vaginal ultrasound procedures before being allowed to terminate a pregnancy. A critical analysis of public discourse surrounding HB1077 might reveal a form of bordering that radically circumscribes women's personhood, juxtaposes regional political ideologies, racializes and factionalizes publics, shunts histories of women's subjugation and liberation away from discussion, and so on. Or, consider the multiple, often violent borderings enacted against queer migrants of color in their daily negotiations of civic imaginaries regulated by heteronormative whiteness. In engaging these and myriad other border rhetorics, the critic's overriding obligation is, unflinchingly, to interrogate the discursive strategies through which bordering is enacted and bordered subjects are affected. Absent this critical commitment, rhetorical border studies abdicates its own ethico-political responsibility toward/for those who most directly experience the violence of bordering acts.

Because borders are consummately human constructions that function to produce social imaginaries (De La Garza, "Critical Eulogy"), *rhetorical border studies should be concerned with how human agency is constrained in and through specific bordering acts.* As a critical project invested in identifying the productive functions of power in disciplining subjects, rhetorical border studies can throw light on the privileging and alienizing mechanisms that condition ways of seeing, feeling, and acting in the world. Such a theory does not presuppose that individuals have agency in any humanist, modernist, or logical sense; nevertheless, actions happen, people matter, influences occur, and things change. While not determined by individuals, or overdetermined by structures, the problematics for how to alter and change those formations is, we think, of paramount concern. Simply arguing that nothing can be done and that it is high vanity, or simply being naive and hopelessly misguided, to believe in individuals, agency, and causality is not sufficient. Suggesting there are no influences, no changes, relating to humans would be akin to Holocaust denial or denying human influences on climate change. Critical border scholars are thus charged with tracking the power-knowledge relation and the disciplinary functions of the border in conditioning bodies, producing subjects, telling truths, and creating worlds.

Rhetorical border scholars have, previously, examined issues concerning human agency primarily through discursive frames of identity, race and ethnicity, citizenship, and (im)migration (see, for example, Chávez; Cisneros, "(Re)Bordering"; DeChaine, "Bordering"; Flores; Holling; Johnson; Ono and Sloop). But, also needed is an attenuated focus on how discourses of law, human rights, gender, medicine, media, sex(uality), capitalism, mobility, biology, art, and technology collude in constraining human thought, value systems, and forms of action that travel beyond the purview of identity frames and civic imaginaries. In pressing border studies to examine how discourses and conjunctures mediate human agency, rhetorical scholars honor a commitment to those whose lives are directly, often profoundly, shaped by the ubiquitous specter of the border.

The materiality of border rhetorics is, in part, constituted by affect and performativity. The differentials in violence between US America's Northern and Southern borders suggest that the militarized buildup occurring on the Southern border is not essential, natural, or static, nor is it inevitable. It is given substance not by cement, concertina, and wooden and metal posts, but by subjects who participate in the formation of consent and the disciplining institutions of repressive state apparatuses. Moreover, as a reciprocal performance of state power and consenting citizen-subjects, bordering mutually implicates the discursive and the nondiscursive in moving bodies toward belief. For these reasons, *rhetorical border studies needs to include a focus on the affective and performative dimensions of border making.* By performativity, we not only mean performance, but also, as Judith Butler theorizes it, repetitive iteration—the unwitting, unrehearsed re-enactments of identity and identity power relations as a social consequence.

Politically, a rhetorical focus on affect involves examining the social stakes of the relation between nondiscursive energy and discourse. The recent turn to affect in rhetorical studies affords researchers of borders opportunities for examining the effects of bordering—the rhetorical practice of ascribing borders onto places, bodies, subjectivities, and social imaginaries—and, in turn, how affectivity shapes individual and collective attitudes about borders. Likewise, the increasing recognition in rhetorical studies of intersectional commonalities with queer studies, gender studies, and performance studies, fields that are deeply invested in theorizing affective and performative dimensions of identity, provides fruitful openings for theoretical collaborations that might lead to a better understanding of how practices of bordering affect and effect bodies and selves. Rhetorical border scholars have a critical stake in extending current theory and research on affect and performativity and in elucidating how structures of belief are mediated by how people *feel* borders in their everyday lives.

While it is clear within critical work that the line between theory and praxis is in fact not a line, and that theory and praxis are co-present and mutually interconnected, nevertheless too much scholarship ends in published journal pages and seminar rooms, and too little of it makes its way into broader realms. Moreover, because we are in the *academy*, the potential for elitism and for not speaking with, to, or beside those without doctoral educations is great. It is for these reasons that *rhetorical border studies (as we have outlined it) considers public pedagogy seriously.* We are not implying that every scholar needs to do public pedagogy or that there are not many ways to do it or that theory itself is not political. However, if we are going to intervene against the violence of borders, part of that endeavor will be to find ways to make at least some of our work relevant and accessible to broader publics. By tactically using our privilege, rhetorical border scholars can reflect and amplify marginalized voices through our teaching and research.

A commitment to public pedagogy is no small thing. It demands self-reflective choices about the kinds of questions we as scholars ask, the issues with which we engage, the audiences we address, the voices we privilege (and those we de-privilege), the metaphors and ideographs we invoke, the languages with which we speak, and the *teloi* to which we obligate ourselves. It means recognizing, in Hall's words, "the deadly seriousness of intellectual work," and of considering the dual function of our theorizing "also as a practice which always thinks about its intervention in a world in which it would make some difference, in which it would have some effect" (286). For rhetorical border scholars, then, our praxis, and hence our commitment to public pedagogy, builds out of our work to theorize, politicize, and historicize both the rhetoricity and materiality of bordering acts and, in so doing, to develop strategies for envisioning and enacting social change. For scholars who take borders seriously a consideration of how theory and research matter in the world can serve as a vital expression of solidarity with and for others.

CONCLUSION

Rhetorical border theory can inform other important areas of research and, as a result, move rhetorical studies in a more socially engaged direction. From discussions of the "disappeared" to those living in exile, rhetorical border theory addresses issues of exploitation, discrimination, legal and policy activism and resistance, transnational global capitalism, violence and warfare, historical exigencies, intercultural relations, and identity. Understanding the history of immigration, the role borders play, and the impact of economics and policy on mobility and socialization, rhetorical border scholars can work to reconfigure communities. In this essay we have argued that rhetorical border studies should not devolve into abstract concepts that suggest every border is equivalent and that, for instance, the border between two offices is similarly consequential to the border between Mexico and the United States. Instead, border studies must recognize the importance of critique, the centrality of power and agency, the affective and performative dimensions of bordering, and a commitment to public pedagogy in whatever practical form it takes. Future scholarship should be positioned to intervene in the structures of power-knowledge that render spectating subjects complicit in the border's violence.

NOTE

1. For a discussion of these terms and their importance to rhetoric, see Black (1980). Black distinguishes an *etic* viewpoint that "approaches a rhetorical transaction from outside of that transaction and interprets the transaction in terms of a pre-existing theory" from an *emic* viewpoint, "which approaches a rhetorical transaction in what is hoped to be its own terms, without conscious expectations drawn from any sources other than the rhetorical transaction itself" (331–32).

WORKS CITED

Alvarez, Jr., Robert R. "The Mexican-US Border: The Making of an Anthropology of Borderlands." *Annual Review of Anthropology* 24 (1995): 447–70. Print.

Anzaldúa, Gloria. *Borderlands = La Frontera*. 2nd ed. San Francisco: Aunt Lute, 1999. Print.

Appadurai, Arjun. *Modernity at Large: Cultural Dimensions of Globalization*. Vol. 1. Minneapolis: U of Minnesota P, 1996. Print.

Black, Edwin. "A Note On Theory And Practice In Rhetorical Criticism." *Western Journal Of Speech Communication: WJSC* 44.4 (1980): 331–36. Print.

Butler, Judith. *Bodies that Matter: On the Discursive Limits of Sex*. New York and London: Routledge, 1993. Print.

Carrillo Rowe, Aimee, Sheena Malhotra, and Kimberley Pérez. *Answer the Call: Virtual Migration in Indian Call Centers*. Minneapolis: U of Minnesota P. 2013. Print.

Chávez, Karma R. "Border (In)Securities: Normative and Differential Belonging in LGBTQ and Immigrant Rights Discourse." *Communication and Critical/Cultural Studies* 7.2 (2010): 136-55. Print.

Cisneros, Josue David. "Looking 'Illegal': Affect, Rhetoric, and Performativity in Arizona's Senate Bill 1070." *Border Rhetorics: Citizenship and Identity on the US-Mexico Frontier*. Ed. D. Robert DeChaine. Tuscaloosa: U of Alabama P, 2012. 133–50. Print.

—. "(Re)Bordering the Civic Imaginary: Rhetoric, Hybridity, and Citizenship in *La Gran Marcha.*" *Quarterly Journal of Speech* 97.1 (2011): 26–49. Print.

DeChaine, D. Robert. "Bordering the Civic Imaginary: Alienization, Fence Logic, and the Minuteman Civil Defense Corps." *Quarterly Journal of Speech* 95.1 (2009): 43–65. Print.

—. "Introduction: For Rhetorical Border Studies." *Border Rhetorics: Citizenship and Identity on the US-Mexico Frontier.* Ed. D. Robert DeChaine. Tuscaloosa: U of Alabama P, 2012. 1–15. Print.

De La Garza, Antonio Tomas. "A Critical Eulogy for Joaquin Luna: Mindful Racial Realism as an Intervention to End Racial Battle Fatigue." *Racial Battle Fatigue: Insights from the Front Lines of Social Justice Advocacy.* Ed. Jeniffer Martin. Praeger, 2015. 177–189. Print.

Demo, Anne. "Sovereignty Discourse and Contemporary Immigration Politics." *Quarterly Journal Of Speech* 91.3 (2005): 291–311. Print.

Flores, Lisa A. "Constructing Rhetorical Borders: Peons, Illegal Aliens, and Competing Narratives of Immigration." *Critical Studies in Media Communication* 20.4 (2003): 362–87. Print.

Gutiérrez, David. *Walls and Mirrors: Mexican Americans, Mexican Immigrants, and the Politics of Ethnicity.* Berkeley: U of California P, 1995. Print.

Hall, Stuart. "Cultural Studies and its Theoretical Legacies." *Cultural Studies.* Eds. Lawrence Grossberg, Cary Nelson, and Paula Treichler. New York and London: Routledge, 1992. 277–94. Print.

Hanisch, Marvin. "Redefining the US-Mexico Borderlands." GRIN Verlag, 2013. Print.

Holling, Michelle A. "Patrolling National Identity, Masking White Supremacy: The Minuteman Project." *Critical Rhetorics of Race.* Eds. Michael G. Lacy and Kent A. Ono. New York: New York UP, 2011. 98–116. Print.

Johnson, Julia R. "Bordering as Social Practice: Intersectional Identifications and Coalitional Possibilities." *Border Rhetorics: Citizenship and Identity on the US-Mexico Frontier.* Ed. D. Robert DeChaine. Tuscaloosa: U of Alabama. 2012. 33–47. Print.

Keating, Ana Louise. "From Borderlands and New Mestizas to Nepantlas and Nepantleras: Anzaldúan Theories for Social Change." *Human Architecture: Journal of the Sociology of Self-knowledge* 4.3 (2006): 3. Print.

Moraga, Cherríe. "Art in America, Con Acento." *Frontiers: A Journal of Women Studies* 12.3 (1992): 154–60. Print.

Nakamura, Lisa. "Don't Hate the Player, Hate the Game: The Racialization of Labor in World of Warcraft." *Critical Studies in Media Communication* 26.2 (2009): 128–44. Print.

Ono, Kent A. "Borders that Travel: Matters of the Figural Border." *Border Rhetorics: Citizenship and Identity on the US–Mexico Frontier.* Ed. D. Robert DeChaine. Tuscaloosa: U of Alabama P, 2012. 19–32. Print.

Ono, Kent A., and John M. Sloop. *Shifting Borders: Rhetoric, Immigration, and California's Proposition 187.* Philadelphia: Temple UP, 2002. Print.

Paredes, Americo. *A Texas-Mexican Cancionero: Folksongs of the Lower Border*. Austin: U of Texas P, 1995. Print.

Pike, Kenneth L. "Etic and Emic Standpoints for the Description of Behavior." *Communication and Culture: Readings in the Codes of Human Interaction*. Ed. Alfred G. Smith. New York: Holt, Rinehart and Winston, 1966. 152–63. Print.

Saldívar, José David. "Chicano Border Narratives as Cultural Critique." *Criticism in the Borderlands: Studies in Chicano Literature, Culture, and Ideology*. Eds. Héctor Calderón and José David Saldívar. Durham, NC: Duke UP, 1991. 167–80. Print.

Saldívar-Hull, Sonia. *Feminism on the Border: Chicana Gender Politics and Literature*. Berkeley: U of California P, 2000. Print.

Santa Ana, Otto. "'Like an Animal I was Treated': Anti-immigrant Metaphor in US Public Discourse." *Discourse & Society* 10.2 (1999): 191–224. Print.

Soderlund, Gretchen. "Running from the Rescuers: New U.S. Crusades against Sex Trafficking and the Rhetoric of Abolition." *National Women's Studies Association Journal* 17.3 (2005): 64–87. Print.

Remapping the Political

10 Peacemaking and the Chancery in Medieval Cairo: Revisiting Medieval Arabic Rhetoric

Rasha Diab

In the past four decades, interest has grown in rhetoric's history and historiography and how they deeply impact the burgeoning studies of rhetoric around the world. This scholarship converges as it calls for reflecting on our assumptions about what counts as rhetoric, who is deemed a rhetor, and what borders we have placed on our rhetoric map. Heeding this call, my study shifts attention to the rhetorical knowledge and practice of Aḥmad ibn ʿAlī al-Qalqashandī, a medieval scholar, Judge, and head of the Chancery in Cairo. Writing about the arts and proficiencies of *al-kātib* (writer/scribe/secretary) in Mamlūk Cairo, al-Qalqashandī has left us with a fourteen-volume encyclopedia titled *Ṣubḥ al-Aʿshá fī Ṣināʿat al-Inshāʾ*, or *The Daybreak for the Sufferer of Night Blindness in Composing Official Documents*.[1] Though the encyclopedia invites numerous rhetorical studies, this article explores only the section devoted to *ṣulḥ*, or peacemaking practices deemed relevant to institutional expression and rhetorical practices of the chancery. The piece argues that al-Qalqashandī provides a unique presentation of peacemaking rhetorical knowledge that is categorized to highlight textual patterns and moves. This unique presentation recognizes and responds to *al-kātib* (chancery writer) consultation needs and literate practices. As such, this piece expands our current knowledge of the arts of letter writing and institutional expression in medieval Egypt.

"New Archival and Rhetorical Frontiers"

Calls for revisiting the rhetorical tradition invite this line of inquiry since they ask us all to explore new frontiers and address absences. To illustrate, scholars (e.g., Agnew et.al.; Ballif; Enos et.al.; Murphy et.al.; Vitanza) ask us to revisit the rhetorical tradition and to remap rhetorical territory, which have remained for so long within the confines of the Greco-Roman traditions. Indeed, Vicki Burton in Octalog III "hope[s] that Octalog III's audiences will go into the wilderness of new archival and rhetorical frontiers with Vitanza's spirit of wildness, with a traveler's curiosity and appetite for knowledge, with Heraclitus' commitment to dwell ethically with texts, speakers, and audiences, and with courage to address the messiness of our times" (Agnew et. al. 130). Her hope converges with similar reflections by medievalists. For example, medieval scholar Martin Camargo invites us to ask *more* and *different* questions about the arts of letter writing and attendant genres, about "what the authors of the fourteenth- and fifteenth-century treatises were trying to do, what needs they sought to satisfy, what sorts of readers they envisioned and the like . . ." (140).[2] Consequently, there has been a rise in recovery scholarship that seeks to shed light on seldom-looked-at texts/rhetorical activities, invisible rhetors, and archives.

Contributing to this scholarship, this article attempts to cross the borders of invisibility of al-Qalqashandī and Arab-Islamic rhetorics and revisits the lands of Mamlūk Egypt, specifically the chancery, to shed light on al-Qalqashandī's fourteen-volume encyclopedia, *Ṣubḥ al-Aʿshā fī Ṣināʿat al-Inshāʾ* (henceforth *Ṣubḥ*). This encyclopedia is dedicated to institutional writing and awaits rhetorical exploration. It is surprising that there are no rhetorical studies on Arab-Islamic institutional peacemaking practices, considering the numerous studies on *ars dictaminis* (e.g., Bazerman and Paradis; Camargo; Perelman; Murphy) and on Arab-Islamic rhetoric.[3] For the past few years, peacemaking rhetoric has been the focal point of my research, which converges with a steady stream of scholarship on the relations among rhetoric, violence and peacemaking, and politics (e.g., Doxtader; Gorsevski; Hatch). Yet, this growing literature, to a great extent, is informed by the Judeo-Christian tradition. As a complementary investment, this study directs attention to Arab-Islamic peacemaking practices. Interestingly, al-Qalqashandī devotes one out of ten essays—Essay Nine—to *ṣulḥ* (a fourteen-centuries-old Arab-Islamic peacemaking practice and tradition) and provides information about different types of *ṣulḥ*, *ṣulḥ* agreements, what's written in *al-ṭurrah* (beginning) and *al-matn* (the body of the document), and concluding formulae. As such, this study sheds light on "new archival and rhetorical frontiers" and calls attention to the tradition of Arab-Islamic institutional writing, which despite its longevity continues to be invisible to rhetoric studies.

Concerned about the arts and proficiencies of *al-kātib*, al-Qalqashandī completed his fourteen-volume (around 6,500 pages) encyclopedia in 818/1415.[4] al-Qalqashandī's goal was to write not a textbook or a manual, which underlines formulae for official correspondence (though he provides many formulae in the process), but rather to compile massive information that could help inform the writing practices of *al-kātib*, a much-needed profession in an increasingly growing administration.[5] In what follows, I contend that Essay Nine (and *Ṣubḥ* more generally) should be recognized as a text worthy of rhetorical attention for its investment in the arts and proficiencies of the writer/secretary. Especially for scholars interested in peacemaking rhetorics, Essay Nine is a treasure trove of *ṣulḥ* formulae and documents. To develop this argument, I explore what Essay Nine has on offer to *al-kātib* in terms of different types of peacemaking practices, examples, and meta-knowledge. This exploration is preceded by a brief introduction to al-Qalqashandī, the rise of *adab al-kātib* (i.e., literature for the development and refinement of the arts and skills of writers of *inshā'*), growing disciplinary interest in selective reading or "consultation literacy," and finally *ṣulḥ*.

AL-QALQASHANDĪ

Born in Qalqashandah—a small village in al-Qalyoubiah, Egypt—in 778/1355 into a family of scholars, Judge al-Qalqashandī (1355-1418 CE) was trained in Islamic law and jurisprudence and teaching until he joined *Dīwān al-Inshā'* (the chancery) as *kātib daraj* under Judge Badr al-Dīn 'Alā' al-Dīn al-'Amrī, who was *kātib sirr*.[6] al-Qalqashandī was multi-lingual (Arabic, Turkish, and Persian). Before joining the chancery, he wrote a *maqāmah*, an autobiographical narrative that represents an internal dialectic about the pursuit of professional life and the choice between working for *Dīwān al-Inshā'* (the chancery) or *Dīwān al-Ḥisbah* (as an accountant). In the *maqāmah*, he introduces *inshā'* and explains the nobleness of the profession and its arts (Musa 9). His *maqāmah* draws on, cites, and evokes a long tradition of investing in *al-kātib* and *inshā'*.

The expansion of Arab-Islamic territory entailed a need for a complex administrative system to link the periphery with the center and a chancery to regulate and oversee all official correspondence and documents. This need led to an investment in *inshā'* (official or institutional expression) and the office of *al-kātib* (writer/scribe). This investment has been well studied by Arab scholars (e.g., Abd al-Karīm), who explain how the rise of official writing as a recognized profession led to and coincided with increased attention to knowledge of writing, genres, book production, Arabic fonts, writing tools, and so forth. More important, there was a complementary investment in articulating standards and compiling formulae that guide writers, including how to begin a letter and what writing skills and techniques are necessary to acquire. This, in turn, led to the rise of *adab al-kātib* (i.e., literature enumerating the arts of the scribe/secretary).

ADAB AL-KĀTIB

With the expansion of governmental bureaucracy—starting from the end of the Ummayyad and reaching its peak in the Mamlūk period (648/1250 through 923/1517), there was a surge in *adab al-kātib*, which refers to specialized literature developed for the training of secretaries (e.g., Van Berkel).[7] The systematic use of correspondence/official writing has roots that go as far back as the seventh century. Then there was an increasing need for religiopolitical and official correspondence, which eventually led to the development of the position/responsibility of letter writer/secretary. In the early days of Islam, Prophet Moḥammad relied on writers/secretaries to correspond with dignitaries. According to Ḥasan Ḥabashī, there were thirty *kātib* (writers/secretaries), which can be considered an early form of the chancery or secretaryship (Ḥabashī). Another important dimension of this line of rhetorical development goes back to the eighth century. The Persian 'Abd al-Ḥamīd ibn Yahyá ibn Wahb al-Qarshī (d. 132/750)—known as 'Abd al-Ḥamīd al-Kātib—was a writer/secretary in the chancery during the rule of the Caliph Hishām ibn 'Abd al-Malik and was well known for his eloquence and style. More important, 'Abd al-Ḥamīd al-Kātib, who is known for a few epistles on a variety of topics, including chess, also wrote a treatise on the responsibilities of the writer titled *Risālah ilá al-Kuttāb* ("An Epistle to Writers") and developing the art of composition, especially epistolary writing. Van Berkel explicates the vision for the writer and the raison d'être of *adab al-kātib* succinctly: "The manner in which the *kātib* is sketched in this treatise, his education in the *adab* disciplines; his character of modesty, trustworthiness, and integrity; and the way in which he should relate to superiors and inferiors set the standard for almost all later *adab al-kātib* manual"("A Well-Mannered" 87-88).

This literature grew during the Mamlūk era as there were numerous encyclopedias devoted to secretarial arts. However, scholars agree that al-Qalqashandī's is the most important. 'Abd al-Ḥamīd's *Risālah ilá al-Kuttāb* precedes and informs al-Qalqashandī's *Ṣubḥ*. According to the estimation of numerous scholars (e.g., Ḥabashī; Van Berkel), *adab al-kātib* was at its peak with al-Qalqashandī's *Ṣubḥ*, which comprises fourteen volumes and is approximately 6,500 pages as noted earlier. Though a feat in itself, it was not al-Qalqashandī's first work on the arts of official writing. Before he held his position as *kātib al-daraj*—al-Qalqashandī wrote a *maqāmah* in praise of the arts of *inshā'* (official writing), his master Badr al-Dīn Ibn Fadl Allāh, and his family of well-known *kuttāb* as noted earlier.[8] This work inspired the encyclopedia, which scholars estimate took him about twenty years to write and was completed in 818/1415 (Ḥabashī; Wansbrough). What makes al-Qalqashandī's stand out is that it combines three different takes on *adab al-kātib*. Rather than settling for providing *al-kātib* with (a) principles of developing proficiencies and skills; (b) the meaning and ends of terms pertaining to *inshā'*; or (c) compilations of examples/formulae for different types of documents and letters to imitate, adapt, or quote, he chose to blend all three. This approach is more consistent with the wide-ranging knowledge and consultation literacy *al-kātib* needs.

CONSULTATION LITERACY

Kuttāb al-inshā'—chancery writers—were expected to "be a walking and talking encyclopedia" (van Berkel, "The Attitude" 163). Put differently, they were expected to have wide-ranging knowledge both secular (e.g., prose, poetry, grammar, history, geography, politics) and religious (e.g., prophetic tradition, *Qur'ān*, and *fiqh*). These high expectations converged with an investment in consultation literacy, or the quick and savvy search for and retrieval of information. Rather than expecting texts to be read in full, there was another type of literacy with which people searched texts for pertinent information. To accommodate this change in literate practices, complex structural and organizational techniques developed to help readers (van Berkel "The Attitude"). These techniques are crucial to navigating a massive resource like *Ṣubḥ*, which comprises explications of *what*, *why* and *how* to write in numerous situations (even rare ones like congratulating one's mother on her nuptials), providing sample letters/documents. Consider, for example, Essay Nine devoted to *ṣulḥ*. It is organized thematically and typologically, covering conditions for and legal/religious bases for peacemaking practices.

ṢULḤ AND RHETORIC

Numerous words in Arabic refer to peace (*salām*) and peacemaking/reconciliation (*ṣulḥ*). *Ṣulḥ* mainly means to reconcile with others, and the term is grounded in an investment in restorative justice as a modality for the realization of relational responsibilities toward oneself and others. Restorative justice—unlike punitive justice—seeks to attend to the needs of all involved parties, including the wrongdoer, as parties work on countering and recovering from violence and injustice. *Ṣulḥ* refers to this investment, and the word also refers to a traditional practice, process, and ritual firmly rooted in the Arab-Islamic tradition. Indeed, one of the highly circulating, vernacular, and condensed references to *ṣulḥ* in modern-day Egyptian Arabic is a section of a verse from the Qur'ān which simply affirms "*ṣulḥ* is good" or "*wa al-ṣulḥ khayr*" ("al-Nisā'" 128), urging people to invest in peacemaking. Across time and space, *ṣulḥ* discourses developed into numerous practices, agreements, and pacts. In *Ṣubḥ*, al-Qalqashandī devotes Essay Nine (approximately two hundred pages) to *ṣulḥ*. The essay, which is partially in volume 13 and partially in volume 14, is divided into a total of six books. These books cover a huge territory, for the discourses of peacemaking are indeed rich and entail varied modes of discursive interaction. As such, it is a crucial resource for people studying Arab-Islamic peacemaking practices, and it is a good place to start exploring institutional expressions of peacemaking.

Essay Nine

Essay Nine begins in the last third of volume 13 (*Ṣubḥ* 321-86) and covers approximately the first third of volume 14 (*Ṣubḥ* 3-123). It covers five main types of peacemaking, terms, formulae commonly used, and principles that guide the process of writing an agreement. Essay Nine demonstrates keen awareness of the intersection of three bodies of rhetorical knowledge: (a) contractual/legally binding writing of *ṣulḥ* pacts; (b) meta-knowledge of institutional, letter/document writing; and (c) textual organization consistent with the demands of consultation literacy. Visually, the most prominent is attention to classification and organization. As al-Qalqashandī compiled information, formulae, and examples of *ṣulḥ*, he organized the information and made it accessible. These different types of information fall into five books (Books 1-5) that address peacemaking relevant to, for example, internal and international business and travel, as well as—in today's terms—foreign relations. Book 6 in contrast is devoted to nullification of agreements. Books 1-3 are in volume 13, and books 4-6 are in volume 14. These books are as follows with Appendix 1 outlining their contents:

> **Book 1:** Safe-Conduct Agreements (guarantees of freedom and safety in relation to religious practice, travel, and business, for example)
> **Book 2:** *Dafn* (Burial Ritual, or ritual for forgiving and forgetting)
> **Book 3:** Pacts with *Ahl al-Dhimmah* (People of Different Confessions)
> **Book 4:** Truce Agreements between Muslims and Non-Muslims
> **Book 5:** *Ṣulḥ* Agreements among and between Muslims
> **Book 6:** Nullification of Agreements[9]

Because of space limitations, the wealth of information the six books provide cannot be fully presented. However, five key features are worth a brief introduction. Essay Nine (a) manifests a multi-dimensional understanding of peacemaking as a discursive activity, (b) sheds light on varied models for initiation of peacemaking as unilateral or bilateral moves and their textual expression, and (c) blends meta-knowledge (i.e., the relations between examples, formulae, and principles that guide ṣulḥ practices) with detailed historical references and provides a compilation of documents that demonstrate peacemaking practices, precedents and articulation of rights (e.g., religious and travel rights and the right to life and safe business transactions) of residents and aliens.[10] Additionally, it (d) addresses grounds for unilateral and bilateral nullification of peacemaking agreements, and it (e) develops a complex yet accessible organizational scheme.

Essay Nine demonstrates a multi-dimensional understanding of peacemaking and provides examples of how peacemaking can manifest as a document, a performative act, and a rhetorical expression. To illustrate, peacemaking can actualize a *hudnah* (truce) that enables people to stop—hopefully not just temporarily—the state of war. Once political parties seize the political will to stop war, they can make use of varied types of *hudnah* documents, including sub-genres. For example, in relation to truce, book 4 (see appendix) helps us see the negotiation of relations among stakeholders and their needs, goals/phases for peacemaking as they issue unilateral or bilateral *hudnah* (truce agreements) and provide formulae and examples of documents articulating both types.

Ṣubḥ also addresses performative and ritualized peacemaking, and, intriguingly, devotes book 2 to *dafn* (burial). As a peacemaking ritual, *dafn* refers to the symbolic burial of someone's wrongdoing (i.e., ritualized forgiving and forgetting).. Under the impression that this is an articulation of individual and private ṣulḥ, I was surprised to find that *Ṣubḥ* lists *dafn* (as pertinent to *al-kātib*'s cultural and relational understanding of ṣulḥ needs). In book two, al-Qalqashandī explains how a recipient of injury/injustice can initiate forgiveness by inviting elders and those the wrongdoer trusts to a process of burying the violation by digging a hole in the ground and stating they have placed in the hole their violation and attendant feelings of hurt and anger. It is not customary—writes al-Qalqashandī in volume 13 (*Ṣubḥ* 351)—to complement this common Arab practice with a record. However, in chapter 2 of book 2, he explains what can be written to complement or replace the process when the pardoning party is a king. Then *dafn* actualizes as a *marsoum* (a decree)—in today's terms, a pardon, articulating a form of public and collective ṣulḥ (*Ṣubḥ* vol. 13 352–4).

Another conspicuous element of *Ṣubḥ* is its careful attention to classification and organization. Every volume has a table of contents, which helps readers get a bird's-eye view of an essay and understand relations between prominent themes of the various books. In addition to the table of contents, there are other organizational tools. Varied peacemaking needs enabled the proliferation of documents, which are introduced and compiled for *al-kuttāb*. Essay Nine is literally packed with information, necessitating an organization that facilitates access to information. The essays are made manageable because of careful attention to arrangement of materials and the use of headings and signposts, which are crucial to help readers spot and study different ways to (a) name a peacemaking document or frame a peacemaking process/event (be it a truce, a burial, an agreement, or a decree); (b) develop a document by going to safe-conduct agreements (books 1 and 2), pacts with resident non-Muslim groups (book 3), or truce/*ṣulḥ* agreements (books 4 and 5); (c) find discrete expressions to begin the document itself by emulating or adapting compiled formulae; or (d) cite precedents using any of the numerous examples—some from centuries earlier. As such, the needs of *kuttāb* to compose documents that initiate or ratify peacemaking agreements are accommodated when headings and signposts are used to direct their work as they consult Essay Nine on *ṣulḥ*.

CONCLUSIONS

al-Qalqashandī was keenly aware of the need for accumulated knowledge and precedents of peacemaking practices, which were crucial for the management of national and international affairs. Not only does al-Qalqashandī come across as a virtuoso, but he also skillfully manages readers' expectations as they navigate the complex information presented in Essay Nine. Refusing to settle for the provision of just compiled formulae or just a treatise on official correspondence, al-Qalqashandī writes an encyclopedia, which is not just thematically organized, but—to accommodate consultation literacy—also develops a complex organizational scheme within and across ten essays. As such, *Ṣubḥ* is an exemplary demonstration of the development of encyclopedic writing blended with an accommodation of consultation literacy. Importantly, *Ṣubḥ* has much more to offer. Recognized as one of the gems of *adab al-kātib*, *Ṣubḥ* provides us with an investment in official correspondence, composition of documents, and a vision for the writer. Considering the discipline's enduring investment in *ars dictaminis*, *Ṣubḥ* leads us to numerous questions: Does *Ṣubḥ* (and *adab al-kātib*) add/change our perception of traditions of letter writing for institutional correspondence? Does it invite us to cross the Mediterranean and explore writing done at the chancery? Since peacemaking is an enduring rhetorical situation and much needed in today's world, *Ṣubḥ* offers a medieval manifestation of peacemaking discourses. What do the documents archived in *Ṣubḥ* have on offer for today's peacemaking practices? I hope these questions pique more interest in al-Qalqashandī and *Ṣubḥ*. Then, we can collectively visit new archives and remap the rhetorical landscape.

NOTES

1. This is van Berkel's translation of the title. I transliterated Arabic words using the LC Romanization guide provided by the Library of Congress, which is available at <http://www.loc.gov/catdir/cpso/romanization/arabic.pdf >."

2. These calls have resulted in new lines of inquiry. To this effect, Denise Stodola writes that "medieval rhetoric as a field has seen a period of transformation and potential redefinition" (42), which has sought to address gaps (conceptual and chronological) and revisit established categories about medieval rhetoric in general and especially letter writing. To illustrate, Malcolm Richardson writes about women's business correspondence in the late Middle Ages

3. The former mainly focuses on Europe (e.g., *Rhetorica*'s 2001 special issue on *ars dictaminis*), whereas the latter mainly focuses on medieval translation and commentaries on Greek rhetorical traditions (e.g., Aristotle); none has focused on Mamlūk Cairo and Arab-Islamic institutional expression (e.g., Baddar; Borrowman; Butterworth; Ezzaher).

4. Referencing Hijrī and Gregorian calendars, respectively, which are often abbreviated as AH and CE.

5. Because of its rich exposition of information relevant to numerous disciplines, the encyclopedia is a well-recognized compendium of knowledge and has been studied by scholars of anthropology, archeology, sociology, history, and Middle East Studies, for example (e.g., 'Abd al-Karīm). Additionally, for a rhetoric scholar, the encyclopedia is exemplary in its classification and organization of information, comprising ten essays that are subdivided into books, chapters, and sections on different topics such as tools, intellectual resources, sciences, and skills the writer needs to invest in. Among the disciplines *al-kātib* needs are geography, lineage and ancestry, oaths, and *ṣulḥ* (peacemaking) pacts, deeds, and practices. All invite rhetorical studies in relation to fluidity of style, clarity of expression, meta-knowledge about writing genres, selection and compilation of exemplars, "archiving" documents now lost to us, enumerating principles that guide *al-kātib's* work, and representing a vision of the perfect writer. Each topic shifts our attention to a new area of exploration of Arab-Islamic rhetoric and extends our current scholarship on medieval rhetoric and, especially, institutional expression in the fifteenth century.

6. There was a hierarchy for the chancery's *kuttāb*. *Kātib al-sirr* is the chief officer, is considered a "confidential secretary," and is higher in rank than *kātib al-dast*, who is higher in rank than *kātib al-daraj*. For more on the changes in and development of the professional hierarchy of *kuttāb* and their varied responsibilities, please see Ḥabashī and Escovitz.

7. The Ummayyads were the second in a sequence of four Caliphates, which was the governance system after the death of Prophet Moḥammad. Their Caliphate (41–132 AH) expanded the territory under Muslim rule. At the time, it reached as far as China to the east and the south of France to the west. The history of the administrative system during the rule of Ummayyad is covered by a lot of scholarship, which explains how their administrative system relied on systems developed by others. For example, they relied on correspondence traditions developed by the Byzantine and the financial administrative system used by the Coptic Church (see, for example, Ḥabashī; Van Berkel, "The Attitude"). However, some scholars like Ḥabashī note the body of correspondence between

Prophet Moḥammad and other rulers of the time as being yet another influential branch of this influence.

8. al-Qalqashandī's *maqāmah* is titled "*al-Kawākib al-Durrīya fī al-Manāqib al-Badrīya*" and is a textual blend of different text types. It blends an autobiographical account of how/why he became a secretary; a comparison between becoming a secretary and an accountant; a reflection on and enumeration of the arts, types of knowledge, and writing skills of the ideal *kātib al-inshā'* (secretary); and a panegyric of *al-inshā'* (institutional writing) in general and his master (and his family of prominent secretaries), Badr al-Dīn ibn Faḍl Allāh. It's worth noting that Badr al-Dīn ibn Faḍl Allāh wrote a manual too, which was titled "*al-Taʿrīf bi-al-Muṣṭalaḥ al-Sharīf.*" For more, please see Durūbī.

9. For an outline of the books and its multi-layered subdivisions, please see Appendix 1.

10. These documents comprise precedents that go back as early as the seventh century.

WORKS CITED

'Abd al-Karīm, Aḥmad 'Izzat. *Abū al-'Abbās al-Qalqashandī wa Kitābuhu Ṣubḥ al-Aʿshá* [*Abū al-'Abbās al-Qalqashandī and His Book Ṣubḥ al-Aʿshá*]. Cairo: Book Institute, 1973. Print.

Agnew, Lois, et al. "Octalog III: The Politics of Historiography in 2010." *Rhetoric Review* 30.2 (2011): 109–34. Print.

al-Qalqashandī, Aḥmad ibn 'Alī. *Ṣubḥ al-Aʿsh'á fī Ṣinā'at al-Inshā'*. Ed. Muḥammad Hussein Shams al-Dīn. 14 vols. Beirut: *Dār al-Kutub al-'Ilmīyah*, 1987. Print.

Baddar, Maha. "From Athens (Via Alexandria) to Baghdad: Hybridity as Epistemology in the Work of Al-Kindi, Al-Farabi, and in the Rhetorical Legacy of the Medieval Arabic Translation Movement." *ProQuest*. 2010. Web. 30 March 2013.

Ballif, Michelle, ed. *Theorizing Histories of Rhetoric*. Carbondale: Southern Illinois UP, 2013. Print.

Bazerman, Charles. "Letters and the Social Grounding of Differentiated Genres." *Textual Dynamics of the Professions: Historical and Contemporary Studies of Writing in Professional Communities*. Eds. Charles Bazerman and James G. Paradis. Madison: U of Wisconsin P, 1991. 15–29. Print.

Borrowman, Shane. "The Islamization of Rhetoric: Ibn Rushd and the Reintroduction of Aristotle into Medieval Europe." *Rhetoric Review* 27.4 (2008): 341–60. Print

Bosworth, C. E. "A *Maqāma* on Secretaryship: Al-Qalqashandī's 'al-Kawākib al-Durriyya fī'l-Manāqib al-Badriyya.'" *Bulletin of the School of Oriental and African Studies* 27.2 (1964): 291–98. Print.

Butterworth, Charles E. "Translation and Philosophy: The Case of Averroës' Commentaries. *International Journal of Middle East Studies* 26.1 (1994): 19–35. Print.

Camargo, Martin. "The Waning of Medieval *Ars Dictaminis.*" *Rhetorica*19.2 (2001): 135–40. Print.

Doxtader, Erik. *With Faith in the Works of Words: The Beginnings of Reconciliation in South Africa.* East Lansing: Michigan State UP, 2009. Print.

Durūbī, Samīr Maḥmūd. *A Critical Edition of and Study on Ibn Faḍl Allāh's Manual of Secretaryship "al-Ta'rīf bi-al-Muṣṭalaḥ al-Sharīf".* Jordan: Mu'tah U, 1992. Print.

Enos, Richard, et. al. "Octalog II: The (Continuing) Politics of Historiography." *Rhetoric Review* 16.1 (1997): 22–44. Print.

Escovitz, J. H. "Vocational Patterns of the Scribes of the Mamlūk Chancery." *Arabica* 23.1 (1976): 42–62. Print.

Ezzaher, Lachen E. "Alfarabi's *Book of Rhetoric*: An Arabic-English Translation of Alfarabi's Commentary on Aristotle's *Rhetoric. Rhetorica: A Journal of the History of Rhetoric* 26.4 (2008): 347–91. Print.

Gorsevski, Ellen. *Peaceful Persuasion: The Geopolitics of Nonviolent Rhetoric.* Albany: State U of New York P, 2004. Print.

Ḥabashī, Ḥasan. "Dīwān al-Inshā': Nash'atuhu wa Taṭawwuruhu [The Chancery: Its Establishment and Development]." *Abū al-'Abbās al-Qalqashandī wa Kitābuhu Ṣubḥ al-A'shá [Abū al-'Abbās al-Qalqashandī and His Book Ṣubḥ al-A'shá].* Ed. Aḥmad 'Izzat 'Abd al-Karīm. Cairo: Book Institute, 1973. 81–96. Print.

Hatch, John. *Race and Reconciliation: Redressing Wounds of Injustice.* Lanham: Lexington, 2008. Print.

Murphy, James, et al. "Octalog I: The Politics of Historiography." *Rhetoric Review* 7.1 (1988): 5–49. Print.

Perelman, Les. "The Medieval Art of Letter Writing: Rhetoric as Institutional Expression." *Textual Dynamics of the Professions: Historical and Contemporary Studies of Writing in Professional Communities.* Eds. Charles Bazerman and James G. Paradis. Madison: U of Wisconsin P, 1991. 97–119. Print.

Richardson, Malcolm. "Women, Commerce, and Rhetoric in Medieval England." *Listening to their Voices: The Rhetorical Activities of Historical Women.* Ed. Molly Meijer Wertheimer. Columbia, SC: U of South Carolina P, 1999. 133–49. Print.

Stodola, Denise. "The Middle Ages." *The Present State of Scholarship in the History of Rhetoric: A Twenty-First Century Guide.* Ed. Lynée Lewis Gaillet and Winifred Bryan Horner. Columbia: U of Missouri P, 2010: 42–82. Print.

Van Berkel, Maaike. "A Well-Mannered Man of Letters or a Cunning Accountant: Al-Qalqashandī and the Historical Position of the Kātib." *Al-Masāq* 13 (2001): 87–96. Print.

—. "The Attitude towards Knowledge in Mamlūk Egypt: Organization and Structure of *The Subh Al-A 'shā* by Al-Qalqashandi (1355-1418)." *Pre-Modern Encyclopedic Texts. Proceedings of the Second COMERS Congress.* Ed. Peter Binkley. Leiden: Brill, 1997. 159–68. Print.

Vitanza, Victor. "Historiographies of Rhetoric." *Encyclopedia of Rhetoric and Composition: Communication from Ancient to the Information Age.* Ed. Theresa Enos. New York: Garland, 1996. 324–25. Print

Wansbrough, John. "The Safe-Conduct in Muslim Chancery Practice." *Bulletin of the School of Oriental and African Studies* 34 (1971): 20–35. Print.

APPENDIX I

ESSAY NINE: THE BOOK ON ṢULḤ OF AL-QALQASHANDĪ'S *ṢUBḤ*

Book 1: Safe-Conduct Agreements (guarantees of freedom and safety in relation to religious practice, travel, and business, for example)

Chapter 1: Safe Conduct with Non-Muslims
Section 1: Cultural and Religious Grounds and Origins, Conditions, and Legal Dimensions
Section 2: Contents, Structure, and Samples
- Beginning Formula 1
- Beginning Formula 2

Chapter 2: Safe Conduct with Muslims
Section1: Origins
Section 2: Contents
- Beginning Formula 1
- Beginning Formula 2
  - Type One: Issued by Caliph
    Formula One
    An Example
    Formula Two
  - Type Two: Issued by Kings
    Formula One: Safe-Conduct
    Style One: In response to a Petition
    Example
    Style Two: Petition not referenced
    Formula Two: Decree
    Old Examples
    Contemporary Examples
    Issued by Sultan
    Issued by Deputies of Northern States

Book 2: *Dafn* (Burial Ritual, or ritual for forgiving and forgetting)
Chapter 1: Meaning and Arab Origins
Chapter 2: What Kings Write

Book 3: Pacts with *Ahl al-Dhimmah* (People of Different Confessions)
Chapter 1: Origins
Section 1: Its Status, Meaning, Qur'ānic and Hadith Grounds
Example

Section 2: What *al-Kātib* needs to know (enumerates 8 different pre-requisites, conditions, and causes for nullification)

Chapter 2: To be written if People of Different Confessions Nullify/Violate Ṣulḥ (provides numerous historical facts and examples of pacts, reasons for their nullification, and what's written to document change/reasons for nullification)

Book 4: Truce Agreements between Muslims and Non-Muslims
Chapter 1: Origins and Principles
Section1: Status, Meaning, and Synonyms
Section 2: Origins
Section 3: Things *al-Kātib* Takes into Account
    Type 1: Truce Agreements between Muslims and Non-Muslims
    Type 2: Similarities between Truce Agreements (between Muslims and Non-Muslims) and *Ṣulḥ* Agreements (between Muslim Leaders)
    • Common Conditions and Terms of Agreements between Kings
    • Required Content: Specification of Terms and Regulations
Chapter 2: What's Written in Truce Agreements and Writers's Different Views
Section 1: Issued by Muslim Kings (copies archived and handed to Non-Muslim Counterparts)
    • Pattern 1: What's Written at the Beginning of the Document
    • Pattern 2: What's Written in the Body of the Truce Agreement
      • Type 1: Unilateral Truce Agreements
        Beginning Formula 1
        Beginning Formula 2
      • Type 2: Bilateral Truce Agreements between Muslim and Non-Muslim Kings
        Beginning Formula 1
        Beginning Formula 2
        Beginning Formula 3
Section 2: Similarities between Truce Agreements Issued by Muslims and Non-Muslims

Book 5: *Ṣulḥ* Agreements among and between Muslims
Chapter 1: Principles of Truce Agreements
Chapter 2: Commonly Written in Truce Agreements between Caliphs and Kings (in relation to succession of nations and pertaining to the Beginning and the Body)
      • Type 1: Multilateral Agreements
      • Type 2: Unilateral Agreements
        Beginning Formula 1
        Beginning Formula 2

Book 6: Nullification of Agreements
Chapter 1: al-Faskh: Unilateral Nullification
Chapter 2: al-Mufāsakhah: Bilateral Nullification

11 "What It Is to Be a Queenslander": The Australian State Parliamentary Motion of Condolence on Natural Disasters as Epideictic and Regional Rhetoric

Rosemary Williamson

The Australian Government describes Australians as a people who are resilient because of their experience of natural disaster (Wells). In late 2010 and early 2011, the Australian capacity for resilience was tested over what former Prime Minister Julia Gillard called the nation's "summer of sorrow" (Gillard). Bushfire, cyclone, and flood wreaked havoc across several of the states and territories into which the country is divided. Among the most devastated was the state of Queensland, which occupies the northeast of the continent and has some five million inhabitants. It suffered extensive and prolonged flooding, and by early February 2011, thirty-five people had died from floodwaters and nine remained missing.

Several motion of condolence speeches were presented to Australian parliaments to commemorate those who died that summer. Two addressed events in Queensland at length. Prime Minister Gillard delivered a speech to Federal Parliament that emphasized Australians' strength in the face of adversity as well as other purportedly quintessential Australian qualities, most notably the heroism and "mateship" (comradeship between friends) that are prominent in Australian political rhetoric, ceremonial events, and popular culture (Williamson, "Home-Grown Heroes"). Gillard made special mention of the then Premier of Queensland, Anna Bligh, who had overall responsibility for the response and recovery effort in her state. Bligh delivered her own motion of condolence speech, to the State Parliament of Queensland, in early 2011. Similarly to Gillard, Bligh praised the strength and tenacity of those affected by the flooding; unlike Gillard, however, she consistently, and almost exclusively, praised the people of a region—Queenslanders—rather than Australians collectively.

Bligh's praise of Queenslanders, which distinguishes the people of a region from their compatriots, invites the question guiding this essay: whether the motion of condolence following natural disasters can be situated within a distinctive tradition of epideictic rhetoric with a regionalist dimension. On one level, Bligh's tendency to exclusivity is pragmatic and attributable to the audience for her speech (members of the Queensland Parliament) and the localized demands of her role as leader of a region. *Region* here is used in the commonly understood sense of a place with formally defined borders. On another level, however, it suggests a more complex and relational shaping of communal identity for Queenslanders based on less overtly defined borders. To borrow from Jenny Rice's elucidation on the nature of regional rhetorics, Bligh potentially "disrupts given narratives of belonging that are framed on a national level and between individuals" and "provide[s] alternative ways of framing our relationships and modes of belonging" (203).

This essay begins by identifying the generic characteristics of the motion of condolence on natural disasters as a form of epideictic rhetoric concerned with articulating and reinforcing regional identity. Those characteristics guide the subsequent reading of Bligh's 2011 speech. To determine whether that speech can be situated within a discernible tradition of regional rhetoric, the essay then moves to what can be considered antecedent speeches from 1974 and 1893. A comparison of the speeches reveals their generic evolution and also serves to extend a body of scholarship on disaster and the rhetoric of resilience.

The Motion of Condolence as Epideictic Rhetoric

The motion of condolence is delivered by a political leader to the Federal Parliament of Australia, or a state or territory parliament. It formally recognizes service to the nation upon the death of an Australian member of parliament or a soldier, or it pays tribute to a group of Australians who have died as a result of catastrophic events, including natural disasters and terrorist attacks. The condolence motion comprises two parts: the motion itself, followed by a speech in support of the motion. In the case of natural disasters, the speech may serve both practical and rhetorical purposes. It may quantify the damage caused, detail the aid provided during and after the disaster, thank emergency services, and outline strategies for recovery and minimizing risk should similar events occur in the future. It also provides an opportunity to praise the collective attributes of those who have died or have helped during the crisis, and it may single out individuals as exemplars of those attributes. Those praised may represent a certain type of Australian who is distinguished from his or her compatriots because of the challenges presented by the natural environment of a region.

Because of these dual purposes, the condolence motion shares similarities with crisis rhetoric prominent in the media at times of disaster. For example, Premier Bligh spoke at a press conference at the height of the Queensland floods in 2011 and provided both "information and inspiration" (Williamson, "Breeding Them Tough" 34) suited to the moment. She reported on the progression of floodwaters and gave practical advice before praising Queenslanders as a resilient people, "the people that they breed tough north of the border . . . the ones that they knock down and [who] get up again" (qtd. in Williamson, "Breeding Them Tough" 34). Here was the combination of "strategic communication that helps to alleviate risk and restore public safety with a deeper, more humanistic communication" (Griffin-Padgett and Allison 377) that is called for when disaster strikes and may be pronounced in statements that respond to the immediate demands of press and people. Unlike the press conference, however, the motion of condolence enables a more considered reflection upon events.

Typically delivered in parliament after the immediate crisis has passed, the motion of condolence speech presents an opportunity to celebrate those attributes of a people that are accentuated during times of peril. It represents the way in which "the argumentation in epid[e]ictic discourse sets out to increase the intensity of adherence to certain values, which might not be contested when considered on their own but may nevertheless not prevail against other values that might come into conflict with them" (Perelman and Olbrechts-Tyteca 51). To achieve this objective and engender a perception of communal belonging based on the sharing of those values, the rhetor uses techniques of "amplification and enhancement" (Perelman and Olbrechts-Tyteca 51). Bligh's 2011 condolence motion is instructive.

2011 MOTION OF CONDOLENCE

The Queensland Parliament met on February 15, 2011, but set aside normal business so that members could discuss the widespread devastation caused by flooding in Queensland that summer. Premier Bligh delivered a motion in six parts. The first three parts concern the flood victims. Bligh moved that Parliament "acknowledges with great sadness the devastation," "extends its condolences and deepest sympathy to the families and loved ones of those killed," and "grieves for those who have suffered injury and who have lost their homes, property and personal possessions and extends . . . support for their recovery." The other three parts concern aid and recovery. Bligh moved that Parliament "places on record its sincerest gratitude for the leadership and the valued contribution" of those who have helped either officially or voluntarily, "sincerely acknowledges" fundraisers and support from home and abroad, and "pledges" ongoing commitment to recovery (1).

After calling for a minute's silence "as a mark of respect" (Bligh 1), Bligh delivered a speech that while long—4,597 words—quickly establishes that Queenslanders' qualities will be revealed through emotive stories. She begins, "The summer of 2010-11 will be remembered as our summer of sorrow." In the next two hundred words, "story" or "stories" appear thirteen times to define the disaster and its legacy; for example, the "summer will be remembered as a story of devastation and of horror, a story of fragility and vulnerability but also a story of hope and inspiration." These stories "characterise our indomitable Queensland spirit," according to Bligh (2).

Tales of destruction and bravery, which permeate the remainder of the speech, provide cumulative evidence of communal unity predicated upon the archetype of the "ordinary" Queenslander. First told is that of the floodwaters' progression: places inundated, days and dates, and damage done. Bligh then conveys the human toll, through images and stories. "Our summer of sorrow," she says, "has a very human face, characterised by powerful and haunting images—images that are both tragic and endearing, appalling and inspiring, heartbreaking and haunting" and are "now etched into our collective psyche" (3). One of several examples is "a family of three—mum, dad and a terrified, almost defeated little boy—trapped on the roof of their car as a boiling river of mud and debris threatened to take them" (3). Acts of bravery are narrated. Some tell of people in official capacities, such as the helicopter pilots "who battled impossible dangerous conditions to rescue [people] from their rooftops"; others tell of "ordinary" people, such as the boy who drowned so that his brother could be saved (4). All are "stories of normal, ordinary Queenslanders who faced and endured an extraordinary ordeal" (3). For Bligh, they are "tales of the Queensland heart and spirit." She repeatedly urges her audience to imagine what people suffered, and to that end uses such emotive descriptions as "appalling ferocity," "unadulterated terror," and "creeping panic" (4).

Even though the speech covers other ground—for example, it details aid provided from within and beyond Queensland—Bligh always returns to praising the "ordinary" people in whom the archetypal Queenslander is manifest. She concludes by thanking "the people of our state—the everyday Queenslanders who confronted these terrible events" and stating her pride in being "one of them" (6). She follows with:

> I knew that we would have to dig deep and we would have to find the very best of ourselves to overcome this ordeal, and that is just what we did. We remembered who we are. As we surveyed all that we had lost, we remembered what it is to be a Queenslander—the ones who today, in every town and city, in every street and suburb, in every farm and business, in every nook and cranny, are proving that when we get knocked down we get right back up again. (6)

Here, Bligh echoes the fundamental sentiment of her January 2011 press conference, when she implored Queenslanders to "remember who we are . . . the people that they breed tough north of the border . . . the ones that they knock down," but that "get up again" (qtd. in Williamson, "Breeding Them Tough" 34). This colloquial expression of resilience distils Bligh's conception of Queenslanders. It also can be seen to allude to Queensland's longstanding rivalry with other states, and perceptions of its inferiority (Williamson, "Breeding Them Tough"; Fitzgerald), and therefore represents a regionalized rhetoric of resilience.

Bligh does not refer directly to regionally-based rivalry, but she does explicitly constitute two communities—one regional, one national— of which the regional is primary. She consistently names flood victims as Queenslanders; indeed, "Australians" appears only when Bligh thanks her compatriots collectively:

> . . . my most heartfelt thanks go to those ordinary Australians— those mums and dads, those children, those families—who have opened their hearts, opened their wallets and opened their piggy banks to donate to our appeal. In times when I know many Australian families are doing it tough, this has meant so much to each and every one of us and so much to those Queenslanders who have been hurt. (6)

While Australians are united in their compassion, they are set apart from, and defined in relation to, Queenslanders. Articulating the values and qualities of Queenslanders remains the rhetor's dominant concern.

1974 MOTION OF CONDOLENCE

Despite Bligh's description of that summer's events being unprecedented, she also mentions "scenes not witnessed in almost 40 years, since the floods of 1974" (2). Queensland had suffered catastrophic flooding previously, including in January 1974, when large parts of capital city Brisbane were ruined and twenty-eight people died across the state. The scale of the disaster was comparable to that of 2010–11. It prompted a condolence motion that formally and qualitatively resembles its 2011 counterpart but overall represents a less fully developed expression of regionally-based resilience.

That this is so is seen early in the 1974 parliamentary record. As in 2011, the condolence motion was a prominent item of business, although to a lesser extent. It too was presented by the Premier to Queensland Parliament's first meeting after the floods, in this case on March 5, but unlike 2011, only after preliminary discussion of other business. Also similarly, the 1974 version comprises the motion followed by a speech in support of it. The then Premier Johannes Bjelke-Petersen moved that parliament "record its deepest sympathy to the families and relatives of those Queenslanders who died in the flood" and "gratitude" (2626) to those at home or abroad who helped Queenslanders. In his supporting speech, Bjelke-Petersen explains that the motions are intended not only "to give thanks where they are due" but also to provide a forum in which members of parliament can "voice constructive criticism" (2626) about the response by emergency services. Here is a marked difference in purpose between the speeches of 1974 and 2011. The latter, by not inviting criticism of emergency services, lacks the implied politicization of natural disaster response seen in 1974.

Another difference is the extent to which stories are used to depict Queenslanders. Premier Bjelke-Petersen tabled files containing official documentation of the emergency. He urges members of parliament to read them "because hour by hour, these files record in its most graphic form the heroism; the courage; the tragedy; the self-sacrifice; the shortcomings; and the human weaknesses; but, above all, the magnificent will of the people of Queensland in what will go down in history as the 'Great Flood'" (2626–27). These sentiments permeate Bligh's speech of 2011, which similarly foregrounds Queenslanders' strength and resilience yet admits their vulnerability, but in another respect, Bjelke-Petersen's speech differs. He admits that he "had intended to outline the story of the flood in detail" but decided not to because it would "take up too much . . . time"; instead, he draws attention to the tabled reports containing "a comprehensive record of the flood" (2627). Bjelke-Petersen's approach to conveying the magnitude of the flood reflects his rather pragmatic view that the condolence motion has dual utility: to commemorate, and to invite criticism of emergency services. His pragmatism may have arisen from exigencies around both the disaster response and parliamentary meetings, and even personal preference, but it also suggests that in 1974 the condolence motion was still evolving generically. It was not yet the sustained celebration of regionalism represented by Bligh's speech of 2011.

That is not to say that stories are entirely absent from Bjelke-Petersen's speech. He acknowledges those organizations and people who provided help in official capacities or voluntarily, then describes more specifically the actions of groups or individuals who typify the "acts of bravery, devotion to duty and self-sacrifice that are unknown except to those concerned" (2627). He singles out, for example, the pilots who flew in perilous conditions to rescue people from floodwaters, as well as those who were employed to represent or serve the people but went beyond what would normally be expected of them. These include members of parliament, such as "The honourable member for Mt. Cooth-tha . . . [who] although shocked, burned and thrown into the water when an amphibious vehicle came into contact with high-tension electricity wires, dived back into the water a few moments later to save another man" (2627). Stories do serve to illustrate "how Queenslanders rose to the crisis" (2627), but they tend to be about the representatives of the people, or those in service organisations, rather than the "ordinary" people who embody the archetypal Queenslander of 2011.

Much of the remainder of Bjelke-Petersen's speech concerns damage done to industries and infrastructure, details of the response and recovery effort, and flood mitigation. Bligh's speech of 2011 similarly covers such pragmatic matters, but Bjelke-Petersen appears to be motivated primarily by his assumption that "what Queenslanders want to know is . . . what is being done to meet future disasters" (Bjelke-Petersen 2629) rather than a concern with evocatively portraying the collective experiences and attributes of "ordinary" people.

This overview of Bjelke-Petersen's speech considers the first 3,057 words, after which is an extended and politically biased debate between the Premier and members of parliament about the adequacy of response and recovery strategies. Members clearly welcomed Bjelke-Petersen's opening invitation to "voice constructive criticism" (2626). His condolence motion speech does not close nor does it refrain from political defensiveness and accusation. From a generic perspective, these judicial elements detract from the essentially epideictic function of the motion of condolence as an expression of region-alism. They differentiate the speech from that delivered by Bligh in 2011.

1893 Opening Speech

Comparing the 2011 and 1974 speeches reveals continuity in the two pre-miers' conceptualizations of Queenslanders as resilient and heroic, despite a thirty-seven year gap in between their terms in office and oppositional politi-cal affiliation. Moving further back in time, to the parliamentary records of colonial Queensland, reveals that Queenslanders of the nineteenth century were less fully described yet nevertheless were seen to display characteristic fortitude when confronted by natural disaster.

Australia comprised a number of separate colonies before becoming a na-tion by federation in 1901. In 1893, the colony of Queensland had existed for only thirty-four years when its economy faced collapse and torrential rain caused severe flooding during what Queenslanders called "Black February." The floods affected various parts of the state, including Brisbane, and caused the deaths of thirty-five people.

Nineteenth-century Queensland had its own parliament with conven-tions derived from those of the British Empire, but these conventions did not extend to routine and discrete commemoration of the effects of natural disas-ter. Queensland Parliament did not meet until May 1893, some three months after the floods. Given this delay and the parlous state of the economy, it is unsurprising that formal recognition of the flooding was brief. There was no motion of condolence; rather, the flood was addressed only in the "Opening Speech" to Parliament by the Governor of the Colony, Sir Henry Wylie Nor-man, which was read to Parliament rather than delivered personally.

Norman's speech comprises only 907 words; the portion devoted to the floods is considerably shorter. Dominating his speech are economic matters and the colony's uncertain future. Early on, Norman mentions the "adverse seasons" (5) responsible for the colony raising less revenue than projected, but the flooding and its effects are not detailed until just over mid-way:

> While the Western pastoral districts have been, and to some ex-tent still are, suffering from a scanty rainfall, the southern coastal districts have been devastated by destructive floods. I have noted with much satisfaction the recuperative powers exhibited by those people who were driven from their occupations and dwellings by the floods, with the loss of their portable property and homes. I have also seen with much pleasure and satisfaction, and gratefully acknowledge, the prompt liberality of our fellow-country-men in all

parts of the world in sending such munificent contributions for the relief of distress. (5)

After moving to other topics, Norman ends optimistically, by expressing hope for "indefinite expansion" in industry, and confidence "that under the blessing of God the result of [parliament's] calm and mature deliberations will be to launch once more the ship of state on the sea of prosperity" (6). As only one of several trials that would test but not destroy the colony, the flood apparently did not merit more than passing comment.

Again, there are similarities with Bligh's 2011 speech, but they are general ones. Norman acknowledges the severity of the flooding, the resilience of victims (albeit through the comparatively understated "recuperative powers"), and the help provided by others. However, his concluding expression of piety and faith in parliament reflect a time when God and Empire, rather than stories of the people, guided the rhetor's sense of appropriateness to occasion. Imperial stoicism is even more pronounced elsewhere when a member of parliament, responding to Norman's speech, refers to the inevitability of Queensland's recovery "because it has never yet been possible to crush a British colony, and it never will" (Kingsbury 9). Norman refrains from naming flood victims collectively, yet elsewhere the parliamentary record from 1893 shows that *Queenslander* was an established term.

CONCLUSION

The Australian parliamentary motion of condolence on death caused by natural disaster is one form of epideictic rhetoric that provides a good, if unwelcome, opportunity to define a citizenry in relation to the challenges presented by the natural environment. From a generic perspective and in the case of Queensland parliamentary statements on flooding, the condolence motion has its origins in the nineteenth century but did not achieve its status as a discrete event until the twentieth century. Transcripts of speeches from 1893, 1974, and 2011 reveal a heightening emphasis on the formal commemoration of death and suffering caused by natural disaster: speeches become longer and more deliberately separated from other parliamentary business, and in 2011 the parliamentary record indicates an opening minute of silence.

A function of epideictic rhetoric is to "increase the intensity of adherence to certain values" (Perelman and Olbrechts-Tyteca 51). In this respect, the three Queensland flood speeches share similarities with responses to disaster elsewhere, whatever the cause of that disaster. Each in its own way praises resilience in the face of adversity, even if "resilience" is not used explicitly. The rhetoric of resilience also occurs in, for example, the portrayal of Britons following major flooding in the 1950s (Furedi, "From the Narrative of the Blitz") and more recently in the description of New Yorkers following 9/11 (Griffin-Padgett and Allison 384) and of Londoners following the 2005 terrorist bombings (Bean, Keränen, and Durfy). As Hamilton Bean, Lisa Keränen, and Margaret Durfy observe, a rhetoric of resilience has the advantage of engendering "a feeling of personal and/or collective well-being, strength, and control" (453). Also similarly to elsewhere, the Queensland speeches of 1974 and 2011 admit the vulnerability of the people. A parallel can be drawn here with the findings of Frank Furedi ("Coping"; "From the Narrative of the Blitz"), who identifies a growing rhetoric of vulnerability around environmentally-based disasters in Britain.

In 1974 and even more so in 2011, the speeches to Queensland Parliament conceptualize natural disaster through narratives of collective experience. Telling stories becomes a prominent device for the "amplification and enhancement" through which the rhetor "establish[es] a sense of communion centered around particular values" (Perelman and Olbrechts-Tyteca 51). From a humanistic viewpoint, story furnishes proof of the agency and irrepressibility of Queenslanders, the "magnificent will" (Bjelke-Petersen 2627) and "indomitable . . . spirit" (Bligh 2) that ensure their recovery and future prosperity in spite of their vulnerability. In 2011, stories "have reverberated across our nation, around the world and . . . will reverberate in our history" (Bligh 4) and so will secure the status of Queenslanders in relation to others, both spatially and temporally.

The epideictic function of the (post-federation) speeches of 1974 and 2011, in portraying the collective qualities and values of Queenslanders, has additional significance when considered from the critical perspective of regional rhetorics. The resilient Queenslander fits within longstanding, populist notions of *Australianness*. It follows, then, that as a named people, Queenslanders constitute a regional (state) community that is concentric with a parent (national) community, with each having the same qualities and values at its center. Supporting this conclusion are acknowledgments in each speech of the benevolence shown to Queenslanders by fellow Australians, which by implying harmony and unity reinforce the assumption of state-nation synergy. Yet as Jenny Rice reminds us, "region is a rhetorical interface" (204) based on relations, but not necessarily concentric ones, between places (206). Region is a complex construct involving more than cartographic borders. Conceptualizing region in this way recalls the purpose of community as advocated by Carolyn R. Miller: community is ideally more than "a geographic or demographic or empirical entity; it is a rhetorical construction, one that is necessary both for emotional solidarity and for political action" (91). Forming emotionally unified and politically active communities may, however, simultaneously give rise to what Rice calls "the tectonic and architectonic impulses of rhetoric," the relational dynamic between places that produces "alternative ways of framing our relationships and modes of belonging" (203) and is the hallmark of regional rhetorics. Behind the naming and depiction of Queenslanders is an oppositional relation to Australians that inevitably fractures national uniformity, no matter how superficially congruent the construct of Queenslander is with its Australian parent. Rhetorical expounding of identity based on regionally-based experience, and the qualities and values defining that experience, necessarily unites a people but separates them from their compatriots.

It is timely to return to Premier Bligh's almost exclusive reference in her 2011 motion of condolence speech to Queenslanders, as opposed to Australians, which inspired this essay. Such exclusivity, which also occurs in Premier Bjelke-Petersen's speech of 1974, reflects cartographic borders as well as political ones that see each state or territory of Australia with its own parliament. Some degree of governmental independence produces distinctive political, economic, and social histories for the nation's states and territories. Bligh's 2011 motion of condolence to Queensland Parliament expresses a sense of regional singularity that is expressed fully in her concluding statement on "what it is to be a Queenslander—the ones who today, in every town and city, in every street and suburb, in every farm and business, in every nook and cranny, are proving that when we get knocked down we get right back up again" (6). While this can be read as yet another iteration of Australian resilience, it can also be read as a regionally situated resilience that alludes to longstanding perceptions of Queensland being denigrated by, or in competition with, other states or territories. Region, therefore, moves beyond the "commonplace" of "a smaller geographic ring to the larger category of nation" (Rice 206) to become an interplay of complex and potentially resistant relations resulting in perceptions of borders of various kinds. Natural disaster, of course, does not respect these borders; however, the motion of condolence on natural disasters provides a formal, epideictic site through which these borders may be remembered, reinforced or even redrawn.

Works Cited

Bean, Hamilton, Lisa Keränen, and Margaret Durfy. "'This is London': Cosmopolitan Nationalism and the Discourse of Resilience in the Case of the 7/7 Terrorist Attacks." *Rhetoric & Public Affairs* 14.3 (2011): 427–64. Print.

Bjelke-Petersen, Johannes. "Queensland Flood." *Official Record of the Debates of the Legislative Assembly (Hansard) Second Session of the Fortieth Parliament.* Vol. 264. Queensland Parliament. Government Printer: Brisbane, 1974. 2626–30. Print.

Bligh, Anna. "Motion: Natural Disasters." *Record of Proceedings: First Session of the Fifty-Third Parliament.* Queensland Parliament, 15 Feb. 2011. Web. 8 July 2014.

Fitzgerald, Ross. "Bligh Tide in Queensland." *Australian* 2 Feb. 2011: 24. Print.

Furedi, Frank. "Coping with Adversity: The Turn to the Rhetoric of Vulnerability." *Security Journal* 20 (2007): 171-84. Print.

—. "From the Narrative of the Blitz to the Rhetoric of Vulnerability." *Cultural Sociology* 1.2 (2007): 235–54. Print.

Gillard, Julia. "Motion of Condolence: Natural Disasters." *PM Transcripts: Transcripts from the Prime Ministers of Australia.* Australian Government, 8 Feb. 2011. Web. 8 July 2014.

Griffin-Padgett, Donyale R., and Donnetrice Allison. "Making a Case for Restorative Rhetoric: Mayor Rudolph Giuliani & Mayor Ray Nagin's Response to Disaster." *Communication Monographs* 77.3 (2010): 376–92. Print.

Kingsbury, John. "Address in Reply." Queensland Parliament 7–9.

Miller, Carolyn R. "Rhetoric and Community: The Problem of the One and the Many." *Defining the New Rhetorics.* Ed. Theresa Enos and Stuart C. Brown. Newbury Park, CA: Sage, 1993. 79–94. Print. Sage Ser. in Written Communication 7.

Norman, Henry Wylie. "The Opening Speech." Queensland Parliament 5–6.

Perelman, Chaim, and L. Olbrechts-Tyteca. *The New Rhetoric: A Treatise on Argumentation.* 1958. Trans. John Wilkinson and Purcell Weaver. Notre Dame, IN: U of Notre Dame P, 1969. Print.

Queensland Parliament. *Official Record of the Debates of the Legislative Assembly during the First Session of the Eleventh Parliament.* Vol. 70. Government Printer: Brisbane, 1893. Print.

Rice, Jenny. "From Architectonic to Tectonics: Introducing Regional Rhetorics." *Rhetoric Society Quarterly* 42.3 (2012): 201–13. Print.

Wells, Kathryn. "Natural Disasters in Australia." *Australia.gov.au.* Australian Government, n.d. Web. 25 June 2014.

Williamson, Rosemary. "Breeding Them Tough North of the Border: Resilience and Heroism as Rhetorical Responses to the 2011 Queensland Floods." *Social Alternatives* 31.3 (2012): 33–38. Print.

—. "Home-Grown Heroes: The Use of Narrative in Prime Minister Julia Gillard's 2011 'Motion of Condolence: Natural Disasters.'" *The Encounters: Place, Situation, Context Papers—The Refereed Proceedings of the 17th Conference of The Australasian Association of Writing Programs.* 25–27. Nov. 2012, Deakin U: Australasian Association of Writing Programs. Web. 8 July 2014.

12 Going Digital: Rhetorical Strategies in the Enhanced State of the Union

Jeffrey A. Kurr

From time to time, the president innovates the State of the Union delivery. In 1923, Calvin Coolidge orated over radio waves. In 1947, Harry Truman appeared on televisions nationwide. In 1965, Lyndon Johnson delivered a primetime address. In 2002, George Bush was streamed live on the Internet. And in 2011, Barack Obama was juxtaposed online with dynamic images and interactive features. Presidents made these innovations in order to expand access to the political process and improve democratic deliberation. Radio allowed the American public to listen to the address live. Television provided a visual accompaniment to the executive's voice. The Internet enabled the globe to watch the delivery. Each of these innovations permitted more of the public to witness the address; however, the online addition of visual images fundamentally altered the message the public received relative to Congress.

Alongside the address's live feed, online users watched a multimedia presentation featuring graphs, images, quotations, and symbols. The television audience and attending members of Congress were not privy to these additional features. The presentation represented an attempt by the president to "enhance" the message the public received. Obama's strategy created a new way of "going public" with legislative items in the annual message, a key feature of the rhetorical presidency (Tulis). Karlyn Kohrs Campbell and Kathleen Hall Jamieson argue that "presidents in the electronic age have attempted to reach both Congress and the people" in order to mobilize the citizenry behind the executive agenda (156). The enhanced State of the Union functioned to digitally engage the public to pressure the legislature.

The effectiveness of presidential agenda setting and public pressure has been studied extensively. Political scientists have reached mixed conclusions analyzing a variety of scenarios (Barabas; Cohen; Cummins; Edwards; Eshbaugh-Soha; Hill; Young and Perkins). In particular, the State of the Union is considered the "primary vehicle" for the "administration's policy priorities" and "regarded as a precious resource" (Yates and Whitford 578). As a result of "the considerable amount of national attention focused on its contents," Jeff Cummins argues, "The evidence presented here provides strong support for the link between the address and the president's policy success" (192). Communication scholars made similar conclusions concerning agenda setting (Tenpas; White). Campbell and Jamieson conclude the State of the Union represents the "greatest opportunity" for the president "to appeal forcefully for congressional cooperation, to buttress such appeals with pleas for popular support, and to link the legislative agenda to cultural values underlying the system of government" (164). This prioritizing function prevents "issues of significant public consequence" from "disappear[ing] into the government technocracy" (Goodnight 223). Hence, legislative items in the State of the Union are more likely to be debated by Congress and highlighted by the media.

As media has developed and become more sophisticated, the ways in which presidential signaling occurs has also changed. Thomas Benson postures, "Use of the Internet by the presidency and citizens offers a prospect of enhancing democracy by reshaping the rhetorical tools and contexts of presidential leadership" (51). Since William Clinton's use of e-mail in the 1992 election, presidents have increasingly used the Internet and new technology. The corpus of literature analyzing these developments is well developed and focuses anywhere from campaigning and fundraising to broadcasting addresses and traditional events. Obama's digital modifications to the State of the Union, which have appeared in his 2011, 2012, 2013, and 2014 addresses, represent the newest evolution in shaping political deliberation. Analyzing the enhanced State of the Union expands on the corpus of literature connecting the presidency and "computer-mediated communication" technologies.

In this essay, I develop the idea of the *digital presidency*, which acts in parallel with the rhetorical presidency, and how digitizing the State of the

Union represents a new strategy of shaping deliberation between the president, Congress, and the American public. I argue that *going digital* in the enhanced State of the Union involves juxtaposing visual images alongside the president's speech and represents an evolution in how the White House attempts to lead political debates. This tactic involves reaching a new online public with the enhanced speech. The address shapes deliberation in the public sphere by linking images with political associations, a strategy similar yet distinct from "subtle iconoclasm" (Finnegan and Kang). This connection attempts to influence public opinion by adopting certain images with specific policy proposals. I proceed in this essay by theorizing how the digital presidency acts in parallel with the rhetorical presidency through the use of interactive online engagement. I then analyze the various ways Obama used images in his enhanced address as a means to shape public debate. I conclude by discussing how the digital presidency and the enhanced State of the Union point to new areas of study in presidential rhetoric.

DIGITAL MEDIA AND THE RHETORICAL PRESIDENCY

Online streaming of presidential addresses had existed for eleven years before Obama "enhanced" the annual message. However, Bush relied on a traditional method of delivery. Streaming on the Internet represented a medium similar to broadcasting on the radio and the television; the president spoke and the public listened. When the president increases his or her outreach through new forms of broadcasting, such as the radio or the Internet, it pushes the presidency "further up the pole of political power" (Becker 10). Obama's "enhancement" provided the public with the ability to interact with the address and to circulate and easily reappropriate its contents online.

Advancements in media technology create new opportunities for the president to "go public," a practice integral to the "rhetorical presidency." Technological changes are critical to the rhetorical presidency because they provide "the president the means to communicate directly and instantaneously to a large national audience" (Tulis 186). While James Ceasar et al. originally focused on radio and television, the rise of the Internet and social media fostered new ways for the president to reach various publics. Stephen Hartnett and Jennifer Mercieca argued that under George W. Bush, the nation "entered an age of a *post-rhetorical presidency*" whereby the president attempted to "confuse public opinion, prevent citizen action, and frustrate citizen deliberation" (600; Mercieca and Vaughn). Rather than viewing the age of social media as "post-rhetorical," the Obama administration has demonstrated that the digital presidency acts in parallel with the rhetorical presidency. Instead of contributing to the explosion of "white noise," the administration attempts to pierce through it by combining the physical and the online (Mercieca and Vaughn 34). The president still stumps on the campaign trail and in town halls, yet at the same time, the White House engages in a digital strategy to engage online publics.

The digital presidency opens up the White House to reach new publics in unique ways. The president through digital circulation has the capacity to "speak to increasingly differentiated and narrow audiences" (Stuckey 45). While the enhanced State of the Union strategy could be classified as part of the "post-rhetorical presidency," the use of digital technology to explain policy positions and persuade a public to their effectiveness does not necessarily "confuse," "prevent," or "frustrate" citizen engagement. For other political figures, such as Hilary Clinton, social media provided "the opportunity to communicate directly with citizens outside of filtered news sites" (Anderson and Sheeler 225). Since politically slanted television channels, such as *MSNBC* and *Fox News*, adapt their messages to suit liberal and conservative ideologies, the president by "going digital" is able to go over the head of television networks, similar to how "going public" allows the president to go over the head of Congress.

The digital presidency relies on the dynamic nature of social media to circulate its message. Mary Stuckey, through her analysis of 2008 campaign events, observed that with "current electronic technologies" any person "could have created their own version" of a major speech based on how the Internet enables dynamic communication (46). "Interactivity" between audience and speaker with respect to online communication has a variety of meanings. "User-to-system" interactivity is the exchange between computers and individuals with regards to information and includes consumption activities, such as clicking on hyperlinks, viewing images, and watching videos (McMillan 174). "Human interaction" occurs when individuals "share the burden of communication equally, subverting hierarchical, linear structures of communication" (Stromer-Galley 117). Online message boards exemplify this type of interactivity as multiple users converse digitally. "User-to-user interactivity" also includes "campaign-to-user or user-to-campaign" based on the authoritative role taken by campaign staffers on political candidate websites, and by extension social media accounts (Endres and Warnick 325). Finally, "user-to-document," occurs when users modify online content and redistribute it through other channels. Initially, this type of interactivity described the act of forwarding e-mails or linking on one's own website (Williams and Trammel). As the power of digital media progressed, this interaction has become exemplified by viral videos and memes (Knobel and Lankshear; Shifman).

Interactivity also enables the president to foster a sense of civic engagement online. Surrounding the 2014 State of the Union address, the White House launched the "Virtual Big Block of Cheese Day." Citing an old legend about Andrew Jackson, the administration invited the public to ask questions about the State of the Union on social media outlets using "#AskTheWH" in their posts (Lindsay). The White House lauded the event as "the most accessible" State of the Union address in history (Lubin). To generate the idea that the president was engaging with the online public, one staff member relayed a question to the president while he was backstage at a speaking event ("Backstage with President Obama"). Obama's answer was uploaded to *YouTube*, a video sharing website, and then circulated amongst other social media outlets.

While the Internet creates the possibility of new ways to engage politically, some critics do not view the developments as beneficial for deliberation. Bruce Gronbeck observed that using the Internet could "operate in grand or lowly ways" ("The Presidency" 47). Similar to their radio and television counterparts, partisan websites, such as *Daily Kos* and *Fox News*, tend to have stories that promote certain "ideological orientations" (Baum and Groeling 359). The polarization problem, while not unique to digital media, becomes particularly salient as social media has the capacity to foster "homogenous enclaves" where like-minded individuals circulate the same opinion amongst themselves (Warner). The digital presidency, through its social media outreach, has the possibility of creating online enclaves where homogenous publics praise or blame the White House's engagement techniques. Prior to the 2014 address, one conservative writer described the president as "setting a political mousetrap" because the virtual block of cheese created a false sense of transparency (Medina). The digital presidency then exists in the same polarized media environment, albeit online instead of over radio or television waves.

Obama's move to provide an interactive State of the Union can be viewed as an initial step in opening up these digital enclaves and foster open deliberation, similar to how previous presidents attempted to control the message in traditional journalism. The webpages for the enhanced State of the Union addresses were embedded streams. Users had the option to generate a link to embed the video, to share the stream via social media, and to download the speech. When sharing the speech, users could provide their own commentary on social media outlets. The 2013 and 2014 enhanced addresses expanded these features and included links at the top of the page to provide additional policy information, offered individuals the ability to "engage" the White House by submitting questions, and provided a transcript of the speech. The transcript enabled users to immediately share or comment on particular lines from the speech through various social media outlets. The digital presidency is tied to each of these features, as they provide new ways for the address to be accessible and the administration to be transparent.

The digital features of the enhanced State of the Union encouraged political participants to recirculate the text and coalesced all three types of interactivity. First, staffers reposted individual comments about certain lines on the official White House *Twitter* feed, a social media site focusing on concise commentary. Second, the audience could instantly find related information on points for either immediate consumption or for later reference. Third, the sharing features sparked conversations between users on other websites over the content of the speech. While each of these interactions existed before these "enhanced" State of the Unions, the online inclusion by the White House attempted to direct audience focus, similar to how the White House press secretary frames his or her answers for media consumption. For example, the entire speech was not posted in entirety on any social media outlet; instead, specific quotes and accompanying images were circulated online. Thus, the White House's use of social media during major speeches is how the digital presidency attempts to control the message received by the public.

Going digital requires the White House to cut through the "white noise" generated by mass media. While the administration may be criticized for contributing to this white noise, the digital presidency needs to pierce the fog in order to reach the public. Before the rise of interactivity on the web, the president set the agenda with the State of the Union address, after which pundits attempted to spin public opinion. As digital media developed, the presidency had to innovate on its tools. The enhanced State of the Union represented this latest development as it allowed the White House to engage the public, as the president was speaking. The instantaneous nature of social media required a variety of methods to foster transparency, and the Obama presidency responded by "enhancing" the State of the Union.

THE PRESIDENT'S POWERPOINT

The enhanced State of the Union relied on the juxtaposition of dynamic images alongside the live stream of the president's speech. Whether they were charts explaining growth, pictures of historical figures, or graphic designs, the images attempted to shape audience understanding of the address. The strategic use of visuals is part and parcel with crafting a presidential ethos. Traditionally, presidents control image making with staged photo opportunities and the circulation of campaign material, either in print or online. Before, the format of the State of the Union provided no avenue to incorporate images. The speech is given in the House chamber at a podium set up right in front of the Speaker of the House. While the set up for a screen or an easel is possible, the addition would detract from the address's traditional focal point: the president.

The "enhanced" State of the Union thus allows the president a way to alter the message suitable for the parameters of digital media. The juxtaposition of dynamic images allows Obama to associate certain visual meanings with his verbal address. Traditionally, the White House crafts political realities through staged photo opportunities, relying on what Keith Erickson describes as "performance imagery" that "attempts to manage and control the citizenry's views of reality by visually imposing interpretive frames that felicitously engage the public's perceptions" (144). The images that were associated with the enhanced State of the Union were an extension of this staging strategy.

The enhanced speech creates a context for the audience to understand the image, which in turn provides clarity and emphasis to the president's address. This strategy intensifies the point being made. David Birdsell and Leo Groarke expand on this idea: "Words can establish a context of meaning into which images can enter with a high degree of specificity while achieving a meaning different from the words alone" (6). Obama's address framed, and was framed by, the images that were juxtaposed in the enhanced version. The duality of verbal and visual cues allows the president's argument to operate over multiple channels. Gronbeck clarifies further: "In multimediated communication, sense-making and inference-drawing depend upon receivers experientially sorting through the symbols in each channel simultaneously, comprehending and interpreting those messages through complex cognitive acts not unlike multitasking" ("Varied Relationships" 175). The primary channels the enhanced State of the Union operates over are visual and audial, which frame the audience's reference point to both the images and the speech.

Whereas the speech may have been intended to create a certain message by itself, the visual image modifies the verbal argument by introducing additional argumentative elements. When the image is structured to be the secondary channel, it can be "used to frame or provide additional meanings" to the speech, a supplementary role (Gronbeck, "Varied Relationships" 175). The address, though, also shapes audience understanding of the visual image because frames, as Michelle Gibbons argues "are internalized, becoming part of one's encounter with images," and, "play such an important role in argument's characteristics features" (186). When fragments of the address were circulated via the Internet, so too were the images. The online public then adopts a distinct message from the television or newspaper publics. Since the State of the Union is traditionally considered an address for "public meditations on values, assessments of information and issues, and policy recommendations," audience expectations of the images are similar to those of the speech (Campbell and Jamieson 139). The images playing a key role in the address are important for the meaning the online public receives. This is a departure from how information is traditionally viewed in public deliberation. Cara Finnegan and Jiyeon Kang note, "Images and vision often are interpreted through a logic of subtle iconoclasm that makes Visuality subservient to dominant linguistic/rational norms" (396). Instead of changing the meaning of an iconic photograph, the speech imports the value from the image into the speech. The selection and circulation of the images provide additional layers for interpretation for the president's address. Hence, the images constitute a visual State of the Union.

The four enhanced State of the Union addresses include two broad visual categories: photographs and illustrative diagrams. In the "photograph" category, most of the images were either political figures or iconic images. There were a few photographs of various objects to illustrate the president's point. For example, when Obama discussed new automobile industry jobs created by Ford, there was a stock image of a Ford vehicle next to him (2013). While these images provide clarity and help illustrate the points being made, the other types of photographs are more salient. The photographs of contemporary figures depict presidential photo-ops. These included Obama in Florida touring a solar power farm (2011), in the situation room monitoring the raid on bin Laden's compound (2012), and in the White House meeting with Olympic athletes (2013). Erickson criticizes photo opportunities as they have the potential to manipulate "visual appeals" and cloud the "distinction between fiction and reality" (139; Grabe and Bucy). Maria Grabe and Erik Bucy observed a similar strategy in the Reagan administration, which frequently used "feel-good imagery to deflect" focus from unpopular agenda items (55). The photographs in the enhanced address function similarly, as they provided positive associations with the president's proposals whether those associations existed or not.

Photographs of historical figures, Robert Kennedy (2011), Abraham Lincoln (2012), and John F. Kennedy (2013), accompanied quotes that the president sampled during his address. The political figure category, both historical and contemporary, was used to create positive associations with the president himself. Obama is either juxtaposed with a popular politician or shown fulfilling the duties of president. Hence, the images helped establish the president's authority to be making the legislative recommendations that he did.

The administration also heavily included photographs that were either iconic images, or contained verbal ideographs. These images attempted to instill a sense of American pride and national identity. In 2011, he used a photo of an astronaut on the moon to illustrate "this generation's Sputnik moment." In 2012, the enhanced version included the flag raising at Iwo Jima as a way to narrate American heroes. In 2013, Obama's presentation included a contemporary manifestation of the V-J Day in Times Square photograph. These images allowed Obama a new way to invoke political icons from the lexicon of American history, and they functioned to create the necessary sense of unity for his legislative agenda.

The second category of images the president used included illustrative diagrams and other infographics. By sheer number, the appearance of these images dwarfed their photograph counterparts, appearing in approximately sixty-five-percent of the slides primarily in the middle of the speech. The 2014 address had the most photographs, on forty-percent of the slides, but bullet points started appearing on the images in the latest enhanced version. The graphs were not used to generate presidential authority or create national identity. The diagrams ranged from bar and line graphs to pictographs. They visually simplified the complexities of economic growth, educational opportunities, governmental agency relationships, and similar issues. These graphs functioned to support the president's legislative agenda, as they favorably depicted various statistical measures. For example, in 2013, a diagram on global surface temperature appeared next to the president when he discussed climate change. To exaggerate the effect of increasing temperatures, the graph extended back to 1880. By including the late nineteenth and early twentieth century, the diagram generated a more dramatic curve in showing increasing temperatures. Since the White House was in charge of making the charts, they were able to control the visual dimension of how the statistical data was displayed. The graphs then prime the deliberation on technical matters, such as climate change or economic policy.

As expected, the images featured in the enhanced address worked part and parcel within the speech's genre. They established the authority of the president to set the agenda, framed the initial discussion of the proposals, and created a unified public to support the policies. The president could be instantly associated with historically popular figures such as Lincoln or Kennedy. Photo opportunities could be redeployed in front of the president's largest audience. Visual diagrams could initially frame complex legislative items. While each of these functions could be achieved by verbal argumentation alone, the images helped frame the address in a positive light.

CONCLUSION

The development of media technologies has required the president to adapt in the past. Roosevelt broadcasted his fireside chats on the radio. Johnson moved the address to the evening to take advantage of primetime television. Bush streamed nearly all of his major appearances on the Internet. Obama's enhancement of the State of the Union is distinct in that it alters how the message is received and then recirculated. The White House is able to set the agenda not only through the address but also shape how publics receive the speech. This represents the act of "going digital," a strategy integral to the digital presidency. Through social media engagement and "enhancing" the address, the presidency attempts to lead policy discussion. Associating images with the speech and encouraging circulation provides additional meaning to the verbal arguments and mitigates attempts by the media to juxtapose their own visuals with the address.

While the Internet may provide more information to individuals than ever before, it also represents a new arena in which the presidency needs to situate its political message. With the explosion of mass media "white noise," the digital presidency requires innovative ways to pierce through the fog and reach the public. The enhanced State of the Union attempts to do this by leading how individuals consumed the message initially and circulated it to other users. In this regard, the digital presidency is not limited to this singular address but rather a new way to understand the ways in which the president reaches the public, one that warrants further study across all genres of presidential rhetoric. The White House is able to craft different messages for distinct audiences through "enhanced" features online. Images are important to this strategy because they have the potential to reframe verbal argument and to be circulated easily online for direct consumption. In so doing, the digital distribution of the enhanced address changes the traditional relationship between the media, the public, Congress, and the president.

WORKS CITED

Anderson, Karrin Vasby, and Kristina Horn Sheeler. "Texts (and Tweets) from Hillary: Meta-Meming and Postfeminist Political Culture." *Presidential Studies Quarterly* 44.2 (2014): 224–243. Print.

"Backstage with President Obama in Pittsburgh, PA." The White House. *YouTube*. 29 Jan. 2014. Web. 10 Dec. 2014.

Barabas, Jason. "Presidential Policy Initiatives: How the Public Learns about State of the Union Proposals from the Mass Media." *Presidential Studies Quarterly* 38.2 (2008): 195–222. Print.

Baum, Matthew A., and Tim Groeling. "New Media and the Polarization of American Political Discourse." *Political Communication* 25.4 (2008): 345–365. Print.

Becker, Samuel L. "Presidential Power: The Influence of Broadcasting." *Quarterly Journal of Speech* 47.1 (1961): 10–18. Print.

Benson, Thomas W. "Desktop Demos: New Communication Technologies and the Future of the Rhetorical Presidency." *Beyond the Rhetorical Presidency.* Ed. Martin J. Medhurst. College Station: Texas A&M University Press, 1996. 50–74. Print.

Birdsell, David S., and Leo Groarke. "Toward a Theory of Visual Argument." *Argumentation and Advocacy* 33.1 (1996): 1–10. Print.

Campbell, Karlyn Kohrs and Kathleen Hall Jamieson. *Presidents Creating the Presidency: Deeds Done in Words.* Chicago: U of Chicago P, 2008. Print.

Ceaser, James W., Glen E. Thurow, Jeffrey Tulis, and Joseph M. Bessette. "The Rise of the Rhetorical Presidency." *Presidential Studies Quarterly* 11.2 (1981): 158–171. Print.

Cohen, Jeffrey E. "Presidential Rhetoric and the Public Agenda." *American Journal of Political Science* 39.1 (1995): 87–107. Print.

Cummins, Jeff. "State of the Union Addresses and the President's Legislative Success." *Congress & the Presidency* 37.2 (2010): 176–199. Print.

Edwards, George C., III. *On Deaf Ears: The Limits of the Bully Pulpit.* New Haven, CT: Yale UP, 2003. Print.

Endres, Danielle, and Barbara Warnick. "Text-Based Interactivity in Candidate Campaign Web Sites: A Case Study from the 2002 Elections." *Western Journal of Communication* 68.3 (2004): 322–342. Print.

Erickson, Keith V. "Presidential Rhetoric's Visual Turn: Performance Fragments and the Politics of Illusionism." *Communication Monographs* 67.2 (2000): 138–157. Print.

Eshbaugh-Soha, Matthew, and Jeffrey S. Peake. "Presidents and the Economic Agenda." *Political Research Quarterly* 58.1 (2005): 127–138. Print.

Finnegan, Cara A., and Jiyeon Kang. " 'Sighting' the Public: Iconoclasm and Public Sphere Theory." *Quarterly Journal of Speech* 90.4 (2004): 377–402. Print.

Gibbons, Michelle G. "Seeing the Mind in the Matter: Functional Brain Imaging as Framed Visual Argument." *Argumentation and Advocacy* 43.3 (2007): 175–188. Print.

Goodnight, G. Thomas. "The Personal, Technical, and Public Spheres of Argument: A Speculative Inquiry into the Art of Public Deliberation." *Journal of the American Forensics Association* 18.3 (1982): 214–227. Print.

Grabe, Maria E., and Erik P. Bucy. *Image Bite Politics: News and the Visual Framing of Elections.* New York: Oxford UP, 2009.

Gronbeck, Bruce. "The Presidency in the Age of Secondary Orality." *Beyond the Rhetorical Presidency.* Ed. Martin J. Medhurst. College Station: Texas A&M UP, 1996. 30–49. Print.

—. "Varied Relationships Between Verbal and Visual Discourses: Jacob Riis' Arguments for Slum Reform." *Engaging Argument.* Ed. Patricia Riley. Washington, DC: National Communication Association, 2005. 174–182. Print.

Hartnett, Stephen J., and Jennifer R. Mercieca. "'A Discovered Dissembler Can Achieve Nothing Great'; Or, Four Theses on the Death of Presidential Rhetoric in Age of Empire." *Presidential Studies Quarterly* 37.4 (2007): 599–621. Print.

Hill, Kim Quaile. "The Policy Agendas of the President and the Mass Public: A Research Validation and Extension." *American Journal of Political Science* 42.4 (1998): 1328–1334. Print.

Knobel, Michele, and Colin Lankshear. "Online Memes, Affinities, and Cultural Production." *A New Literacies Sampler*. Ed. Michele Knobel and Colin Lankshear. New York: Peter Lang, 2007. 199–227. Print.

Lindsay, Erin. "The First-Ever Virtual 'Big Block of Cheese Day'—The White House is Open for Questions." *The White House*. 29 Jan. 2014. Web. 10 Dec. 2014.

Lubin, Nataniel. "The Most Accessible and Interactive SOTU Yet." *The White House*. 27 Jan. 2014. Web. 10 Dec. 2014.

McMillan, Sally J. "Exploring Models of Interactivity from Multiple Research Traditions: Users, Documents, and Systems." *Handbook of New Media*. Ed. Leah Lievrouw and Sonia Livingstone. Thousand Oaks, CA: Sage, 2002. 163–182. Print.

Medina, Victor. "It's a Trap! Obama White House plans 'Big Block of Cheese Day.'" *Examiner*. 28 Jan. 2014. Web. 10 Dec. 2014.

Mercieca, Jennifer R., and Justin S. Vaughn. "The Post-Rhetorical Legacy of George W. Bush." *Perspectives on the Legacy of George W. Bush*. Ed. Michael Orlov Grossman and Ronald Eric Matthews Jr. Newcastle upon Tyne: Cambridge Scholars Publishing, 2009. 31–52. Print.

Obama, Barack. "The 2011 State of the Union Address." *The White House*. 24 Jan. 2011. Web. 10 May 2014.

—. "The 2012 State of the Union Address." *The White House*. 25 Jan. 2012. Web. 10 May 2014.

—. "The 2013 State of the Union Address." *The White House*. 12 Feb. 2013. Web. 10 May 2014.

—. "The 2014 State of the Union Address." *The White House*. 28 Jan. 2014. Web. 10 May 2014.

Shifman, Limor. "An Anatomy of a YouTube Meme." *New Media & Society*. 14.2 (2012): 187–203. Print.

Stromer-Galley, Jennifer. "On-line Interaction and Why Candidates Avoid It." *Journal of Communication* 50.4 (2000): 111–132. Print.

Stuckey, Mary. "Rethinking the Rhetorical Presidency and Presidential Rhetoric." *Review of Communication* 10.1 (2010): 38–52. Print.

Tenpas, Kathryn Dunn. "The State of the Union Address." *The President's Words: Speeches and Speechmaking in the Modern White House*. Ed. Michael Nelson and Russell L. Riley. Lawrence: UP of Kansas, 2010. 147–205. Print.

Tulis, Jeffrey K. *The Rhetorical Presidency*. Princeton, NJ: Princeton UP, 1987. Print.

Warner, Benjamin R. "Segmenting the Electorate: The Effects of Exposure to Political Extremism Online." *Communication Studies* 61.4 (2010): 430–444. Print.

White, Eugene E. "Presidential Rhetoric: The State of the Union Address." *Quarterly Journal of Speech* 54.1 (1968): 71–77. Print.

Williams, Andrew Paul, and Kaye D. Trammell. "Candidate Campaign E-mail Messages in the Presidential Election 2004." *American Behavioral Scientist* 49.4 (2005): 560–574. Print.

Yates, Jeff, and Andrew Whitford. "Institutional Foundations of the President's Issue Agenda." *Political Research Quarterly* 58.4 (2005): 577–585. Print.

Young, Garry, and William B. Perkins. "Presidential Rhetoric, the Public Agenda, and the End of Presidential Television's 'Golden Age.'" *The Journal of Politics* 67.4 (2005): 1190–1205. Print.

13 REDRAWING THE GOP BORDERS? WOMEN, REPRODUCTION, AND THE POLITICAL LANDSCAPE OF THE 2014 MIDTERM ELECTION

Lora Arduser & Amy Koerber

In this essay we continue an analysis that we began in our 2014 *Women's Studies in Communication (WSC)* article, "Splitting Women, Producing Biocitizens, and Vilifying Obamacare in the 2012 Presidential Campaign." That article examined Republican discourse about women's reproductive rights during the 2012 US Presidential campaign. Here we extend the article's analysis to consider the 2014 aftermath of what came to be known in 2012 as the latest phase of a "Republican war on women."[1]

In "Splitting Women," we traced how anti-Obamacare sentiments based on a neoliberal anti-government political philosophy were articulated with anti-reproductive rights sentiments. The articulation of these two contradictory ideas led Republicans to advocate severe government intervention in the most intimate aspects of women's lives. In this essay, we extend our analysis to investigate how these trends are shifting (or not shifting) in the discourse that emerged after 2012 by examining how they are represented in two texts that have appeared since the 2012 election: the "Growth and Opportunity Project" report (GOP Report) and the conservative website Woman Up! USA (Woman Up!).

To trace this thread of campaign discourses, we employ a theory of articulation. Articulation encompasses a relationship or connection between disparate elements when such a relationship becomes naturalized or starts to seem like a reflection of an underlying order (Hall). We find this concept useful in examining recent Republican discourse because it explains how such obviously contradictory ideas come to be connected in ways that seem logical or natural to some segments of the voting population. These connections, as Nathan Stormer explains, "delineate form and establish the boundaries and substance of a body, whether textual, corporeal, institutional, social, or natural, by arranging its elements" (264). Thus, thinking of political rhetoric in terms of articulation means acknowledging that, as a political message communicates a particular version of truth it also articulates the speakers, identities, audience, and rhetorical situation of those who are subject to that truth.

The 2014 Midterms

In the 2012 campaign discourse the woman voter was articulated through a contradictory set of discourses as a split subject—on the one hand, a citizen free to enjoy the same freedoms as any other citizen, but on the other hand, a biocitizen whose reproductive capacities were subjected to increasingly stringent forms of restrictions. As Nikolas Rose and Carlos Novas note, these biological identifications are coupled with biological presuppositions that "shape conceptions of what it means to be a citizen, and underpin distinctions between actual, potential, troublesome, and impossible citizens" (440).

Unlike the biological presuppositions that Republicans made about women, contraception, and abortion in their 2012 arguments, in the 2014 midterm articulations were made that shifted from a focus on gender roles related to women's reproductive rights to identities that assume women are part of traditional families with husbands and children. Such reconfigurations are possible because "[A]rticulation is about how radically different rhetorics emerge historically in the ever-churning segregation and hybridization of things and discourse" (Stormer 260-61). As such, in conservative discourse since the 2012 campaign, the troublesome "split woman" of 2012 became a Republican vision of what it might mean to make women whole again. This reconfiguration is evident in the GOP Report and the Woman Up! website. In these texts, women are re-articulated as caregivers, family breadwinners, and mothers who can easily hold all these roles simultaneously and will rally around the political issues that Republican strategists deem most important. Thus, in addition to re-articulating the woman voter, Republicans also try to re-articulate the rhetorical situation in which political discussions will unfold; they are trying to redraw this situation in a way that excludes reproductive rights as an issue that matters to women voters.

THE GOP REPORT

After the Republican's 2012 presidential defeat, Republican National Committee (RNC) Chairman Reince Priebus set up the independent review panel called the Growth and Opportunity Project. The project's purpose was to make recommendations for growing the party and winning more elections. Toward this goal, a five-person panel worked for three months conducting surveys, focus groups, and one-on-one meetings with over fifty-two thousand individuals (Barbour, Bradshaw, Fleisher, Fonalledas, and McCall). The resulting recommendations centered around three areas: 1) engaging more (and more diverse) voters through a nationwide, permanent field operation, 2) updating and providing digital technologies to state parties and campaigns to reach out to voters, and 3) updating the presidential primary, debate, and convention process in 2016 to strengthen the eventual Republican presidential nominee (Barbour, Bradshaw, Fleisher, Fonalledas, and McCall, par. 5).

Given the widespread recognition that Republicans' losses in 2012 occurred because of their failure to attract women and minority voters, re-articulating the woman voter in ways that would compel women to vote Republican was clearly an important goal for the Party. Reflecting this goal, the one-hundred-page GOP Report includes a sub-section entitled "Women." We specifically focus on this sub-section to show how the document recirculates some of the same arguments that split women's reproductive rights from other rights and ultimately alienated many women voters in the 2012 election. The report does so by re-articulating the rhetorical situation in a way that excludes reproductive rights as a legitimate concern of women voters. This re-articulation is expressed through language that circulated in the 2012 election concerning the Republican "war against women." The phrase "Republican War Against Women" was first used in a 1996 memoir by Tanya Melich, a lifelong, active Republican who became disillusioned when the party shifted focus in the 1960s toward an openly anti-women's rights, anti-choice perspective. But during the 2012 campaign, Democrats took control of this language and effectively used it to call out Republican candidates at all levels who made contemptible remarks about women. As just one example, Democratic activists effectively used social media when Todd Akin made his horrific comments about pregnancy and rape to ensure that women voters across the nation heard these comments and identified them with a Republican Party that was coming to be seen as increasingly misogynistic.[2]

Similar language is evident in Recommendation 5 of the "Women" subsection of the report:

> Republicans should develop a more aggressive response to Democrat rhetoric regarding a so-called "war on women." In 2012, the Republican response to this attack was muddled, and too often the attack went undefended altogether. We need to actively combat this, better prepare our surrogates, and not stand idly by while the Democrats pigeonhole us using false attacks. There are plenty of liberal policies that negatively impact women, and it is incumbent upon the party to expose those and relentlessly attack Democrats using that framework. (20)

Because the rhetorical situation is "an event that makes possible the production of identities and social relations" (Biesecker 126), by shifting the battle lines in the report from a war on women to one against Democrats, the Democratic Party is constituted as the enemy and the "so-called" Republican war on women does not exist. It is a lie or "false attack" by the Democrats. By re-circulating the battle language and aiming it at the Democratic Party, reproductive rights stay off of the battlefield altogether. In fact, the lengthy GOP Report does not once mention the words abortion, contraception, or reproduction. As such, we might say the rhetorical situation that is articulated in the report also shifts women's subjectivities.

These re-articulations of women voters' identities are evident, for example, in the report's ten recommendations on how to "include female voters and promote women to leadership ranks within the committee" (19). These recommendations are as follows:

1. Communicate, organize, and win the women's vote as a part of all activities the RNC undertakes.
2. Implement training programs for messaging, communications, and recruiting that address the best ways to communicate with women.
3. Develop a surrogate list of women based upon areas of policy and political expertise.
4. Be conscious of developing a forward-leaning vision for voting Republican that appeals to women.
5. Develop a more aggressive response to Democrat rhetoric regarding a so-called "war on women."
6. Talk about people and families, not just numbers and statistics.
7. Understand that women need to be asked to run.

8. Make a better effort at listening to female voters, directing their policy proposals at what they learn from women, and communicating that they understand what a woman who is balancing many responsibilities is going through.
9. Reevaluate the committee member process to help incentivize more women in leadership roles rather than solely in the "committee-woman" slot.
10. Use Women's History Month as an opportunity to remind voters of the Republican Party's historical role in advancing the women's rights movement.

Taken as a whole, the list emphasizes that even as the Republican Party tries to make women voters/citizens whole, it separates women voters and women politicians from their male counterparts through a process of othering—a process that ultimately represents women as 'not one of us.' This process results in a revised form of biocitizenship from that of 2012. Now women are not troublesome by virtue of their reproductive capacities; they are troublesome because they are difficult to understand and difficult to communicate to for vague, unspecified reasons. For example, women presumably need to be reached through an intermediary (another woman) who can translate Republican policies to them (Recommendations 3 and 8). In fact, women are so different that entire new training programs have to be designed and implemented for messaging, communications, and recruiting (Recommendation 2), and they must be *asked* [our emphasis] to run for elected office (Recommendation 7).

At first glance, this representation of women being different from men might be viewed as an antagonism. An antagonism, as Kevin DeLuca explains, "occurs at the point of the relation of the discourse to the surrounding life world and shows the impossibility of the discourse constituting a permanently closed or sutured totality" "(336). In other words, acknowledging that women are different than men might seem to re-articulate discourse in a manner that would better engage women voters. By moving reproductive rights off the battlefield and out of the realm of discussion, however, the antagonism becomes foundational. As a foundational antagonism (Laclau and Mouffe), a simple difference that cannot be changed by the ability to question the discourse surrounding an idea, linkages are not contingent and Republicans are able to begin welding together a representation of women voters whose identities are established through relationships to others (children and families) rather than individuals with citizenship rights.

While this shift may speak to the Republican base, it is a questionable move in light of the 2012 election results. According to NBC News national exit polling from 2012, 67 percent of unmarried women said they voted for Obama (Fox). According to the GOP Report itself, in 2012 President Obama won women by 11 points, whereas Governor Romney won married women by 11 points (19). However, the GOP Report also notes that 40 percent of female voters are single and that Obama won single women by 36 percent (19). The GOP Report skips past any discussion of reproductive freedom, assuming that women Republican voters have children and families. For instance, the GOP report states that to reach women voters "Republicans need to talk about people and families, not just numbers and statistics," and it refers to women as "the caregivers for their families" (20).

The efforts to re-articulate the woman voter in the GOP Report still perpetuate the idea of women as biocitizens (i.e., their reproductive citizenship split from their citizenship as voters who enjoy basic rights and freedoms). In the discourse in 2014, however, the reproductive woman is re-articulated to issues of economics, as evident in the language of Recommendation 6 of the GOP Report: "Female voters want to hear the facts; many of them run the economies of their homes and understand economics better than the men in their families" (20). In other words, the new woman voter that Republicans seem to be articulating is a voter who is free, and even encouraged, to hold political office, enjoy professional success, and be her family's caregiver at the same time. At the same time, this voter is assumed to be happy filling all of these roles simultaneously; there is no longer a need to worry about reproductive choices because these have been made for her.

Woman Up! USA

The website Woman Up! seems designed to help achieve some of the activist goals that the GOP Report recommends for engaging women voters. Although the origin of the website's name is not specified, it is logical to assume that the YG Network intended it to be empowering because of the positive connotations of the word "up" and the idea of having a voice. Woman Up!, however, is also an appropriation of the more familiar phrase "man up," which is generally affiliated with the characteristic of bravery. According to the web-based Urban Dictionary, two definitions for the phrase "woman up" are to "be a courageous and strong mature woman by appropriately taking action and responsibility" and "pay your own way and stop freeloading off guys and your female friends" (Woman Up).

This characterization echoes the discourse of the GOP Report in a much more concrete way. Here, instead of women simply "balancing many responsibilities," which is the language used in Recommendation 8 of the GOP report, women are family breadwinners. Similar to the way anti-Obamacare ideas became visible and concrete through the articulation with women's bodies and reproductive rights in the 2012 election, the Woman Up! website's articulation of women voters with the identities of an individual paying her own way and being the family breadwinner also makes the more abstract concept of the Republican Party's platform on social and economic issues more concrete. These breadwinners, unlike the infamous "welfare queen" referenced by Ronald Reagan in his 1970 campaign speeches, do not need to use (or take advantage of) federal aid through programs that Republican politicians have characterized as excessive entitlement programs (Caff-Thoughts). Dis-articulating the Republican woman voter from the identity of a single woman on welfare is yet another way in which this current Republican rhetoric masks reproductive rights issues behind a veil of economics (i.e., the good mother is able not only to produce the children but also to support them economically). As such, the Republicans are able to find a way to both support a pro-life agenda and an economic policy that advocates for cutting entitlement programs like welfare.

If the woman voter of 2012 was split between her reproductive capacities and her rights as a free citizen, the Republican woman of 2014 is made whole again through Republicans' repeated emphasis on the idea that today's woman can have it all; she need not worry about controlling her reproductive capacity because that capacity does not have to get in the way of her freedom to earn money and participate in politics. This economic identity of women as breadwinners, an identity outlined in Recommendation 6 of the GOP Report as well, is woven throughout the Woman Up! site. Recommendation 6 of the GOP Report says

> Female voters want to hear the facts; many of them run the econo-
> mies of their homes and understand economics better than the men
> in their families. But they are also the caregivers for their families.
> Women need to hear what our motive is—why it is that we want to
> create a better future for our families and how our policies will affect
> the lives of their loved ones. Those are things that cannot be com-
> municated well in graphs and charts—and we need to do a better
> job communicating why our policies are better, while using female
> spokespeople to do it. (20)

In this recommendation we see women articulated as breadwinners, a role that has been stereotypically assigned to the male, but in this case, assigning the breadwinner identity to women does not make women equal to or the same as a male breadwinner. In fact, the language in this recommendation "others" women in the same manner as the GOP Report recommendation summaries that we discussed above. Unlike the discourse of the 2012 election cycle, in which women were articulated with bodies that were biologically different, here women breadwinners are different (and separate) because it is not just about "facts," "economics," and "charts." The recommendation is saying that "we" (the male Republican leadership) need to talk to women differently because they are different even if they hold similar roles such as breadwinners or politicians. According to the report, for women, it is also about "loved ones" and caregiving.

The "About" page of Woman Up! articulates women in a similar manner, as the two following examples illustrate:

> There is a better way; America deserves 21st century policies that encourage economic growth, investment and opportunity. Leaders who understand that government doesn't create real, sustainable job growth, entrepreneurs, small businessmen and women, and investors do.
>
> Nearly 40 percent of working wives out-earn their husbands and in another 20 years it is expected that a majority of women—not men—will be the ones who bring home the most bacon for their families."

These examples are interesting on two levels. The first, which echoes the language of much of the GOP Report by focusing on women as "business women," continues to be consistent with discourse in the 2012 election in which Republicans tried (but ultimately failed) to shift focus away from reproductive rights issues toward economic issues. The second example implies that we do not need to worry about the "equal pay" issue anymore because it is becoming increasingly common for wives to out-earn their husbands. At the same time, the language in the second example ("bring home the most bacon") seems particularly retrograde, bringing to mind the 1980 Enjoli perfume advertisements that included the lyrics: "I can bring home the bacon / Fry it up in a pan / And never, ever, ever let you forget you're a man" (MMacG1167). Again, in the new world order that Republicans "redraw" (which, ironically, resembles that of the 1980s), the woman voter need no longer concern herself with the troublesome issues that took center stage in 2012. Interestingly, outside of GOP politics these retrograde ideas have been questioned in the news. A recent example is that of Indra K. Nooji, the CEO of PepsiCo. In answering a question in an interview with *The Atlantic* owner David Bradley, she stated: "I don't think women can have it all. I just don't think so" (Friedersdorf). By focusing on women as family caregivers and breadwinners, however, both the GOP Report and the Woman Up! website begin to etch in political borders that would seem to transform reproductive issues such as contraception and abortion into "non-issues." In the discourse we examine, choice is not about having children or not having children. Having children is a given, so women's bodies are not particularly troublesome anymore. As with the economy, the question then becomes: *how are we going to pay for it?* These articulations and dis-articulations are apparent in the language of both Woman Up! and the GOP Report in the places where these documents refer to women as caregivers. The website highlights political issues that would affect women's families from an economic perspective. A prominent example can be found in the results of "National Female Survey" on the website.[3] The topics included in the survey covered questions on the economy, education, immigration, the deficit, health care, government spending, taxes, and energy, all of which can be seen as impacting families from an economic perspective. Parents, for example, deal with rising college costs for their children and rising health care costs that affect the entire family. Reproductive rights issues are absent from the survey. This exclusion echoes a similar omission in the list of the website's issues. Note that the issues do not list reproductive rights. Instead they list: 1) economic growth and job creation, 2) low-cost, patient-centered healthcare, 3) reduced energy prices, 4) affordable higher education, and 5) welfare-to-work reforms to help the neediest. Unlike the 2012 campaign discourse that articulated a moral imperative to regulate women's reproductive capacities with an economic imperative to maintain a healthy economy, this list echoes the language in the GOP Report, which articulates women to identities such as politically engaged breadwinners, caregivers, and mothers. In other words, women can have it all.

As Republicans attempt to re-articulate the woman voter they want to attract, they are also trying to re-articulate the rhetorical situation in a way that places reproductive rights outside the boundaries of what should concern voters. In fact, neither the web page called "Women" on the Woman Up! site nor the web page called "Healthcare" have any posts about reproductive health. The topic does not come up on the Woman Up! website blog, "Moms are Cool," either. In the literature, mommy blogs have been seen as potentially building communities and challenging dominant representations of "the good mother that has dominated our media, with its impossible demands and assumptions about women" (Lopez 742-43). The "Moms are Cool" blog imitates this genre. However, rather than challenging dominant representations of motherhood, this blog reinforces what Susan Douglas and Meredith Michaels (2004) described as "new momism": "The insistence that no woman is truly complete or fulfilled unless she has kids; that women remain the best primary caretakers of children; and that to be a remotely decent mother, a woman has to devote her entire physical, psychological, emotional, and intellectual being, 24/7, to her children" (4). A quick scroll through the topics of the "Moms are Cool" posts illustrates how the blog re-articulates the notion of motherhood to the good mother role:

- Announcing the YG Woman Up "My Mom Is Cool Because..." Essay Contest
- The Latest in General Study: Children Exposed To Violent Video Games Retain Aggressive Behavior, Thoughts
- More Moms Staying at Home
- Study: Middle School Sex Harassment Widespread
- Autism More Common Than Thought
- Helping Your Kids with Homework Doesn't Help, Study Says
- Watch these amazing iPod-based magic tricks. Then show your kids!
- Having Children Major Driver of Spending Patterns in US
- "Global Moms Relay" Shares the Strength of Motherhood Around the World
- Cities Your Recent College Graduate Should Avoid

By articulating women voters with this representation of motherhood—mothers who help with homework and stay home to take care of their children—and dis-articulating them from reproductive rights as a political interest, the website not only supports the Republican pro-life agenda but adds one more task for mothers to undertake—creating new conservative voters. In the 2012 Republican Presidential campaign, women's role as biocitizens was related to women's potential for producing future citizens in general. By focusing efforts on "moms" after the election, conservative discourse seems to be articulating women's role as mother to educating her children to be a particular *kind* of citizen that eventually votes a particular way.

This contrast in the political discourse becomes clearer if we go back to language in the 2012 campaign that characterized the state as a healthy, and moral, place for babies to be conceived and born (which, of course, necessitated that women's reproductive and sexual capacities be strictly controlled as biocitizens). In the discourse of the "Moms are Cool" blog, on the other hand, women are dis-articulated from their generally troublesome pregnant bodies and re-articulated to the responsibilities of biocitizenship that require them to focus on managing future bodies (their children) in terms of providing for them financially and educating them rather than managing their own unruly bodies.

CONCLUSION

In the 2012 election cycle, the Republicans' rhetorical strategies failed them, at least on the national level, and the election was touted as a victory for feminists and other progressives. The loss led the Party to take a hard look at its vulnerabilities, which were reported in the GOP document. The Woman Up! website is one example of conservative efforts to address these vulnerabilities and "redraw" the GOP Party borders in a way that is more inclusive to what the Report refers to as its "demographic partners" (12).

As we have argued, however, one consequence of these efforts has been that these new political borders exclude reproductive rights from the political landscape. Feminist rhetorical scholars can draw attention to what is being presented through these new shapes, conjunctions and disjunctions. As the "Growth and Opportunity Project" report makes especially clear, the GOP has not rethought its actual beliefs about women's rights or about gender equity. Rather, they have repackaged the same ideas in ways that they hope will be more appealing to women voters. Perhaps there will be different spokespeople (as they initiate their efforts to get more "female spokespeople") and perhaps they will make better use of technologies to deliver the message, but we probably cannot expect much change in the content of the message itself.

The value of examining these texts in light of the 2012 and 2014 political campaign discourses is twofold. First, because both of the texts we examine here attempt to make the Republican Party's conservative ideas more appealing to women, they provide an excellent opportunity to explore how the articulations that were so prominent in the 2012 Republican campaign discourse were revised and reconstituted for the 2014 midterm elections and, ultimately, may be apparent in the 2016 presidential campaign. Just as importantly, an analysis of the ways in which women are imagined as an audience for political messages helps better equip feminist scholars to critically engage with political discourse targeting women voters and to explore some of the larger implications of such appeals.

NOTES

1. Tanya Melich first used the phrase "War Against Women" to characterize the Republican Party's shift in the 1960s toward an openly anti–women's rights, anti-choice perspective. On the recent resurgence of this term, see Miller.

2. In an interview on the *Fox News* show The Jaco Report, Representative Akin, the Republican nominee for Senate in Missouri, told the interviewer, "First of all, from what I understand from doctors, [pregnancy from rape] is really rare. If it's a legitimate rape, the female body has ways to try to shut that whole thing down" (Jaco Report).

3. It may be beneficial that women are not interested in charts and graphics, as suggested by the GOP Report, because the graphs and charts used to display the survey results do not add up in terms of total number of participants. For example, the table labeled "Economic Matters Most" it looks like a total of 96 women

responded. The following bar chart "Growing Free Market Economy and Private Sector Beats Larger Federal Government" shows a total of 100 responses, and the next chart, "Majority Says Deficit and Debt Hurting Jobs and the Economy" shows 131. The reason for these discrepancies is difficult to parse because the survey does not indicate the total number of participants.

WORKS CITED

Arduser, Lora, and Amy Koerber. "Splitting Women, Producing Biocitizens, and Vilifying Obamacare in the 2012 Presidential Campaign." *Women's Studies in Communication* 37.2 (2014): 117–37. Print.

Barbour, Henry, Sally Bradshaw, Ari Fleisher, Zori Fonalledas, and Glenn McCall. "The Growth And Opportunity Project: A One-Year Check-Up" *Real Clear Politics*. Real Clear Politics, 17 Mar. 2014. Web. 5 May 2014.

Biesecker, Barbara A. "Rethinking the Rhetorical Situation from Within the Thematic of Différance." *Philosophy and Rhetoric* 22.2 (1989): 110–30. Print.

CaffThoughts. "Rick Santorum Interviews with CaffeinatedThoughts.com." Online video clip. *YouTube*. YouTube, 18 Oct. 2011. Web. 25 Oct. 2012.

DeLuca, Kevin. "Articulation Theory: A Discursive Grounding for Rhetorical Practice." *Philosophy and Rhetoric* 32.4 (1999): 334–48.

Douglas, Susan J. and Meredith W. Michaels. *The Mommy Myth: The Idealization of Motherhood and How it Has Undermined All Women*. New York: Free P, 2004. Print.

Fox, Maggie. "New Voter Bloc Emerges: Single Women." *Today*. NBC News, 7 Nov. 2012. Web. 10 May 2014.

Friedersdorf, Conor. Why PepsiCo CEO Indra K. Nooji Can't Have It All." *The Atlantic*. The Atlantic Monthly Group, 1 July 2014. Web. 14 Dec. 2014.

Growth and Opportunity Project. *Growth and Opportunity Project*. The Republican National Committee, 2012. Web. 5 Apr. 2014.

Hall, Stuart. "On Postmodernism and Articulation: An Interview with Stuart Hall." *Journal of Communication Inquiry* 10 (1986): 45–60.

Jaco Report. Full interview with Todd Akin. 19 Aug. 2012. Web. 10 Oct. 2012.

Laclau, Ernesto, and Chanul Mouffe. *Hegemony and Socialist Strategy: Towards a Radical Democratic Politics*. London: Verso, 1985. Print.

Lopez, Lori. 2009. "The Radical Act of 'Mommy Blogging': Redefining Motherhood Through the Blogosphere." *New Media & Society* 11(5): 729–47. Print.

Melich, Tanya. *The Republican War Against Women: An Insider's Report from Behind the Lines*. New York: Bantam, 1996. Print.

Miller, Sunlen. "Birth-Control Hearing Was 'Like Stepping into a Time Machine.'" *ABC News*. ABC News Internet Ventures, 17 Feb. 2012. Web. 18 Sept. 2012.

MMacG1167. "Enjoli—1980." Online video clip. *YouTube*. YouTube, 7 July 2009. Web. 14 Apr. 2014.

Reagan, Ronald. Ronald Reagan Radio Commentary on the Welfare Queen, October 1976. *Slate Voice*. Slate, n.d. Web. 20 Dec. 2014.

Rose, Nikolas. *The Politics of Life Itself: Biomedicine, Power, and Subjectivity in the Twenty-first Century*. Princeton, NJ: Princeton U P, 2007. Print.

Rose, Nikolas, and Carlos Novas. "Biological Citizenship." *Global Assemblages: Technology, Politics, and Ethics as Anthropological Problems*. Ed. Aihwa Ong and Stephen J. Collier. Oxford: Blackwell Publishing, 2005: 440–63. Print.

Stormer, Nathan. "Articulation: A Working Paper on Rhetoric and Taxis." *Quarterly Journal of Speech* 90 (2004): 257–84.

Woman Up. *Urban Dictionary*. N.p., 2014. Web. 14 May 2014.

Woman Up! USA. "About." *WomanUpUSA.org*. Woman Up USA, 2014. Web. 17 Feb. 2014.

Woman Up! USA. "National Female Survey." *WomanUSA.org*. Woman Up USA, 2014. Web. 17 Feb. 2014.

Contesting Boundaries: Science, Technology, and Nature

14 LOCALIZED SCIENCE SENTINELS: TEDx AND THE SHARED NORMS OF SCIENTIFIC INTEGRITY

Ron Von Burg

When a reporter asked Representative John Boehner (R-OH) about the Obama Administration's EPA carbon emission regulations, Speaker Boehner responded, "Well, listen. I am not qualified to debate the science over climate change. But I am astute enough to understand that every proposal that has come out of this administration to deal with climate change involves hurting our economy and killing American jobs" (qtd. in Sheppard). Other Republican lawmakers have echoed similar responses—"I am not a scientist"—distancing themselves from judgments about climate science in favor of criticizing the economic effects of climate change regulations. While these specific statements are likely cynical and strategic gestures from conservative politicians concerned with surviving primary challenges, they are also sentiments echoed by sincere and sympathetic non-scientists who find scientific discourse distant and alienating. The appeals of "I'm not a scientist" simultaneously position scientific expertise as an important feature in public discussions of science while absolving the non-scientist from proffering judgment on scientific claims. Yet, non-scientists continue to make judgments on technical matters in which they also lack expertise. As in the case of Boehner, the Speaker bypassed judgment on climate change science only to defer to the claims of climate change skeptics and economic and political experts condemning global warming legislation. This disposition reveals a complex, and often troubling, relationship between non-scientists and scientific expertise in public discourses of science, where traditional notions of expertise are either valorized or problematized depending on the types of expert appeals needed in putative public debates. Navigating this turbulent relationship lies at the heart of science studies scholars Henry Collins and Robert Evans' attempt to resuscitate scientific expertise amidst growing public distrust and alienation in science. In the spirit of Collins and Evans' work to reconceptualize articulations of expertise, this essay examines how framing non-experts as guardians against dubious science and pseudoscientific prophets offers an avenue for enfranchising non-scientists in discussions with putative scientific experts, with the hope of improving public deliberations on scientific matters.

The inability and, in the case of some politicians, unwillingness for non-scientists to engage science experts reveals not only a lack of understanding about science, but a disenfranchisement with the scientific process and its practitioners. Democratic deliberations and its purported norms of openness, equity, and accessibility often operate in tension with concepts of scientific and technological expertise where the expert voice is privileged over the contributions of the non-expert. For rhetorical scholars whose loyalties often lie with democratizing deliberations, this presents a disquieting dilemma. On one hand, rhetoric's roots in democratic promises of persuasion present a problematic relationship with discursive and epistemic practices that functionally exclude a wide swath of interlocutors. To wit, Thomas Goodnight's landmark essay identifies how scientific and technical discourses colonize public spheres by framing social problems in technical terms that require technical expertise, thus alienating non-experts and positioning specialists at the center of a decision-making process. On the other hand, scientific expertise is a necessary, even if not sufficient, feature to persuasion and decision-making in the modern world. Credible evidence and trustworthy testimony enable sound reasoning, and the persuasive appeals polluted by bad argument and unreliable data undermine good judgment. Therefore, it comes as no surprise that public discussions of science often leave scientists, and sympathetic rhetorical critics, rather unsettled when bad scientific arguments populate deliberations and non-experts, already feeling disenfranchised from interactions with experts, are unable to distinguish between legitimate science and its charlatan counterparts. Climate change skeptics, vaccine doubters, and intelligent design advocates, to name a few advocates that invoke appeals to scientific expertise, often advance "bad" and pseudoscientific claims that comport with preexisting ideologies or extant political interests instead of claims grounded on scientific merit. With scientific expertise challenged on democratic grounds, claims that run counter to legitimate science can find themselves in public discussions of science on grounds of openness and fairness. The animating question, therefore, is how to navigate the disenfranchising and anti-democratic dimensions of scientific expertise in public deliberations without undermining the value scientific and technical knowledge brings to the deliberation process.

The 2012 open letter from TEDx Director Lara Stein and TED.com editor Emily McManus encouraging TEDx organizers to be more vigilant in selecting speakers provides such a template for enfranchising non-experts.[1] Stein and McManus acknowledge that most TEDx organizers lack the scientific expertise necessary to distinguish legitimate scientists from the purveyors of pseudoscience. Although this essay is not a defense of the "TED talk" or a referendum on this type of science popularization, I argue that the TEDx letter offers constructive strategies for non-scientists to assess scientific expertise by leveraging a non-scientist's ability to judge social behaviors. The Stein and McManus letter weaves together a layperson's capability to detect suspicious behavior, what Collins and Evans call "transmuted expertise" based on "ubiquitous discrimination," with basic guidelines for differentiating legitimate science from pseudoscience to create an opportunity for enfranchising non-scientists in discourses involving scientific expertise. Specifically, I suggest that the letter empowers non-scientists as sentinels protecting the boundaries of legitimate science against its charlatan counterparts, thereby investing non-scientists in improving public scientific discourse. In presenting this case, I first examine the extant literature on the tensions between expertise and democratic deliberations, namely through the work of Collins and Evans. Second, I offer a rhetorical analysis of the Stein and McManus open letter, examining how they position non-scientists as guardians of legitimate science. I conclude with some observations on the opportunities and limitations of transmuted expertise in assessing scientific expertise and advancing democratic deliberations on scientific matters.

DEMOCRACY AND THE PROBLEM OF SCIENTIFIC EXPERTISE

In the "Third Wave of Science Studies," Collins and Evans introduce the idea of Studies of Expertise and Experience (SEE), a line of science studies research that explores expertise within a liberal democratic space, one that balances the credentialed and constructed nature of expertise with experiential knowledge that largely falls outside the bounds of traditional notions of expertise. If expert, technical claims reside with an elite few, there are problems of political and social legitimacy on the grounds that such deliberations lack a democratic ethos. As a result, the tendency, in the name of democratizing knowledge, is to dissolve the boundaries between experts and non-experts. Furthermore, the linguistic turn in science studies—what Collins and Evans dub the "second wave" of science studies—reveals the socially and rhetorically constructed nature of scientific knowledge, thereby diminishing the privileged epistemic position of the scientific expert. In other words, not only is science undemocratic but it also fails to live up to its own claims as an objective insight into the natural world.

Collins and Evans, however, argue that contemporary assessments of expertise have gone too far in undermining the substantive and epistemic value of expertise, requiring a rehabilitation of expertise that better comports with certain democratic sensibilities. The SEE approach asks the fundamental question as to why scientific expertise ought to be valued and how it can become politically and socially legitimized within a specific deliberative context. To that end, Collins and Evans provide a taxonomy for understanding expertise—the Periodic Table of Expertise—that differentiates the types of expertise and the contexts in which they possess legitimacy.

In *Rethinking Expertise*, Collins and Evans offer a systematic assessment of expertise, noting that non-experts are often asked to judge expert claims or competing claims of experts. This presents a distinctive challenge when non-experts lack the epistemic resources to offer such judgments on the merits of scientific knowledge. In expanding the Periodic Table of Expertise, Henry Collins and Martin Weinel recognize the challenges of non-experts assessing expert claims, given the "asymmetry of technical understanding between experts and non-experts" (401). Collins and Weinel further argue that one such strategy is for non-experts "to judge the social position or social performance of experts" (402). Collins and Evans describe this process as transmuted expertise, a type of social expertise utilized by non-technical experts to render judgment of technical expertise. Transmuted expertise employs "ubiquitous discrimination," or the "practical applications of our regular judgments about friends, acquaintances, neighbors, relations, politicians, salesperson, and strangers, applied to science and scientists within Western scientific society" (*Rethinking Expertise* 45–6). In other words, one uses her or his understanding of social interactions to render judgment on a technical or scientific matter.

Collins and Evans are careful to note that such discrimination "is not part of the *legitimate* methods of science. . . . [and when used by the public] it does not, and should not, be accepted as a legitimate input to scientific method" (Rethinking Expertise 52, emphasis original). Even if we accept that transmuted expertise lacks import in the actual knowledge-making process of scientific investigation, a statement that is certainly subject to debate, that does not suggest transmuted expertise lacks value in public deliberations of scientific matters. The transmuted expertise of the non-scientist could help improve the quality of public discussions of science, especially when such public deliberations are infused with problematic scientific and pseudoscientific claims. By leveraging existing social knowledge, non-scientists can gain a foothold in distinguishing scientific expertise from non-scientific or pseudoscientific experts who adorn their claims with all the accouterments of seemingly legitimate scientific discourses. The seductive appeal of pseudoscience highlights the importance of demarcation, identifying boundaries that separate legitimate science from the scientific imposters.

Like Collins and Evans, many sociology and rhetoric of science scholars who engage in studies of scientific boundary work, such as Thomas Gieryn and Charles Taylor, trace the rhetorical maneuvers of scientists to construct such boundaries, excluding the role of non-scientists in assessments of pseudoscience and expertise. Many other rhetorical and argumentation scholars, in an effort to broaden the role of non-scientists, have identified avenues for expanding studies of expertise by using the tools of rhetoric. To wit, Zoltan Majdik and William Keith turn to *phronesis* to conceptualize expertise as a type of argument, focusing it around questions of judgment that empowers those affected by expert assessments. In a similar spirit, Jean Goodwin borrows from SEE and argumentation studies to advance a normative understanding of expertise that illuminates how non-experts must rely on indirect, yet argumentative, methods of evaluating expertise.

As *phronesis* and judgment are central to the use of expert testimony and the valuation of expert claims when rendering a decision, there are opportunities for improving the rhetorical awareness to help non-experts assesses expertise, especially in the effort to parse out science from its pseudoscience imposters. I suggest that attention to the rhetorical performances of expertise offers a viable and accessible heuristic for non-experts to differentiate between scientific experts and peddlers of pseudoscience, one that calls upon transmuted expertise to empower non-scientists to render technical judgment.

The open letter sent by TEDx Director Lara Stein and TED.com editor Emily McManus encouraging TEDx organizers to be more cautious in assessing expertise relies on non-experts attending to the rhetorical performances of experts. Instead of offering clear criteria for classifying pseudoscience, Stein and McManus highlight the argumentative and rhetorical behaviors of pseudoscientists. Stein and McManus's letter attempts to embolden and enfranchise non-scientists to perform such boundary work by rearticulating standards of scientific judgment to better comport with a non-scientist's native expertise. By empowering non-scientists with ways to adjudicate scientific argument, I suggest that Stein and McManus share the burden of scientific integrity with non-scientists.

JUDGING (PSEUDO-) SCIENCE AND THE INTEGRITY OF TEDx

The central feature of the TED event, the "TED talk," possesses numerous generic features: a 15-18 minute memorized speech flush with engaging visual aides and rife with thought provoking "ideas worth spreading." The TED talk epitomizes the role of an individual expert disseminating information to a passive and likely lay audience. The speaker commands the stages precisely because her or his expertise is deemed worthy of public consumption.

In 2006, capitalizing on this engaging form of science popularization, TED launched TED.com, an online repository of TED talks for the connected world to share. Success followed, as the videos have been viewed well over a billion times collectively. Despite TED's success in providing a popular public platform for promoting scientific innovation, TED is not without detractors. Critics note, quite fairly, that TED talks often "dumb down" science, offer simple solutions to complex problems, privilege sales and consumption, and elevate entertainment at the expense of education (Bratton, Robbins). Despite such criticisms, TED has enjoyed significant success as a conduit for science popularization, leading to the creation of the TEDx franchise, locally organized conferences modeled after the main TED conference. Since its inception, TED has sanctioned over ten thousand TEDx events; but such successes have presented new challenges and criticisms.

In late 2012, the news and social networking site Reddit exploded with concerns over pseudoscientific and bad science talks presented at local TEDx events. Talks about crystal therapy and the medicinal attributes of natural food raised the ire of Internet scientists concerned that TEDx provided a platform for legitimizing pseudoscientists. In an effort to address the problem, TEDx director Lara Stein and TED.com Editor Emily McManus penned an open letter calling upon TEDx organizers to vet properly speakers and serve as quality control agents.

Stein and McManus' letter blends a conversational, playful style (complete with emoticons) with an inviting, yet assured tone that emphasizes the importance of quality control. The letter unfolds in four parts: a short, working definition of pseudoscience (marks of good and bad science); ways to spot bad and pseudoscience (problematic [red flag] topics, because they often attract pseudoscientists); red flag behaviors that are symptomatic of pseudoscientists; and suggestions for researching possible speakers. They open with a clear charge to the TEDx organizers. Stein and McManus note:

> It is your job, before any speaker is booked, to check them out, and to reject bad science, pseudoscience and health hoaxes . . . . Vetting your speakers is hard work, and can lead to uncomfortable moments. But as TEDx organizers, your audience's trust is your top priority, over and above any other personal or business relationship that may have brought this speaker to your attention. It is not your audience's job to figure out if a speaker is offering legitimate science or not. It is your job.

They follow these appeals by outlining the consequences of failing to vet properly the speaker, specifically noting how the Andrew Wakefield vaccine-autism hoax left millions of children susceptible to deadly diseases.

From the opening appeal, Stein and McManus place the burden of trust, grounded in a sense of scientifically accepted expertise, upon the organizers. By foregrounding the question of trust, Stein and McManus not only enfranchise organizers as vanguards to the TED brand but also as sentinels for the public expressions of science. Stein and McManus concede that identifying pseudoscience presents a difficult challenge as non-experts may not be able to parse the claims cloaked in the discourses of science. In framing the challenge as a question of trust and not one of scientific expertise, Stein and McManus deputize the organizers as important figures in the health of public scientific discourse by asking them to marshal their innate social knowledge—how to gauge trust—to judge putatively technical, expert claims.

Stein and McManus cultivate a supportive tone throughout the letter, identifying with non-expert organizers on the inherent challenges of levying judgment on self-assured experts. Instead of offering suggestions as to how to evaluate the content of one's purported expertise, Stein and McManus point to the rhetorical markers of good science and pseudoscience. The "marks of good science" rely on the expected, institutional markers of scientific expertise: the speaker possesses bonafide credentials from an accredited university, the research is published in peer-reviewed journals, and that the claims have support from other experts. Stein and McManus bolster such features of credible expertise by pointing organizers to markers of a legitimate scientific process: the claims can be tested and verified and the research does not "fly in the face of the broad existing body of scientific knowledge." They also note that practitioners of good science are secure enough to weather doubts and calls for further investigation.

In addition to lacking the features of good science (reproducible studies, support of peers), the "marks of bad science" highlight a series of rhetorical dimensions that are more detectable using ubiquitous discrimination. Notably, they warn of arrogant fringe experts who speak dismissively of mainstream science and combine simplistic interpretations of legitimate science with "imprecise, spiritual or new age vocabulary." The markers of good and bad science offer a blend of credentialed and experiential appeals coupled with some basic understanding of well-worn science studies. The letter imports both Popperian sensibilities of *falsifiability* and Mertonian *norms of doubt and skepticism* to articulate an image of credible scientific practice.[2] The appeal to scientific consensus as a partition between good and bad science presents a unique challenge to the TED brand, as TED's ethos resides in innovative, boundary-pushing science. As non-experts may encounter difficulties in judging competing scientific claims, Stein and McManus directs attention toward the discourses and behaviors exhibited by "experts" when advancing scientific claims. The humility and openness to criticism of scientists promoting good science versus the arrogance and dismissiveness of scientists peddling bad science presents organizers with an additional resource for judgment. As evident in their opening statements, an assured expert asserting that the organizers lack the expertise necessary to judge the scientific merits of his or her claims might intimidate non-experts unable to assess the merits of certain technical claims.

In addition to the marks of good and bad science, Stein and McManus identify "red flag" topics that often attract pseudoscientists. They are careful not to suggest that such topics are "banned" (as that would not fit TED's ethos of openness to innovative ideas worth spreading), but vetting these topics require even greater scrutiny, including asking local university experts for their input on the submitted talk. The first two sections—markers of good and bad science and the red flag topics—are rather standard fare in public conversations around parsing pseudoscience from good science. The third section places identifying behaviors of pseudoscientific speakers and hoaxers as the centerpiece for enfranchising organizers to assess the claims of the claims of putative experts.

Stein and McManus present an extensive list of twelve bullets points that caution organizers about the typical behaviors and rhetorical techniques of pseudoscientists. While such markers are not always signs of pseudoscientists, they ask organizers to practice due diligence if any potential speakers exhibit such suspicious behaviors. The suggestions roughly fall into two categories: interpersonal behaviors in response to rejection and explicit appeals to putatively scientific expertise.

Stein and McManus note that pseudoscientists are often wont to display arrogance and antagonism. They argue that pseudoscientists appeal to their own unique insights, knowledge that no one else possesses, and when further scrutinized will often act upset or antagonistic. Furthermore, Stein and McManus note that a pseudoscientist often "acts oddly persistent about getting to your stage. A normal person who is rejected for the TEDx stage will be sad and usually withdraw from you. A hoaxer, especially one who sees a financial upside to being associated with TEDx, will persist, sometimes working to influence members of your team one by one or through alternative channels." This observation highlights two expected signs of pseudoscientist behavior: the response to rejection and the desire for financial gain. While these actions are not inherently problematic, within the context of this decision-making process, such behaviors warrant greater caution.

Stein and McManus further call attention to how pseudoscientists will use seemingly scientific appeals to cultivate an ethos of expertise to intimidate the non-scientific expert organizers. For example, they caution organizers against information overload, barraging organizers with general, and often irrelevant, data. The data will often include self-referenced website anecdotes and testimonials from single individuals. While one could assume the avalanche of data as evidence of expertise and legitimate science, Stein and McManus assure the non-scientist organizers that such behaviors are indeed compensating for an epistemological shortcoming.

Stein and McManus note that the scrutinized pseudoscientists typically resort to threats against the credibility of TED and TEDx. These attacks largely play upon the tropes of good science and the self-created ethos of TED. They argue that pseudoscientists often accuse the organizers of curtailing their freedom of speech by not allowing them to present "both sides of an issue." One's democratic leanings and desire for scientific objectivity would likely find such calls for balance appealing. However, pseudoscientists have used such appeals in helping legitimize their voice for non-expert public audiences. Appeals to openness, even representation of non-mainstream views can play into the laudable sensibilities of scientific inquiry, and without any checks on the epistemic validity of such claims, those same calls for openness and balance become increasingly problematic when used by charlatans to contest legitimate scientific expertise. Stein and McManus attempt to assuage elitist concerns by reinforcing the relationship of relevance between institutional accreditation and the area of expertise. For example, an engineer who wishes to speak on matters of physics or a medical researcher who lacks a relevant terminal degree or MD should be greeted with caution. As Stein and McManus note, "this is not snobbery; if a scientist truly wishes to make an advance in their chosen field, they'll make an effort to engage with other scholars." This reinforces issues of openness as a norm scientific inquiry, and rhetorical performances of purported experts that fail to engage the scientific community are the ones who violate the scientific norms of openness, fairness, and skepticism.

The letter concludes with reassurances that organizers need not become experts in all fields of science by offering some concrete suggestions for researching potential speakers. Each suggestion is shrewd in its ordinariness: browse the web, including Wikipedia; consult a professor at a local university; visit the library; fact-check with a journalist; and if still uncertain, email TEDx for assistance. While one would likely find undergraduates in a public speaking or an introduction to composition class utilizing such research methods, Stein and McManus sanction these actions as necessary bulwarks against pseudoscientific claims. By framing commonplace and achievable research practices as avenues for navigating claims of purported scientific expertise, Stein and McManus enfranchise non-scientists as gatekeepers of good public scientific discourse. They reinforce such a gesture in their final plea to organizers: "As a member of the community, if you do come across a talk on the TEDx YouTube channel or at a future event that you feel is presenting bad science or pseudoscience, please let us know."

Conclusion

Public discussions of science often suffer from the lack of engaged and informed interlocutors. Without a doubt, many non-scientists find scientific discourses alienating and disempowering. As the cynical utterances from Congressional leaders demonstrate, the disavowal of expertise does little to advance public debate and oftentimes invites bad scientific argument and problematic appeals to expertise. The challenge, therefore, is how to provide non-scientists an avenue for engaging scientific expertise utilizing the resources they already possess. As Goodwin argues, non-experts are unable, and perhaps too intimidated, to challenge self-generated appeals to one's own expertise. As a result, non-experts must turn to indirect markers for determining or evaluating expertise. I argue the Stein and McManus TEDx open letter directs non-experts to evaluate expertise by parlaying their ability for ubiquitous discrimination, a type of transmuted expertise, with a rudimentary understanding of the scientific process. This blending of commonplace social judgment and familiar research methods with basic understandings of standard scientific practice invests non-scientists as public guardians of legitimate science.

To be sure, the Stein and McManus letter is by no means a complete treatise on enabling non-experts to parse out pseudoscientific from scientific claim. The letter still places the scientific expert as the final arbiter of legitimate scientific claims. Furthermore, the TEDx organizer is already invested in the process of assessing scientific expertise. Despite the explicit limitations, the Stein and McManus letter does provide a series of accessible guidelines for not only evaluating the content of questionable talks but also the notable rhetorical dynamics of displaying expertise. Collins and Evans argue "in the absence of suitable specialist experience, the citizen can make technical judgments only through the transmutation of expertise that starts with the social expertise of ubiquitous and local discrimination—a matter of choosing *who* to believe rather that *what* to believe" (139). The Stein and McManus letter identify a way of making such distinctions, and perhaps more importantly, it identifies the stakes in assessing expertise, enfranchising non-experts in the process of vetting and assessing expertise, as a necessary feature in improving public scientific discourse.

Notes

1.TEDx is the local franchise of TED, an acronym for Technology, Education, and Design. TED began in 1984 as a showcase conference for technological innovation, and has since expanded to include locally organized conferences.

2. Karl Popper argues that a statement can only be considered scientific if it can be subject to falsification, possible tests or experiments that could disprove the claims. Sociologist of science Robert Merton contends that there are a series of norms, what he dubs as CUDOS (Communalism, Universalism, Disinterestedness, and Organized Skepticism), that determine whether a practice is properly scientific.

Works Cited

Bratton, Benjamin. "We Need to Talk About TED." *The Guardian*. Guardian News and Media Ltd., 30 December 2013. Web. 17 Feb. 2014.

Collins, Henry and Robert Evans. "Third Wave of Science Studies: Studies of Expertise and Experience." *Social Studies of Science* 32.2 (2002): 235–96. Print.

—. *Rethinking Expertise*. Chicago: U of Chicago P, 2007. Print.

Collins, Henry, and Martin Weinel. "Transmuted Expertise: How Technical Non-Experts Can Assess Experts and Expertise." *Argumentation* 25.3 (2011): 401–13. Print.

Gieryn, Thomas. *Cultural Boundaries of Science: Credibility on the Line*. Chicago: U of Chicago P, 1999. Print.

Goodnight, G. Thomas. "The Personal, Technical, and Public Spheres of Argument: A Speculative Inquiry Into the Art of Public Deliberation." *Journal of the American Forensics Association* 18 (1982): 214–27. Print.

Goodwin, Jean. "Accounting for the Appeal to the Authority of Experts." *Argumentation* 25.3 (2011): 285–96. Print.

Majdik, Zoltan P. and William M. Keith. "Expertise as Argument: Authority, Democracy, and Problem-Solving." *Argumentation* 25.3 (2011): 371–84. Print.

Circuitry. "The TED Name is Being Dragged Through the Mud in Valencia, Spain, where a TEDx-approved event is promoting pseudoscientific stuff like (and I quote) crystal therapy, Egyption psychoaromatherapy, healing through the Earth, homeopathy and even 'basic mind control'" *Reddit*. Reddit Inc., 2013. Web. 17 Feb. 2014.

Robbins, Martin. "The Trouble with TED Talks." *New Statesman*. 10 September 2012. Web. 17 Feb. 2014.

Sheppard, Kate. "John Boehner: 'I'm Not Qualified To Debate The Science Over Climate Change.'" *The Huffington Post*. HuffingtonPost.com. 29 May 2014. Web. 20 June 2014.

Stein, Laura and Emily McManus. "A Letter to the TEDx Community on TEDx and Bad Science." *The TEDx Tumblr*. 7 December 2013. Web. 17 Feb. 2014.

Taylor, Charles Alan. *Defining Science: A Rhetoric of Demarcation*. Madison, WI: University of Wisconsin Press, 1996. Print.

15 Citizen Science in Lower Hood Canal: The Emergence of the Lower Hood Canal Watershed Coalition (LHCWC) as a Forum for Environmental Education, Policy Development and the Shaping of Political Will

John Angus Campbell

Citizen Science carries two distinct but inter-related meanings. In the first, and most generally accepted meaning, a citizen *scientist* is a kind of *scientist*. In this meaning, a person not formally accredited by any technical discipline may contribute to science, usually through making empirical observations, and thus be considered an honorary scientist (Ashley Kelly, ch.2). A *citizen* scientist in the second sense is primarily a *citizen* who, while occasionally engaging in citizen *science,* uses technical or scientific knowledge to formulate or critique public science policy, initiate environmental restoration programs, or conduct the research needed for their development. The first meaning places *science* in a privileged position over citizenship. The second meaning reverses this emphasis and places *citizenship* in a privileged position over technical knowledge. Technical knowledge in this second sense is significant not because it advances human understanding *per se* but because it is useful or necessary to formulating wise public policy and advancing the common good.

In its second sense, *citizen* science stands to science as do the subjects that everyone needs to know about in order to deliberate, or to judge deliberations, that Aristotle discusses in Book I of the *Rhetoric*. (*Rhetoric*. Bk. 1. 4–15). Because taxes, fortifications, etc. are all subjects citizens need to know about to participate in, or judge public debate and discussion, these subjects, when approached from the standpoint of public policy, no longer belong exclusively to specific sciences. The incorporation of these technical subjects into the values, norms, passions and cultural projects of a self-governing, deliberating community—even when the information presented by advocates is accurate—makes them no longer the property of technical expertise but part of the knowledge proper to citizens.

The Lower Hood Canal Watershed Coalition (LHCWC) while occasionally engaging in citizen *science* in the primary sense, is principally an example of *citizen* science in the second. The primacy of citizens in LHCWC's approach to science is reflected in its membership: "The LHCWC is a group of local citizens, businesses, and representatives from governmental agencies and the Skokomish Tribe who work for clean water and sustainable natural resources." In this ordering, citizens and local businesses come first, governmental agencies and the tribe follow. The citizens and businesses are LHCWC's core constituency; governmental and tribal agencies provide scientific, water-management, planning, and regulation expertise. The primacy of citizens is also evident in LHCWC's mission statement: "Our mission is accomplished through thoughtful review and inclusive discussions of water-related issues at monthly meetings or through proposing corrective actions to local citizens, County, State, Tribal and Federal agencies" (LHCWC. 2). "Thoughtful review" affirms the competence of ordinary citizens to sit with experts and understand and critique their policy proposals. "Corrective actions" indicates LHCWC's work as clean-water ambassadors and teachers. LHCWC shares with neighbors best practices for maintaining beach or stream-side property, oyster health, the maintenance of septic systems, and the dangers and sources of run-off. Similarly, since LHCWC members are citizens, taxpayers, and active voters they have credibility with neighbors, state agencies, or commissioners independent of credentialed expertise.

Despite its importance as a citizen-based environmental forum and its track record in facilitating significant regional water quality initiatives, LHCWC is not an arm of government or a 501 (c) (3) non-profit organization. LHCWC dispenses no grant monies, nor does it have a website. LHCWC meets on the first Monday of every month at 6:00 pm in the board room of the North Mason School District. The rent for the meeting room is paid by one or the other of its joint co-chairs, Bob Hagar and Constance Ibsen, both resident retirees. Incidental printing expenses for the handouts distributed at its meetings are either absorbed by the co-chairs or occasionally provided gratis by a visiting agency. The organization has an e-mail list of eighty individuals, though some never attend. An ordinary meeting will range anywhere between 5–10 individuals at the lower end and 20–25 at the upper (Hagar).

What unites LHCWC members as *citizen* scientists is water: its quality, where it flows, whether fish in the canal or shellfish on private (or public) beaches are safe to eat, and whether the canal is clean enough for swimming, boating, and water sports. For rhetoricians of science, LHCWC is of interest for how it serves as a forum where laypeople in their role as citizens argue, deliberate, politic and form coalitions with scientific and/or government agency professionals, educate their neighbors, and shape local political will.

I begin with a brief description of Hood Canal as a physical object that occasions and constrains *citizen* and scientific discourses on its water quality. The narrative then charts LHCWC's origin as a *citizen* group that became knowledgeable of water science and the canal's challenged water quality under the name the Lower Hood Canal Management Committee (LHCMC) and the *Action Plan* (*LHCMAP*, 1985) it produced. A summary of LHCWC's development and activities through two subsequent official advisory committees will clarify the genesis and mission of the current organization. This section will examine how LHCWC's identity grew from its role as an organization of *citizens* concerned about clean water, who were also knowledgeable about the sources of pollution, rather than from the activities of many of its members as citizen *scientists*. The conclusion will briefly consider how LHCWC illustrates the unique role of and need for *citizen* science. It will note that while the roles of *citizen* science and citizen *scientist* overlap, it is as a *citizen* science forum that LHCWC has been able to shape government policy, public practices and even the research agenda of professional science.

An Exigency Marked By Urgency: Citizen Science, Hood Canal and the Water Quality Debate

Citizen science in its first or second sense may have made an early and enduring, if inadvertent, impression on contemporary Hood Canal water-quality debates. Through a slip of mind or pen an inattentive early draftsman changed the name Captain Vancouver assigned to the waterway in 1792—

Hood's *Channel*—to Hood *Canal*, (Michael Fredson, introduction). To state the obvious, Hood Canal is not a human-made passage. What is true under either name is that Hood Canal is a narrow body of marine water. The name substitution may have been prescient. In the instant between one's first encounter with the name and the realization that Hood Canal is not a "canal" one thinks of it as a work of human engineering. The tension between seeing the Canal as a channel produced by self-shaping/healing nature and as a human artifact requiring maintenance and restoration is central to the exigence driving the urgent contemporary stakeholder arguments over restoring and protecting water quality. To grasp how citizens mobilizing the resources of science might reverse Hood Canal's problematic water quality one must begin with the constraints imposed on description by the object.

Hood Canal is approximately sixty miles in length and generally varies from a mile to a mile-and-a-half in width. The Canal begins in the north at Admiralty Inlet, between Tala Point and Foulweather Bluff, and travels forty-five miles southwest to the great bend. At the great bend where the Skokomish river empties into it Hood Canal turns east and travels in an east/west plane another fifteen miles to the estuary of the Union River (Hood Canal Coordinating Council).

Hood Canal is a fjord—and the only one in the lower forty-eight States. In common with all fjords, Hood Canal has high sills at its entrance, and thus, the sea water coming in from Admiralty Inlet does not replace the old water returning from the southern portions of the canal with each tide. One estimate places the partial flushing of canal water back into Puget Sound at Admiralty Inlet at over 260 days. (Messman 2) Even minus human habitation, simply because of their structure, fjords are prone to periods of low dissolved oxygen.

A cycle of forces combine to make portions of Hood Canal periodically lethal to sea-life. Because of its incomplete and lengthy flushing, sediments and organic pollutants from the numerous riverways that empty into the canal from the Olympic Mountains or the streams from the Puget Sound Basin are neither completely carried away nor significantly diluted by the tides. Further, the stable stratification of fresh and salt water, particularly in lower Hood Canal, inhibits mixing of the deeper, heavier saline water with the lighter surface freshwater and produces the pre-conditions for low dissolved oxygen.

Given these pre-conditions, the crucial balance-tipping ingredient is algae blooms. Algae blooms form in Hood Canal all year round. When the blooms sink and decompose they remove oxygen from the bottom of the waterway. Especially in the late summer and fall, given the right pattern of southerly winds, algae blooms contribute to creating a dome of oxygen-depleted water—particularly in lower Hood Canal. As these domes expand and rise from the canal floor, deep-water fish can be seen gasping for air on the surface. When the dome is complete, even for a short time, the result is a massive fish kill. (Messman, 4-7, HCCC).

Any attempt by humans to "fix" the problem of poor water quality in the Canal has to contend with the natural tendency of the waterway—without any help from humans and even before the arrival of Europeans—to become "rotten with its own perfection." (Kenneth Burke, 16) There is, however, a margin of human-caused contributions to poor water quality, which, if reduced, could help tip natural forces back from the fish-kill brink. The human-caused sources of low dissolved oxygen include: on-site septic systems, storm-water runoff, logging practices, and waste disposal practices. All of these contribute silt and organic matter to the waterway. The water-born loads from these dispersed sources, rather than concentrating pollution at a single location, are identified as "non-point pollution" (*LHCWAP.* ii). While animal waste is also a factor, non-point pollution is primarily human caused. Non-point pollutants also contribute to the toxins ingested by shellfish, particularly in the shallow waters of Lynch Cove in Lower Hood Canal (*Benthic Invertebrate Communities*). In the space between the natural causes of low water quality endemic to fjords and their augmentation by human contributions, science can provide the technical analysis that gives *Citizen* science the margin from which to launch its cultural and political appeal.

Citizen Science Intervention in Lower Hood Canal: The Intersection of Nature and Culture

The need for *citizens* to take a leading role in improving water quality, particularly in Lower Hood Canal, began to be recognized in the 1970's. During this decade the assumption that nature was a super-abundant resource began to be challenged by a new awareness that nature had limits, was fragile, and required human stewardship. To meet this challenge science and citizenship had to become more closely aligned. For lower Hood Canal, the first step in this process was the Lower Hood Canal Watershed Action Plan (LHCWAP).

The genesis of the citizen-centered LHCWAP began with the Puget Sound Water Quality Authority (PSWQA) established in 1985 (*LHCWAP*, i). A central objective of the PSWQA, created by the Washington State Legislature, was to develop and coordinate an overall state-wide plan for addressing the growing problem of pollution (*LHCWAP.* 1-1-2-1). The Lower Hood Canal Watershed Action Plan authored by the Lower Hood Canal Management Committee may be considered the *Bible*, *Constitution*, or founding document of the modern day LCWC. Virtually everything the contemporary *citizen*-science coalition discusses or does takes its rationale from this document (Hagar).

CITIZENS, SCIENCE AND POLITICAL POWER

The PSWQA illustrates the distinctive orientation of *citizen* science as opposed to citizen *science* in addressing their shared interest in improving environmental health. Though scientific expertise is necessary to diagnose the causes of poor water quality, in a democratic society expertise alone, even if it is widely distributed among citizens, cannot solve a problem created by the confluence of nature and the human cultures it has attracted and nourished. The demands of science, even when they are known, must be weighed against material cost and the social cost of change. Wisely, the PSWQA did not impose a uniform plan on all of Puget Sound. Instead as the *LHCWMAP* illustrates, the PSWQA designed a process in which local citizens with an interest in water quality were authorized to draw up a plan sensitive to the particular needs of their particular area. In *LHCWMAP*, we see citizens informed by technical knowledge negotiating the social boundary conditions in which science can be effective.

Though county governments, in this case primarily Mason but also Kitsap county, were responsible for the ordinances and regulations of their own jurisdictions, twenty-three representatives of the people of Lower Hood Canal (though unelected) drew up the local plan of action (*LHCWAP* i) under the PSWQA. Though the PSWQA was careful to respect the sovereignties of the counties under its authority, its procedures facilitated the development of a complicated redistribution of policy-making power. Parallel to the "separation" of powers in the Federal Constitution, the LHCWAP positioned citizens as a counter-balancing force to various official agencies. The agencies retain official jurisdiction and have scientific expertise, but LHCWAP provides citizen monitoring. Politically, the LHCWAP can be understood as is a kind of intra-agency federalism. LHCWAP authorizes the county, other agencies, and citizens to act on, through, and with one another in a variety of ways.

LHCWAP was decisive for the development of *citizen* science in Lower Hood Canal because by taking the technical information sequestered in numerous scientific reports and piece-meal governmental-planning documents and assembling it into a unified Action Plan, it turned knowledge into power. With the authorization of this plan by citizens, science-based knowledge became *common knowledge*. When citizens disseminated this information/knowledge, it gained local credibility not because it was based on science but because it was backed by the *ethos* of neighbors. Because this new citizen authority invested facts with meaning and sensitivity to local civic values, it lent to otherwise inert data persuasive power. Whereas citizen *science* is guided by the concerns of particular disciplines and written in a technical language, *citizen* science is motivated not by a desire to advance knowledge but by the need to translate it into the vernacular, adapt it to local conditions and realize its potential for the common good.

The Lower Hood Canal Action Plan As Citizens Managerial Rhetoric: Brevity, Bullet Points, Lists and Reiteration

The unanswered question of citizen science is how can amateurs direct professional science? The answer of the LHCWAP is to summarize the science in terms accessible to laypersons and then turn technical knowledge into issues of management. Though written in the form of a short book with sequential chapters, and with an iconic aqua-colored cover with a drawing of a heron fishing amid cat-tails, the LHCWAP is less a work to be read than a manual to be consulted. The document has just enough narrative to reduce major water quality issues to an understandable story line while confining detail to segregated, compacted or expanded lists that inform the reader without bogging him or her down in detail. While we cannot provide a complete outline, an overview will help clarify the persuasive power of its tight integration of form and content.

By vesting power in an unelected lay committee and reducing technical information to procedures of governance and oversight, LHCWAP legitimized an informal group of unelected citizens to act as civic watchdogs of the technical/scientific planning work of experts and governmental agencies. The LHCWAP was not only well-crafted for motivating and legitimating its original committee of citizen scientists but had the good fortune to be inherited by two successor committees whose citizen scientist members had a stake in continuing its legacy.

Table 13.1. Summational Style: The Visual Rhetoric of LHCWAP

The document is short	58 pp. Comment letters from agencies in appendix 47 pp.
It is easily readable	Opens with executive summary, no technical terms, few paragraphs longer than 10 lines, numerous bullet points.
The chapters (except Ch. 4) approach the same problem from different angles with different levels of detail.	An executive summary presents the 2 general and 9 specific "causes" of non-point pollution. General: 1) Overall water quality, 2) Citizen Education, Specific: i) On-site Septic, ii) Ground water, iii) Aquatic recreation, iv) Agriculture, v) Forestry, vi) Erosion & storm water, vii) Landfill, viii) Illegal dumping, ix) Wildlife
Chapter 1	Background on PSWQA, description of Watershed Committee in 3 pp.
Chapter 2	General & Specific causes (above) reframed as "Problem Identification," "Problem Statements," for 11 causes.
Chapter 3: Almost entirely a series of lists.	Renames 11 causes "Control Strategies," followed by bullet point "Objectives," & numbered "Actions."
Chapter 4: "Action plan implementation" 4pp. Shortest in document.	After each "Action Step" is an agency responsible for carrying it out. At 28 pp. longest chapter in document
Stand alone segment divided into two parts	Divided into 8 boldfaced heads: **Coordination by Lead Agencies, Coordination other Programs, Schedule Implementation, Tasks and Resp Agencies, Funding , Public Involvement During Implementation, Evaluation and Annual Plan Review.**
Appendix	"Schedule of Implementation of the LHCWAP: Recommended Action Steps." (1 p.) "Matrix of Recommended Actions and Implementing Entities." (2 pp.) Approval of Mason County Department of Health, concurring letters, with occasional caveats, from various agencies, but in the case of Mason County outright disagreement. (47 pp.)

1993–1998 CITIZEN SCIENCE PHASE #2: LOWER HOOD CANAL CLEAN WATER DISTRICT ADVISORY COMMITTEE.

The need for *citizen* science to address the problems of Hood Canal and prod a slow-moving county bureaucracy to action was demonstrated almost before the ink on LHCWAP was dry. On February 2, 1993 the Department of Health, following routine inspections, closed Lower Hood Canal to shellfish harvesting. The closure included not only Toten Inlet in Hood Canal but also North Bay in the Puget Sound Watershed and Oakland Bay In the Oakland Bay Watershed (*Consent Order*. 2). The consent order required Mason County to take at least some of the actions that the Citizens Management Committee had recommended in its *Action Plan*, which had been completed in 1992 though not formally approved by the Washington State Department of Ecology (DOE) until 1994. LHCWAP had urged Mason County to form a clean water district. The county did nothing until the consent order from the DOE required them to act. Happily, the initial *LHCWAP*, even before it was formally approved, provided the framework for its successor committee—the Clean Water District Advisory Board (LHCCWDAB).

Following its founding in July, 1993, the Advisory Board, with its leadership of local citizens, held monthly meetings to determine the most promising approach to cleaning up the waters of Hood Canal. Whereas a spending-averse county would hesitate to pay for new programs that their immediate constituents were not demanding—the citizen Advisory Board had no such hesitation. The Board recommended the county initiate and finance testing of all parcels of land on Hood Canal and associated fresh waterways. Under the Advisory Board's plan, failed sites were identified and put on a course of repair. The inspections were carried out by the Department of Health. At the suggestion of its citizen Advisory Board, the county also developed and adopted (June 6, 1996) an on-site septic management plan (*Operation and Maintenance*).

In its initial stage of work with the county, the citizen-led Advisory Board was largely successful. In October of 1993, the septic inspection and repair program enabled the Department of Health to reopen part of the South Shore of Hood Canal for shellfish harvesting, but the success was limited. Approximately five hundred parcels of land were not surveyed because the owners refused to allow inspectors on the property or because they had not responded to a certified letter from the County. Given the established failure rate of ten percent, there was good evidence that at least fifty sites were still failing (*Refused Access*. 1). The mixed results revealed an early tension between the county and its lay committee. While the County was happy to declare an eighty-nine percent improvement a success, members of the citizens committee remained unsatisfied. With the continuing pollution of the ten percent (up-dated to eleven percent), the citizens committee faced a problem neither it nor the county knew how to address.

Despite this tension, in December of 1996 the county authorized the committee to monitor and report to it the county's progress on the *Watershed Action Plan* developed by the earlier management committee. This additional responsibility led to the reconstitution of the committee in 1998 as the *Lower Hood Canal Implementation Committee* (*Minutes*).

1998–2005 Citizen Science Phase #3: Lower Hood Canal Implementation Committee

Beginning approximately in its third incarnation as the Implementation Committee, committee members and the agencies with which they were now familiar took a more entrepreneurial approach to their mission—presaging the contemporary LHCWC—and formed informal *citizen* science/science partnerships to encourage Mason County to act. To address the problem of fecal coliform entering Hood Canal from the Union River, members of the committee began collaborating with Dave Garland of the Department of Ecology. By practicing citizen *science*, members of the committee contributed to the preliminary scientific water sampling and fact-finding necessary for a grant. By practicing *citizen* science when the county took no action, the committee members wrote the grant and persuaded the county to submit it. A result of this grant was a major cleanup of the southern portion of the Union River that runs through Mason County and empties into Hood Canal.

The most spectacular *citizen* science/science partnership of the group that finally became LHCWC began with a conversation, in the late '90's or early 2000's, between the Oceanographer Jan Newton and long-term member of the Advisory and Implementation Committees Bob Hagar. Conversation with Newton and relevant players in state and non-profit environmental agencies (especially the Hood Canal Salmon Center) resulted in the formation of the Lower Hood Canal Dissolved Oxygen Project. When Norm Dicks, Hagar's neighbor on the South Shore's highway 106 and long-time member of the US House of Representatives, got on board, the subsequent project developed into one of the most extensive scientific studies and, ultimately at thirteen million dollars, certainly the most expensive ever done of Hood Canal.

CITIZEN SCIENCE IN HOOD CANAL PHASE #4: DISSOLUTION OF THE LHCIC AND THE BIRTH OF LHCWC

The dissolution of the LHCIC in April of 2005 by Mason county followed the issuing of what turned out to be the committee's final report in 2003. The dissolution marked not an end of the organization but the pivotal moment in its evolution as an independent voice for *citizen* science. As early as 1999, Debbie Riley of the committee of the Mason County Department of Health wrote the committee a memorandum suggesting the committee focus on education—effectively ending the survey and inspection program overseen by the committee (*Change of Focus*). Given the historic reluctance of Mason County to lead in water cleanup efforts, its comparatively small population and its low tax base, the dissolution of the Implementation Committee was not unexpected. Commissioners had many state agencies to which they had to answer, and an unpaid group of policy-informed citizens, while occasionally useful, could also be an irritant. When one of the committee members took the potentials of citizen so seriously as to run against one of the sitting county commissioners and came within a few votes of defeating him, the potential of the committee to be a political liability was evident.

From the standpoint of the members of the committee, the work that remained to be done and their experience of the constant need for involvement and oversight to get it done made them reluctant to abandon their role as citizen champions of Hood Canal water quality. When one considers the working relationships the committee had formed over the years with various state and regional public and non-governmental agencies—it seemed evident that official status, or even grant-giving power or credentialed expertise, was not necessary to carrying forward the committee's key functions.

CONCLUSION

LHCWC emerged in response to the need for a citizen voice in improving water quality in Hood Canal. The PSWQA recognized not only the inability of science to mobilize its resources without the direction of government but also the inability of government to carry through its own policies without a strong and independent civic culture to support it. Drawing on the legacy of the LHCWAP, the subsequent advisory board and management committees that eventuated in LHCWC further developed the role of a citizen voice in water quality by their interactions with government, the public, and technical science.

What is unique or distinctive about LHCWC as an example of "citizen science" is that though some of its members are scientists or citizen *scien-*

tists, LHCWC does not ground its authority on its scientific standing. The authority of LHCWC to speak on issues of water quality is grounded on its translation of science into civics and thus on the right and responsibility of citizens to deliberate about the common good. Building on its civic foundation LHCWC has defined a role for itself in uniting what neither technical knowledge nor government alone can reliably perform.

WORKS CITED

Aristotle. *Rhetoric.* Trans. G. Kennedy. *Aristotle On Rhetoric: A Theory of Civic Discourse.* 2nd ed. Oxford: Oxford U P, 2007. Print

Burke, K. *Language As Symbolic Action.* Berkeley and Los Angeles:U of California P, 1966. Print.

Fredson, M. *Hood Canal.* Charleston, SC: Arcadia Publishing, 2007. Kindle file.

Hagar, B. Personal Interview. 9 May. 2014.

Hood Canal Coordinating Council. *Hood Canal Geography.* N.p., n.d. Web.7 June 2015.

—. *The Hood Canal Watershed: Where Humans and Nature Coexist.* N.p., n.d. Print.

Ibsen, C. Personal Interview. 13 Mar.. 2014.

Kelly, A. R. "Hacking Science: Emerging Parascientific Genres and Public Participation in Scientific Research." Diss. U of North Carolina, 2014. Print.

Lower Hood Canal Clean Water District Advisory Board. *Refused Access or Non Response to Requests for Inspections.* N.p.7 Oct. 1996. Print.

Lower Hood Canal Management Committee. *Lower Hood Canal Watershed Action Plan: Working Towards Protecting and Improving Our Water Quality.* N.p., 1994. Print.

Lower Hood Canal Watershed Coalition. *The Future of Hood Canal Is in Our Hands.* N.p., 8 Jan 2010. Print.

Mason County. *On-Site Sewage Operation and Maintenance Program.* N.p. 6 June 1996. Print.

Mason County Commissioners. *Resolution.* No. 57–98. N.p. 2 June 1998. Print.

Mason County Department of Health. *Change of Focus.* Debbie Riley, 28 June 1999. Print.

Messman, S. A. *South Hood Canal: A Water Quality Issue Paper.* Washington Department of Ecology, Jan. 1991. Print.

Washington State. Dept. of Ecology. Consent Order No. DE 93 WQ-S194. 9 June 1993. Print.

Washington State. Dept. of Ecology. Dutch, M., *et. al. The Influence of Sediment Characteristics and*

Dissolved Oxygen on Benthic Invertebrate Communities in Hood Canal, Olympia: DOE 20007. Web. 7 June 2015.

16 THE "NATIVE" AS NOT SO CREATIVE COMMONPLACE IN THE BORDERLAND OF ENVIRONMENTAL WRITING

Alexis F. Piper

[The Indian] begins where we leave off . . . so much the more divine; and anything that fairly excites our admiration expands us. Not only for strength, but for beauty, the poet must travel the logger's path and the Indian's trail, to drink at some new and more bracing fountain of the Muses, far in the recesses of the wilderness.

—Henry David Thoreau, *The Maine Woods*

S
even years before his premature death, in July of 1857, Henry David Thoreau walked into the "wild Maine woods" with his cousin Ed Hoar and a Wabanaki guide by the name of Joe Polis. This trip is recounted in the final essay of Thoreau's *The Maine Woods*, a book that distinctly navigates multiple borders: borders between countries and geographical demarcations, between conceptions of wilderness and civilization, between nineteenth-century delineations of "Indian" and "Euro-American", between "nature" and "culture", between Western science and traditional ecologi-

cal knowledge (or TEK), and between epistemologies and worldviews. *The Maine Woods* is representative of a larger trend evident in nature writing for at least the last 150 years. Following Thoreau's enduring influence on American nature writing[1], since the mid-nineteenth-century nature writers have assumed the ethos of a lone, intrepid, sage adventurer who helps their audiences navigate borders.

Consequently, American nature writing remains a site where borders interact, overlap, and vie for creative, constructive influence. Put another way, American nature writing is a border rhetoric where differing rhetorical appeals, epistemologies, rhetorical genres, arguments, and orientations compete for contested territory. My first objective in this paper is to illustrate the various ways American nature writing is a unique, transformative border rhetoric. Then, I will argue that within this borderland of Western "nature writing," Native eco-orientations and alternative environmental ethics frequently function as commonplaces. However, I will also contend they are not as productive of a commonplace or creative site of invention as they could be because Anglo-American nature writers often fail to engage with the writing of Native authors. Finally, I will contend that a more productive border rhetoric could be constructed if the actual words of Indigenous peoples were to be more ethically and thoughtfully engaged.

Environmental rhetoricians have frequently described environmental rhetoric as a borderland (Herndl and Brown 10-13, Cantrill and Oravec 4, Killingsworth and Palmer 11, and Waddell 55). For example, rhetorician Louis Ulman defines nature writing as a genre that exists on the "borderland" (47) between scientific writing about natural history and autobiographical writing about the way individuals relate to the natural world (46-80). Also speaking to the borderland state of contemporary writing on the environment, Carl Herndl and Stuart Brown insist that:

> Nature writing often combines a scientific knowledge of nature with a desire to reenchant science, to connect scientific knowledge to a spiritual sense of nature and its beauty. Thus, nature writing often uses conventions and forms more characteristic of poetic discourse and appeals to pathos as well as to reason (12).

Therefore—perhaps even more pointedly than in other literary genres—the rhetorical appeals of pathos, logos, and ethos interact and alternatively accede to prominence in Western writing on the natural world. As is evident throughout the genre, appeals to logos and pathos overlie one another: scientific, rationality-based appeals and emotional, personal-experience-based appeals are frequently interwoven. For instance, throughout his considerable body of work environmental author Barry Lopez alternates between deriving his ethos from personal, felt, spiritual encounters in nature to shaping it through a detached observation of nature—between his own emotionally-incited observations and those of scientific and academic specialists. In Lopez's *Arctic Dreams*, for example, he weaves scientific and historic research on Antarctica into emotional reactions to the stark beauty and mystery of the landscape (6, 14, 38, 297). Lopez is adept at alternately drawing from both logos and pathos to appeal to his audiences and develop his environmental ethos.

In addition, in *Green Culture* Carl Herndl and Stuart Brown describe how rhetorical appeals overlap and interact with one another by providing a rhetorical model for environmental discourse that they configure as a triangle with ethos at the apex and pathos and logos forming the base (11). Herndl and Brown illustrate how these appeals and their specific corresponding characteristic discourse border one another[2]. "Successful environmental writing," write Herndl and Brown, "often combines the styles, forms, and rhetorical appeals of more than one of these discourses" (12). Additionally, although they insist on the necessity and preeminence of logos, environmental rhetoricians James Cantrill and Christine Oravec also point out the importance of bordering, interconnected appeals in environmental discourse and nature writing (4). These scholars of environmental communication conceive of the ways we communicate about the "natural" world and nature writing as a borderland where multiple appeals and discourses are folded in on one another.

The environmental ethos employed by nature writers also derives its authority both from scientific knowledge and a personally-experienced, emotional knowledge of the "natural" world. Therefore, nature writing is also often the site where epistemologies border one another. For example, in Terry Tempest Williams' influential autobiographical text *Refuge*, she struggles with the question of whether Western science and medicine can offer her the knowledge and awareness she seeks during her mother's death or whether her pathetic, spiritual experiences with the Salt Lake landscape of her youth can offer her "True" knowledge of death, dying, and rebirth. Similar to Lopez's interweaving of rhetorical appeals, Williams draws from different epistemologies that combine to construct a complex Truth through scientific and humanistic principles. Therefore, both Williams and Lopez seem to realize the reality Craig Waddell highlights when he writes, "Our ability to address successfully many of the most pressing problems we face today . . . requires sophistication in both scientific and humanistic disciplines" (55) as well as the knowledge or epistemologies that those disciplines entail. Thus, both environmental authors construct epistemological borderlands in their texts.

American nature writing also frequently navigates between the borders of deliberative and forensic rhetorical genres as described by Aristotle in *The Art of Rhetoric* (85). In other words, nature writing is increasingly the site where the analysis and evaluation of future (deliberative) and past (forensic) eco-orientations take place (Corbett xiv). For example, as George Myerson and Yvonne Rydin point out, the ethos associated with environmental debates regarding global climate change and overpopulation is most frequently established by looking forward (122), while the rhetoric of wilderness historians and philosophers such as Paul Shepard and Max Oelschlaeger often turns to the past to make judgments and to establish authenticity and authority. As evidence of this, Myerson and Rydin look to the future for answers to our current environmental crisis, while Shepard and Oelschlaeger turn to our pre-agricultural revolution, Paleolithic past to imagine a more egalitarian relationship with "nature" (for example *Coming Home to the Pleistocene* by Shepard, *The Wilderness Condition* by Oelschlaeger, and, additionally, *In the Spirit of the Earth* by Martin Calvin Luther).

In addition, Aldo Leopold and Edward Abbey's work often combines the strategies of exploring past environmental legislation and collective actions in ways that pivot from forensic judgments of past actions to deliberative assessments of future actions taken on behalf of the environment. For instance, in *A Sand County Almanac* Leopold questions (and ultimately condemns) the laws and practices of wolf eradication and the related problem of deer overpopulation with an eye towards future actions and attitudes (223). By comparison, Abbey laments and condemns past legislation allowing the introduction of sheep in the American West, also with an eye toward future legislation and collective action (189). Leopold and Abbey employ deliberative and forensic rhetorics to affect the hearts and minds of their audiences, thereby participating in the construction of the borderland rhetoric of American nature writing.

The ways we deliberate and construct the "natural" world through language is also a borderland where rhetors and audiences must navigate multiple arguments. Myerson and Rydin, for instance, have repeatedly pointed out the polyphonic nature of environmental discourse, claiming that the ways we communicate about the environment will evolve into a public, deliberative space in which multiple arguments vie for and achieve rhetorical and political "success" (11). The implications for nature writing are that multiple arguments can be used to win, persuade, or identify with a wide variety of different audiences. There need not be one overarching argument, and there need not be one means to achieve one end. The ends and the means of nature writing and of environmental cognizance can be disparate and diffuse. In *Deliberative Acts* Arabella Lyon points out the profoundly fragmentary effects of globalization on audience and argument. Audiences of American nature writing are also becoming increasingly globalized and fragmented. Following Lyon's thrust, Myerson and Rydin contend that, "In modern culture, argumentation is multiplied and diverse. Any argument cuts across many different media . . . [the ways we communicate, especially about the environment] are everywhere linked and always fragmenting" (8). In a diverse yet connected context for arguments, claims, proofs, and positions interact in what Myerson and Rydin have termed the *argumentative environet*, which they contend is "a central fact of contemporary culture" (11). Therefore, the persuasion and identification strategies of nature writing are also a borderland where audiences must interact, engage, and identify with a variety of interwoven arguments.

In addition to the borders already discussed, there is another borderland I believe contemporary, Western nature writing continues to explore. Writing on and on behalf of the "natural" world also marks a border where ecocentric and anthropocentric worldviews interrelate, pull, push, and border one another. In other words, nature writing is where human-centered and biosphere-centered orientations ebb, flow and overlap. "Anthropocentrists," according to Oelschaleager, "see the human species as the most significant fact of existence, and accordingly evaluate all else from a human standpoint" (293). Within anthropocentric orientations, the "natural" world has no inherent rights and is valuable only in how it serves the wants and needs of humankind. Anthropocentrists envision, reason, and argue exclusively from a human-centered perspective. Other species and the planet are given little to no ethical, moral, or empathetic consideration beyond their usefulness to humankind. By comparison, ecocentrism is, "an egalitarian attitude on the part of humans toward all members of the ecosphere" (Ulman 68). Ecocentrists view all life as possessing rights, intrinsic worth, and ethical consideration. The human species is part of the larger picture of life on this planet, and the interdependence of all beings—including human beings—is acknowledged and esteemed. Environmental historian Carolyn Merchant writes, "An ecocentric ethic is grounded in the cosmos. The whole environment is assigned intrinsic value" (57). Within an ecocentric ethic, humanity is not the pinnacle of creation—not the only life form that matters. I believe that nature writing often navigates the borders between these two orientations. In fact, the genre often draws from the dominant narrative of anthropocentrism, meeting their audiences where they are, and striving to move them towards ecocentrism. My own survey of American nature writing from the last two centuries suggests that environmental writing can be characterized as a creative border site where anthropocentric and ecocentric worldviews are articulated, sometimes identified with, and sometimes disavowed or dis-identified with—thereby audiences can walk the borderland between the two paradigms.

In addition, there is further evidence that the ways we communicate about the natural world is a borderland between the established rhetorics of anthropocentrism and the transformative rhetorics of ecocentrism. For example, in their extensive analysis of environmental rhetoric, *Ecospeak*, Jimmie Killingsworth and Jacqueline Palmer coined the term *developmentalist* to describe the worldviews and the discourse of those "who seek short-term economic gain regardless of the long-term environmental costs" (9), those who reason and deliberate purely from an anthropocentric, "nature as resource" perspective. Developmentalism, Killingsworth and Palmer contend, continues to dominate the mainstream conversation, including controlling cultural discourse and paradigms. In fact, throughout *The Death of Nature* Merchant contends that anthropocentric, domination-and-manipulation-of-nature orientations have held sway since the eighteenth-century Enlightenment (11). Scholars from Oelschlaeger to Shepard to Calvin to Lynn White have traced this anthropocentric mentality back even further to the turn from a hunter-gathering existence to agriculture and the subsequent foundation of monotheistic, Abrahamic religious traditions. Thus, given the historic dominance of anthropocentrism, contemporary Western nature writing is a unique borderland where the radical, counter-cultural rhetoric of ecocentrism vies for an alternative voice within the long-established discourse and cultural ideology of anthropocentrism. Put another way, nature writing is the borderland between established and transformative rhetorics. In this endeavor, the genre strives to articulate then transform millennia of ecocidal tendencies made possible by anthropocentric thought and language. Therefore, at its best, American nature writing continues to be a border rhetoric.

Possibilities for a More Productive Borderland

As Gloria Anzuldúa has so eloquently established, borderlands are often places of volatility, clashing identifications, conflict, and even violence (*Borderlands* 30). According to Anzuldúa, the volatile nature of borderlands is what gives them their transformative potential. Borderlands are places of change—places pushing toward transformation. American nature writing should strive to achieve this transformative objective. However, in a borderland, because it is a site of volatility and potential transformation, sojourners in the ever-morphing landscape often construct and cling to commonplaces as points of stability that reinforce group identifications. I am arguing that this is frequently how Native eco-orientations continue to be rhetorically employed in Anglo-American nature writing.

Rhetoric's first office, invention, has long been conceived of as a way to develop proofs and as a method for discovering the unknown. And the commonplace, according to Richard McKeon, plays an integral role in invention. For instance, commonplaces can serve as places of collective, widely shared meaning and recognition that can be used to make new meanings and incite new recognitions of symbolic significance. In fact, in his philosophical speculation on creativity, "Creativity and the Commonplace," McKeon asserts that "Memory is the basis of invention, invention provides the materials for memory, and commonplaces are the devices of both invention and memory" (199). Therefore, commonplaces are integral to McKeon's theory of invention. Yet, strategies for invention that rely exclusively on the commonplace without making new meaning, without discovering the unknown, can become stale, and consequently counterproductive. McKeon warns that commonplaces can lose their productive, creative, new-argument-inciting function by pointing out how, at different historical periods and particularly during the height of Roman Rhetoric and rhetorical theory, "Commonplaces ceased from time to time to be ways to the new and unknown, and commonplaces became collections of aphorisms and verses rather than arts of invention" (202). In short, commonplaces can morph, over time, from strategies for invention and innovation—ways to explore the unknown—to proselytizing and mindless repetition (207). They can devolve into stereotypes and comfortable, worn re-articulations of the old (207). Reifying stereotypes and reiterating unproductive commonplaces within a borderland hinders the site's volatile, transformative potential—its potential to change discourses and paradigms, to move thinking.

For centuries, American environmental authors have consistently turned to Indigenous orientations as commonplaces—first, to the physical bodies, and later, to the cultural traditions and worldviews of Native Americans. As an example representative of nineteenth-century nature writing, John Muir writes in *The Mountains of California*,

> Occasionally a good countenance may be seen among the Mono Indians, but these, the first specimens I had seen, were mostly ugly, and some of them altogether hideous. The dirt on their faces was fairly stratified, and seemed so ancient and so undisturbed it might also possess a geological significance. The older faces were, moreover, strangely blurred and divided into sections by furrows that looked like the cleavage-joints of rocks, suggesting exposure on the mountains in a castaway condition for ages. Somehow they seemed to have no right place in the landscape, and I was glad to see them fading out of sight (72).

By describing the countenances (humankind's singular feature that often defines and expresses our humanity) of the Mono Indians in topographical terms, by depicting the faces of the Monos as geological features, Muir dis-identifies with the Natives and renders them as essentialized, physical bod-ies that belong to a timeless landscape. Thereby he constructs an alternative place in the natural world for the Monos that differs from his own Anglo-Eu-ropean place. It is clear from this example that "Indian" is "other"; "Indian" is landscape; "Indian" is on the "nature" side of the nature/culture divide. This would have been a commonplace that Muir's nineteenth-century audi-ence presumably would have recognized.

Over one hundred years later, Gary Snyder employs the opposite rhetori-cal strategy of consubstantial identification when he pens the following in *Turtle Island*: "Some American Indian cultures have 'mature' characteristics . . . The return to farmland on the part of longhairs is not some nostalgic replay. Here is a generation of white people finally ready to learn from and become the Elders . . . All Natives of Turtle Island . . . This isn't as difficult as you might think" (105). Snyder encourages his readers to form consub-stantial identifications with his romanticized construction of Native eco-ori-entations. By turning to the ecological Indian as commonplace, Snyder so-lidifies identifications within his predominantly Anglo-American audience while also offering them an alternative, idealized environmental ethic. Here Muir and Snyder offer representative examples of late-nineteenth- and late-twentieth-century environmental writers turning to Indigenous worldviews and environmental ethics as commonplaces.

This longstanding tradition of turning to Native understandings of the "natural" world continues today and is apparent in the work of numerous contemporary environmental writers such as Lopez (411), Williams (154), Annie Dillard (114), Charles Wohlforth (107) Scott Russell Sanders (361), and Wendell Berry (50, 84-85). Native relationships to and conceptions of the natural world frequently serve as a commonplace used to evoke and imagine more environmentally conscious and egalitarian attitudes. In this way, the imagined, simulated construction of Native relationships to land-scape serve as a marker, a place of collective identifications, affinities, and knowledge shared by author and audience, a community of the environmen-tally concerned and cognizant.

As a number of scholars have shown (Baird and Callicott and Harkin and Lewis, for example), many Native tribes do ascribe to an environmen-tal ethic that differs from Western conceptions of the "natural" world. Yet, scholars have also demonstrated that an idealized, romanticized, Western-construction of the ecological Indian are a part of our common discourse and American culture (Owens 220). When juxtaposed with Western devel-opmentalist society, the ecological Indian serves as a significant common-place for the environmentally concerned. As Cherokee author Louis Owens points out for example, it is a popular tactic for environmentally conscious Euro-Americans—in a wholesale, oversimplified fashion—to identify and align themselves with the myth of the "American Indian as a genetically predetermined environmentalist" (220); and as a result, the complexity and significance of Native beliefs articulated and vivified by Native peoples for generations have been further denigrated (220-21). Similar to the "vanishing Indian," the "bloodthirsty warrior," and the "noble savage" stereotypes prevalent in nineteenth-century literature and consciousness (Owens 13), the ecological Indian is often found in American nature writing. For example, Snyder writes the following in his essay "The Wilderness":

> I think there is wisdom in the worldview of primitive peoples that we have to refer ourselves to, and learn from . . . What we must find a way to do, then, is incorporate the other people—what the Sioux Indians called the creeping people, and the standing people—into the councils of government (108).

In the same way, Lopez evokes the *ecological Indian* in an overly simplistic, indiscriminate fashion when he writes, "The aspiration of aboriginal people throughout the world has been to achieve a congruent relationship with the land, to fit well in it. To achieve occasionally a state of high harmony or reverberation" (297). As another example, Williams equates her own construction of Native cultural traditions with more ecologically minded, in-tune-with-nature—yet vanished—Indigenous perspectives when she writes, "Yes, the actions of life are recorded, here, now, through the hands of the Anasazi, the 'ancient ones,' . . . Their spirits have never left. One feels their intelligence held in the rocks, etched into the rocks" (56). Thus, we see that the ecological Indian has long served and continues to serve as a commonplace in American nature writing.

This tradition and rhetorical strategy has historically served different purposes within the borderland of American nature writing. However, now "the Native" in American nature writing needs to move from a reductive to a productive, constructive commonplace. It needs to move more towards articulating the intricate complexities of diverse Indigenous cosmologies, mythologies, and orientations—towards more direct, sophisticated engagement with the actual words of Native authors who have long articulated an alternative, more ecocentric environmental ethic. At its worst, this commonplace of the Western-constructed ecological Indian is a trite, simplistic, reduction of Native eco-orientations that does little to challenge and transform audiences. The invocation of commonplaces reinforces group identifications and identities; yet commonplaces are often reified and re-articulated within the community without being challenged or critically questioned. It seems to me that the latter may often be occurring in the construction of Native eco-orientations within the context of contemporary American nature writing produced by Anglo-Americans. While simulations of Indigenous eco-orientations serve to reinforce group identifications in environmental circles, these simulations are frequently failing to function as the heuristic of invention that they have the potential to be because Anglo nature writers rarely directly engage the work of Indigenous writers who have long voiced alternatives to Western, developmentalist, anthropocentric rhetoric and worldviews.

For example, although the non-Native nature writer Lopez is frequently cited as being the most mindful and inclusive of Native eco-orientations (Blaeser 97), particularly in his most expansive work *Arctic Dreams*, nowhere in this text does he actually engage with Native writing. As we have seen throughout this paper, although Lopez consistently constructs consubstantial identifications and non-identifications with his understanding of Native relationships to the natural world, he does not actually engage with or incorporate the words of Native authors who have articulated these relationships. As another example, in *Red*, Williams, repeatedly draws from her understanding of the mythology and cosmology of the Navajo, or Dinè, people (4, 24), yet she does not draw directly from, interpret, or engage with contemporary Dinè writing. For example, Williams appropriates what she perceives as the "message" of Dinè songs (31) as well as Dinè trickster, coyote, and Kokopelli myths, but does not directly engage with Dinè writing. In a chapter titled "Coyote's Canyon" Williams writes,

> Just when you believe in your own sense of place, plan on getting lost. It's not your fault—blame it on coyote. The terror of the country you thought you knew bears gifts of humility. The landscape that makes you vulnerable makes you strong . . . The trickster quality of the canyons is Coyote's cachet. When the Navajo speak of Coyote, they do so hesitantly, looking over their shoulders . . . Their culture has been informed by Coyote. He is profane and sacred, a bumbler and a hero (24).

Although multiple Native authors have vivified and drawn from the complexity of coyote mythology (Owens, for example, as well as Thomas King and, perhaps most notably and consistently, Gerald Vizenor), Williams does not engage with these writers, or any Dinè writing.

I suggest that relying on commonplaces of constructed Native conceptions of the natural world *without actually engaging with those conceptions as they have been articulated in Native writing* seldom contributes to moving the traditionally transformative borderland genre of American nature writing forward. However, if environmental authors would engage the writing of

Native authors such as Winona LaDuke, Linda Hogan, and Jeanette Armstrong, the commonplace of imagined, simulated Native eco-orientations could be outgrown and reimagined. These Native authors are innovating and re-imagining a new, ecocentric environmentalist ethos and ethic, one grounded in communitarianism and social justice. Given this reality, Anglo nature writers should more carefully engage with the full complexity of their thinking and with the alternative eco-orientations they vivify in their writing. Then, given what we've established regarding "the Native" within American nature writing as currently under-productive commonplace, the alternative orientation exhibited in Native writing could potentially move from the reductive and Anglo-constructed to a more viable and productive heuristic for invention, for both Native and Anglo authors and their audiences.

This re-imagining of the Native within environmental writing is more in line with the revolutionary rhetoric and transformative ecocentric purposes of the borderland genre described by Merchant, Oelschlaeger, Shepard, and others. Directly engaging with Indigenous eco-orientations will also help further navigate the borderland between anthropocentric and ecocentric orientations. Direct engagement also has the potential to contribute to nature writing's important project of exploring and constructing borderlands and transforming thought—but only if nature writers move beyond stereotypes toward engagement with the long-articulated complexities of Indigenous eco-orientations as one possible strategy for moving audiences. Direct engagement could also continue the rhetorical borderland tradition by exploring borders between "Native" writing and "nature" writing.

Invention theorists such as Anne E. Berthoff and Karen Burke LeFevre (116) remind us that language itself is the great heuristic. According to Berthoff, "Language, words enables us to make the meanings by whose means we discover further meaning" (II). In addition, McKeon tells us that, "the commonplaces of creativity operate *in the interpretation* of texts as well as in the writing of texts" (209) [emphasis added]. Therefore, I am arguing that a more productive, creative commonplace for the borderland of American nature writing and for environmental rhetoric in general would be to engage with the language, the words, and the writing of Native authors who are innovating and offering their own integral alternatives to anthropocentric worldviews and rhetoric. Consciously and closely engaging with and interpreting Native writing would be a more useful heuristic of invention—one with the transformative potential the borderland genre of nature writing sought in the time of Thoreau and should continue to seek today.

NOTES

1. For example, Max Oelschlaeger remarks that "It is no exaggeration to say that today all thought of the wilderness flows in Walden's wake" (171) and Scott Lyon who credits Thoreau with founding the genre of American nature writing (xi).

2. In Herndl and Brown's model ecocentric discourse or "nature as spirit, poetic discourse" corresponds to pathos; ethnocentric or "nature as resource, regulatory discourse" corresponds to ethos; and anthropocentric discourse or "nature as object, scientific discourse" corresponds to logos (11).

WORKS CITED

Abbey, Edward. *Desert Solitaire: A Season in the Wilderness*. New York: Ballantine, 1968. Print.

Anzuldùa, Gloria. *Borderlands/La Frontera: The New Mestiza*, 4th ed. San Francisco: Aunt Lute, 2012. Print.

Aristotle. *The Art of Rhetoric*. London: Penguin, 2004. Print.

Armstrong, Jeannette. "Land Speaking." *Speaking for the Generations: Native Writers on Writing*. Ed. Ortiz, Simon. Tuscon: U of Arizona P, 1998. Print.

Berry, Wendell. *A Continuous Harmony: Essays Cultural and Agricultural*. San Diego: Harcourt Brace Jovanovich, 1972. Print.

Berthoff, Anne E. *Reclaiming the Imagination: Philosophical Perspectives for Writers and Teachers of Writing*. Upper Montclair: Boynton/Cook, 1984. Print.

Blaeser, Kimberly. "Centering Words: Writing a Sense of Place." *Wicazo Sa Review* 14.2 (1999): 92– 108.

Callicott, J. Baird and Michael P. Nelson. *American Indian Environmental Ethics: An Ojibwa Case Study*. Upper Saddle River: Pearson, 2003. Print.

Cantrill, James G. and Christine L. Oravec. *The Symbolic Earth: Discourse and Our Creation of the Environment*. Lexington: UP of Kentucky, 1996. Print.

Corbett, Edward. *Classical Rhetoric for the Modern Student*. Oxford: Oxford UP, 1999. Print.

Harkin, Michael E. and David Rich Lewis, eds. *Native Americans and the Environment: Perspectives on the Ecological Indian*. Lincoln: U of Nebraska P, 2007. Print.

Herndl, Carl G., and Stuart C. Brown, eds. *Green Culture: Environmental Rhetoric In Contemporary America*. Madison: U of Wisconsin P, 1996. Print.

Hogan, Linda. *Mean Spirit*. New York: Ivy, 1990. Print.

—. *Dwellings: A Spiritual History of the Living World*. New York: W.W. Norton, 1995. Print.

Killingsworth, M. Jimmie, and Jacqueline S. Palmer. *Ecospeak: Rhetoric and Environmental Politics In America*. Carbondale: Southern Illinois UP, 1992. Print.

King, Thomas. *The Truth About Stories: A Native Narrative*. Minneapolis: U of Minnesota P, 2003. Print.

LaDuke, Winona. *All Our Relations: Native Struggles for Land and Life*. Cambridge: South End, 1997. Print.

—.*The Winona LaDuke Reader: A Collection of Essential Writings*. Minneapolis: Voyageur, 2002. Print.

LeFevre, Karen Burke. *Invention as a Social Act*. Carbondale: Southern Illinois UP, 1987. Print.

Leopold, Aldo. *A Sand County Almanac*. Oxford: Oxford UP, 1966. Print.

Lopez, Barry. *Arctic Dreams: Imagination and Desire in a Northern Landscape*. New York: Bantam, 1987. Print.

Lyon, Thomas J., ed. *This Incomperable Lande: A Book of American Nature Writing*. Boston: Houghton Mifflin, 1989. Print.

Martin, Calvin Luther. *In the Spirit of the Earth: Rethinking History and Time*. Baltimore: Johns Hopkins UP, 1992. Print.

McKeon, Richard. "Creativity and the Commonplace." *Philosophy and Rhetoric* 6.4 (1973): 199–210.

Merchant, Carolyn. *The Death of Nature: Women, Ecology, and the Scientific Revolution*. New York: Harper and Row, 1989. Print.

—. "Environmental Ethics and Political Conflict: A View from California." *Environmental Ethics* 12.1 (1990): 45–68.

Myerson, George and Yvonne Rydin. "Environmental Communication: The Future of Environmental Rhetoric." *Critical Studies in Media Communication* 14.4 (1997): 376–379.

Nash, Roderick Frazier. *The Rights of Nature: A History of Environmental Ethics*. Madison: U of Wisconsin P, 1989. Print.

Oelschlaeger, Max. *The Idea of Wilderness*. New Haven: Yale UP, 1991. Print.

—. ed. *The Wilderness Condition: Essays on Environment and Civilization*. Washington, DC: Island, 1992. Print.

Owens, Louis. *Mixedblood Message: Literature, Film, Family, Place*. Norman: U of Oklahoma P, 1998. Print.

Sanders, Scott Russell. *The Force of Spirit*. Boston: Beacon, 2001. Print.

Shepard, Paul. *Coming Home to the Pleistocene*. Washington, DC: Island, 1998. Print.

Snyder, Gary. *Turtle Island*. New York: New Directions, 1974. Print.

Thoreau, Henry David. *The Maine Woods*. New York: Penguin, 1988. Print.

—. *Walden*. Roslyn, NY: Walter J. Black, 1942. Print.

Ulman, H. Lewis. "'Thinking Like a Mountain': Persona, Ethos, and Judgment in American Nature Writing." *Green Culture: Environmental Rhetoric In Contemporary America*. Ed. Carl G. Herndl and Stuart C. Brown. Madison: U of Wisconsin P, 1996. 46–81. Print.

Vizenor, Gerald, ed. *Survivance: Narratives of Native Presence*. Lincoln: U of Nebraska P, 2008. Print.

Waddell, Craig. *Landmark Essays on Rhetoric and the Environment* Vol. 12. Mahwah: Hermagoras, 1998. Print.

White, Lynn. "The Cultural Basis of Our Environmental Crisis." *Environmental Ethics: Readings in Theory and Application*. Ed. Louis P. Pojman. Belmont, CA: Wadworth/Thompson Learning, 2001. 13–18. Print.

Williams, Terry Tempest. *Red: Passion and Patience in the Desert*. New York: Knopf Doubleday, 2002. Print.

—.*Refuge: An Unnatural History of Family and Place*. New York: Random House, 2001. Print.

Wohlforth, Charles. *The Fate of Nature: Rediscovering Our Ability to Rescue the Earth*. New York: Macmillan, 2011. Print.

17 Technologies of Mediation and the Borders and Boundaries of Human-Nonhuman Animal Relationships in Marine Species Advocacy

Amy D. Propen

In 2009, the California power company, Pacific Gas and Electric (PG&E), applied for a twenty-year license renewal for the Diablo Canyon nuclear power plant, which is located about halfway between Los Angeles and San Francisco. In the summer of 2011, just after the March earthquake and tsunami that caused the nuclear disaster in Japan, PG&E asked the Nuclear Regulatory Commission to delay issuing the license renewal until seismic testing was conducted to assess earthquake faults near the plant. Diablo Canyon sits on an eighty-five-foot cliff overlooking the Pacific Ocean and is situated within three miles of two fault lines. The Hosgri Fault lies several miles offshore of the plant and was discovered in 1971 after the plant was near completion. Then, in 2008, geologists discovered the Shoreline Fault, which runs less than one mile offshore of the plant. While Diablo Canyon was designed to withstand a 7.5 magnitude earthquake, based on under-standings of what the Hosgri fault is *potentially* capable of, there is new concern that the two faults could work in tandem to produce a much larger earthquake than the plant could potentially withstand (*California Coastal Commission*, "*Offshore*"; *PG&E*, "*Seismic Safety*"). Further complicating the issue, and of main interest to this project, is the fact that the planned seismic testing *itself* is perceived as presenting a risk to coastal life and marine mammals in the region.

With these ideas in mind about the impacts of seismic testing on marine life, and grounded in an ongoing analysis of texts and media articles about the debate, this project explores how human/nonhuman animal relationships are mediated by and constituted through hybrid systems of nature-cultures that eschew what Bruno Latour (1993) and Donna Haraway (2008) see as the modern tendency to create distinct ontological boundaries between humans and nonhumans, in this case, relative to arguments about seismic testing. Interestingly, that is, even though there is consensus among stakeholders that the faults must be assessed prior to Diablo's license renewal, there has been much debate—perhaps even greater debate—over the potential impacts of the seismic testing itself. Seismic testing involves the use of sound cannons that are thought to disturb local marine life, including seals, sea lions, and otters. While PG&E stated that they would implement mitigation measures to monitor the effects of the testing on marine mammals like sea otters, stakeholders and members of the public were nonetheless skeptical that marine life and subsequently local industries would avoid harm (Sahagun, "PG&E Plan"). The proposed seismic testing then sparked a public debate about risk to marine species in the region—namely, the Southern Sea Otter and Harbor Porpoise. Moreover, the US Fish and Wildlife Service requested that PG&E track and monitor sea otters and harbor porpoises, in order to gauge whether the seismic testing would impact their feeding, breeding, and migration patterns (Sneed, "Research"). This mitigation measure itself drew negative public response, as citizens and environmentalists viewed tracking as yet another possible disturbance to species and questioned the value of further harassing these species in order to then gauge how they would respond to the already disturbing seismic tests.

In recent years, in fact, there has been so much local and statewide debate about the potential impacts of the seismic tests on marine life, that in November 2012, the California Coastal Commission voted to deny PG&E's permit for seismic testing, stating that the company did not provide enough information about the effects or adequately mitigate for them, thus putting a temporary halt to seismic testing. Thus, there exists an already-skeptical public, one that seems to value marine species on both intrinsic and extrinsic levels. Notably, as cited in several media outlets, "[t]he concern that crystallized opposition to the sonic blasting was the harm it could do to marine life.

Two of the most vulnerable species are sea otters and harbor porpoises, both of which are territorial and most vulnerable to harm if displaced by the loud noises or exposed to them for an extended period" (Sneed, "PG&E"). Most interesting in terms of this research project is the public's perception that the threat to marine mammals from seismic testing overrides the potential threat to the public from not conducting the tests near Diablo Canyon.

The range of risks used to constitute the threat to marine mammals include both extrinsic and intrinsic rationales, and in many ways represent the concerns of human and nonhuman species as highly intertwined. Some stakeholders cite concerns that are more focused on impacts to local fishing and tourism industries. Other scientists and environmentalists, concerned more so with the wellbeing of marine mammals and the potential disturbance to species, suspect that sound cannons can cause marine mammals to experience "acoustical trauma," become confused and strand themselves, or look for other areas in which to feed (Polom, "The Seismic Effect"). As one member of the Monterey Bay National Marine Sanctuary Advisory Council put it, there is great concern that the negative impacts for marine life "far outweigh any beneficial information" that the seismic testing would reveal (Etling, "More Critics"). Another article described the public's more extrinsic valuing of marine life: "[O]pposition to the seismic surveys is steadfast among environmentalists, fishermen, and county residents, who fear the surveys could harm the local economy. A common theme among opponents is the belief that the damage the sonic blasts will do to the ocean outweighs whatever new earthquake fault information the process will generate" (Sneed, "Nearly"). A member of the North Coast Advisory Council also voiced a pervasive theme in the debate when she said: "This feels like a runaway train. I have a lot of concern the negative impacts would outweigh any beneficial information the testing would yield. . . . We have no information that this will change what they do at Diablo. No way to evaluate the risk/reward" (Etling, "More Critics"). This range of perspectives then begins to illuminate not only the various ways that the public perceives their relationship to marine mammals but also how the public perceives and articulates the potential risks of technology relative to the benefits it would yield; in this case, the risks and benefits of technology are understood largely through the lens of potential impact on marine species. Again, this debate reflects a public that implicitly understands the concerns of human and nonhuman species as enmeshed with one another.

In addition, local publics *already* perceive risk from the Diablo Canyon facility, given its controversial history related to early design and architectural problems that required re-building part of the plant. In 1981, seismic supports were retrofitted to account for the Hosgri fault that was discovered in 1971; however, the blueprints for the retrofit were interpreted incorrectly, and so the retrofit had to be re-retrofitted. In 2011, it was discovered that emergency cooling pumps had been disabled for eighteen months and operators had not noticed. (Maddow, "The 'Diablo' in Nuke Plants Details"). Then in 2012, the plant was temporarily knocked offline when jellyfish-like creatures called sea salp clogged the plant's cooling water intake cove (CalCoast News, "Diablo Canyon"). In essence then, based on history and available evidence or lack thereof, the vast majority of stakeholders perceive that the benefits of seismic testing for human knowledge-making do not outweigh the *risks* that it poses for marine species. This reflects a sort of cost-benefit analysis, in which seismic testing may be viewed as not worth the risk for *any actors*—human or nonhuman; thus, the boundaries between human and nonhuman animal values become blurred. These themes of risk perception and the impacts of risk for human and nonhuman species then underpin my analysis.

RISK, DISCOURSE, AND MEDIATING TECHNOLOGIES

As sociologist Ulrich Beck has described, a "risk society" occurs when the "speeding up of modernization has produced a gulf between the world of quantifiable risk in which we think and act, and the world of non-quantifiable insecurities" (40). I suggest that the seismic testing debate reflects this sort of risk society and falls within the space of this gulf. That is, in this case, the development of a nuclear power plant situated along fault lines has given rise to the perceived need for seismic testing. However, the acceleration of modernization reflected in seismic testing technologies (namely, the use of sound cannons or air guns) has not yet yielded quantifiable data on the risks to marine life, or at least, such data has not been credibly recorded in the eyes of the scientific community. Thus, the potential impact of sound cannons and air guns on marine species is hotly debated among scientists and concerned publics. In February 2012, for example, a mass stranding of dolphins on the northern coast of Peru made the national news, largely because the cause was unknown; many speculated, however, that nearby seismic testing could be the cause (Polom, "The Seismic Effect"). On the one hand, stakeholders question whether the benefits of conducting the seismic testing outweigh the risks. Critics, for example, argue that the negative impacts for marine life "far outweigh any beneficial information" that the seismic testing would reveal" (Etling, "More Critics"). On the other hand, some argue that the potential benefits of the testing do not receive enough attention. William Lang, a marine-mammal expert and former program director for the NSF's ocean sciences environmental operations, says that for all the "hype on risks to [marine species] from seismic research," the benefits get little attention, and "[t]he risk to people for not pursuing this type of research is simply not part of the story" (Zaragovia, "Is Ocean Seismic Testing"). Further, State Senator Sam Blakeslee, "who has expressed concerns about the techniques" used in the testing, has nonetheless noted that "We don't know when stresses on these faults will cause them to fail, with potentially devastating results" (Lambert, "County Supervisors"). Again, the seismic testing debate reflects and perpetuates a sort of risk society, in which a gulf exists between known risks and non-quantifiable insecurities related to such variables as nuclear power and environmental uncertainties, the subsequent use of seismic testing technologies, and the risk of that testing for the environment and human and nonhuman species.

The risk society reflected and perpetuated through the seismic testing debate is, moreover, a product of discourse. As Jeff Grabill and Michelle Simmons have similarly noted, "The 'truth' about risk is also a product of disputes within the public arena, in which experts make a bid for citizen approval" (423). For Beck, risk is a cultural construct where, "the *perception* of threatening risks determines thought and action" (213). In the seismic testing debate, the cultural values of local communities along California's central coast and the intrinsic and extrinsic value of marine species for those communities influence perceptions about whether seismic testing is worth the risk. Risk then becomes part of a larger discourse in which citizens are at the center of knowledge claims. In this sense, risk displays overtones that stem from Michel Foucault's idea of *governmentality*. Policy theorist Daniele Navarra sees Foucault's concepts of *governmentality* and *risk* as compatible. Navarra notes, for example, that since the sixteenth century, knowledge about the public has been gained through demographic statistics and used to calculate life expectancy, mortality, and birth rates, and "to deploy and prioritise resources, assign tasks and produce technologies aimed at the well-being of the population. Therefore, Foucault's idea of governmentality, even if not directly aimed at explaining risk, understands it as a 'discourse' which places the citizen at the centre of a net of expert systems of knowledge" ("Conceptualising Risk"). These knowledge systems then perpetuate the "language of [what counts as] socially appropriate or risk-free behaviour" (Navarra, "Conceptualising Risk"). How citizens might respond to or interpret what counts as the most appropriate or risk-free behavior related to seismic testing, then, is tied to discourses about perceived risk to human and nonhuman animals from the technology.

Seismic Testing as Mediating the Boundaries
of Human/Nonhuman Relationships

From a cultural studies of science vantage point, or as Bruno Latour and Donna Haraway might see it, seismic testing is always already a product of discourse, and likewise functions as a meditating or compound technology (Haraway 250). Haraway understands technologies as always comprised of multiple, active, interpretive agents at play with one other, when she writes:

> They are composed of diverse agents of interpretation, agents of recording, and agents for directing and multiplying relational action. These agents can be human beings or parts of human beings . . . machines of many kinds, or other sorts of entrained things made to work in the technological compound of conjoined forces. (250)

Indeed, part of the significance of the seismic testing debate is the multiplicity of voices being represented through what seems to be a clear focus on marine mammals through the lens of a risk society. Moreover, arguments for protecting marine species appear to be both extrinsic and intrinsic; that is, there exists the concern about harm to local fisheries and economies, but there is also intrinsic concern for the future welfare of species like the sea otter in particular. As one veterinarian for the Monterey Bay Aquarium described when referring to the potential harassment of sea otters: "When you are handling wildlife . . . you don't want to take any shortcuts. The otters deserve better" (Sneed, "Research"). As one geophysicist and supervisor for the Coastal Commission put it, "When you have whales and nuclear power in the same conversation, you need to proceed with caution" (Cuddy, "Planned Seismic Tests"). Stakeholders in this debate, then, seem to voice a sense of responsibility for these species, reflecting the implicit values of these local communities, and perhaps even conveying what Diane Davis has referred to as a "post-humanist ethics" (19). That is, as Davis has noted, "an ethics of decision in a world that has lost its criteria for responsible action begins with straining to hear the excess that gets drowned out, sacrificed for the clarity of One voice, One call, One legitimate position. A post-humanist ethics ought not be about shutting down the flow but about opening it up, pulling back the stops" (19). In building on these points, I suggest here that the dissolving boundaries between human and nonhuman animals reflect a qualitative, palpable shift in the form and scope of the discussion—of what counts as perceived risks and for whom. The whom, here, becomes especially significant—we are not dealing with a primarily human "whom"; what we are seeing is a sort of posthuman advocacy, in the form of risk perception, coming from humans but incorporating nonhuman animals into the fold and accounting for them as part of the conversation and as implicated in a risk society.

Similarly, geographers who study human-nonhuman animal relationships have recently begun to explore the distribution of nonhuman animals within society, often citing the sort of tensions produced by questions of what counts as the most appropriate ways for humans to understand and interact with nonhuman species (Michael 281). As Mike Michael describes in his cultural study of roadkill, for example, humans have long been enculturated to understand animals as having certain places or purposes within society: "As pets, or as laboratory, wild or feral, and as farm animals, they culturally and physically are situated in particular ways: There are, in other words, some quite standardized views about what sort of animal belongs in what sort of space. . . . Animals move across . . . spaces in a number of ways" (281-82). In moving across spaces, animals create what geographers Jennifer Wolch and Jody Emel call "borderlands," in which "humans and animals share space, however uneasily" (*xvi*). I suggest here that the seismic testing debate illustrates this sort of unease in negotiating these shared spaces. On the one hand, there is an interest in opening up the conversation to include and account for the welfare of marine species; on the other hand, ideas about how to best account for their welfare vary among stakeholders. A public mistrustful of Diablo Canyon and nuclear power rejects the idea that seismic testing is worth the risk; state officials and scientists who support the idea of seismic testing must then address concerns about potential harm to marine species—the main focus of the risk.

TRACKING SPECIES TO MITIGATE THE IMPACTS OF MEDITATING TECHNOLOGIES

If there is one marine species that exemplifies not only Wolch and Emel's point that "humans and animals share space, however uneasily" (*xvi*), but also the tensions and risk society that characterize the seismic testing debate, it is the Southern Sea Otter. Recent efforts by biologists to track the otter in an attempt to gauge the effects of the testing on their breeding and migration habits have drawn much public criticism. The tracking, proposed as a mitigation measure, drew negative public response, as it was viewed as yet another possible disturbance to species. Again doubting that the benefits of tracking the otters would outweigh the risks, concerned publics questioned the value of further harassing this species in order to gauge how they would respond to the already disturbing seismic tests. Moreover, I suggest here that the perceived need to track the otters also reflects implicit ideas about how we understand, value, and interact with nonhuman species co-implicated in a risk society.

The Southern Sea Otter in particular is a vulnerable species, protected within California, after having been hunted to near extinction in the 1800s (Sneed, "Research"). As a keystone species, the otter is often considered the benchmark of what is considered an acceptable impact on the environment, and local groups have long been monitoring populations of sea otters and their perceived responses to human and environmental changes. To study the impacts of the seismic surveys on the otters, a team of veterinarians and scientists have been monitoring otters along the Central Coast in an attempt to learn how they will react to the tests. This is an invasive process that involves the capture, anesthetizing, and, in the case of otters, surgical implantation of locator devices. (With porpoises, whales, and other pinipeds the process can be slightly less intrusive.)

While acknowledging the risks of the capture and tagging procedures, some scientists nonetheless convey an interest in the knowledge gained through monitoring otter and porpoise populations and see a value in better understanding these species' responses to what they view as the inevitable task of seismic testing—whether it happens now or down the road. As the director of the organization Friends of the Sea Otters in Monterey stated, "If these surveys are [eventually] going to get green-lighted, it's important to have in place something that will measure the effects" (Sneed, "Research"). Interestingly, one biologist interviewed about the seismic testing controversy described what she perceived as an unintended benefit of tracking harbor porpoises: "It increased awareness of a cryptic species. . . . You can't appreciate something you don't see" (Sneed, "PG&E"). Likewise, as Etienne Benson describes in his book *Wired Wilderness*, recent conversations about tracking wildlife reflect shifting understandings of the technology and its uses: "[S]cientists could now be seen as mediators of a kind of virtual intimacy between individual animals and mass audiences, or even as audiences themselves" (190). Indeed, these rationales for tracking the otters, and the perceived benefits of doing so, in many ways situate scientists as advocates for a species that would otherwise be unable to advocate for themselves. This advocacy, however, is complicated in its embrace, for it assumes a need to make visible that which we do not know needs or wants to be made visible. In doing so—in advocating through processes of seeing and revealing—the lives of these nonhuman species are being mediated in ways that may also be understood as intrusive.

The technological mediation of the sea otter, albeit intrusive, also arguably helps work against distinct ontological binaries of human and nonhuman, to foster what Latour refers to as social hybridities. According to Latour, as Michael describes, "we moderns have kept separate society and nature: In contrast to premodern cultures, modernity fundamentally has been concerned with purifying what he sees as the constitutive hybridity of the social. Thus, we moderns routinely have indulged in dualism" that tends toward continued binaries but also contains "multitudes of hybrids" (Michael 282). Animal bodies are the quintessential example of the hybrid, as they are "at once material, symbolic, physical, technological, and cultural" (Michael 284). The role of the otter in the seismic testing debate perhaps exemplifies the idea of the animal body as hybrid. The perceived need to track the otter, and the intrusion that such tracking requires, in many ways represents human ideas about what constitutes the best way to advocate for nonhuman animals at this cultural moment. The best way to advocate for the needs of the otter then involves some form of human technological mediation and intervention into the world of the nonhuman animal. Thus, as Latour describes, it has become impossible to avoid the merging of humans and nonhumans: "when we find ourselves invaded by frozen embryos, . . . sensory-equipped robots, . . . whales outfitted with radar sounding devices, . . . and so on, . . . something has to be done" (49–50). At this point, Latour says, our attempts at purification no longer hold up, and hybrids become the majority; the question then shifts to the nature of the relationship between these practices of purification and mediation (Latour 50-51).

Such a view perhaps raises more questions than it answers, in terms of responsibility, accountability, and as Haraway puts it, "hermeneutic agency" (262). In questioning, for example, whether marine mammals have agency in the fact of their being tracked to learn more about their habits and habitats, we might consider the words of Haraway, who writes: "There is no general answer to the question of animals' agential engagement in meanings, any more than there is a general account of human meaning making" (262). As Haraway discusses, technologies and humans adapt to and "cohabit each other in relation to particular projects or lifeworlds" (262). She reflects on the notion that

> "In so far as I use a technology, I am also used by a technology."
> Surely the same insight applies to the animal-human-technology
> hermeneutic relation. ... In so far as I (and my machines) use an
> animal, I am used by an animal (with its attached machine). I must
> adapt to the specific animals even as I work for years to learn to
> induce them to adapt to me and my artifacts in particular kinds of
> knowledge projects. (262)

This sort of adaptation dilemma and its social and cultural implications indeed seem to be at the heart of the debate about seismic testing and risk to marine species. How have humans perceived and adapted to or addressed the needs of marine species in light of this debate? We may question the cultural and communicative implications of using locative media, for example, to track and monitor marine species' responses to seismic tests. We may also question the various ways in which we conceptualize our relationship to and accountability toward marine species when we acknowledge both the need for and the risk inherent in seismic testing.

CONCLUSION

On the one hand, then, we can consider these questions of co-adaptation raised by Haraway and ask, for instance, whether inducing marine mammals to adapt to us (by way of tracking) then requires that they make themselves visible in order to be justly appreciated. On the other hand, interestingly, the seismic testing debate also appears to be adapting to the perceived needs and welfare of marine species. Does this adaptation then signal a shift toward a more explicit acknowledgement of hybridity and the co-construction of human/nonhuman animal agency? Does it reflect the values of a local community that understands marine species as valuable on multiple levels? Or is this shift a byproduct of the public's skepticism for the speeding up of modernization, as expressed through a risk society that views nuclear technology as outpacing more ethical concerns and that ultimately wants to see Diablo Canyon decommissioned? As Quinn Gorman writes in an essay about photography and environmental representation, "ultimately, from the perspective of environmental action, one must admit that cultural meaning and categories are the human tools that allow us to take substantive, positive steps toward change. We can only act based upon our understanding of what nature is and how we might protect it—however limited, constructed, imaginary, and flawed that understanding might be" (254). As we continue to explore the rhetorical components of the debate about seismic testing and the various implications and mitigation measures for stakeholders, both human and nonhuman, we may understand the debate as an illustrative case through which to explore how the cultural relationships between humans and nonhuman animals are mediated by technologies of recording, archiving, and visualization that eschew what Latour sees as the modern tendency to create "entirely distinct ontological zones" of humans and nonhumans (10). Further yet, we might question the broader cultural implications about what is reflected in the perceived need to mediate nonhuman animal bodies with technologies of visualization in an effort to best advocate for them. This case, then, not only helps us to conceptualize humans and nonhuman animals as co-implicated in arguments about contemporary environmental issues but also how technologies mediate our continually shifting understandings and experiences of animals in our worlds.

Works Cited

Beck, Ulrich. "Risk Society Revisited: Theory, Politics and Research Programs." *The Risk Society and Beyond: Critical Issues for Social Theory.* Ed. Barbara Adam, Ulrich Beck, and Joost Van Loon. London: Sage, 2000: 211–229. Print.

—. "The Terrorist Threat: World Risk Society Revisited." *Theory, Culture & Society* 19 (2002): 39–55. Print.

Benson, Etienne. *Wired Wilderness: Technologies of Tracking and the Making of Modern Wildlife.* Baltimore: John Hopkins UP, 2010. Print.

"Diablo Canyon Nuclear Power Plant Temporary Shut Down." *CalCoast News.* Cal-Coast News. 26 Apr. 2012. Web. 21 Jun. 2014.

California Coastal Commission. "Offshore Seismic Survey Project Background Materials." *Coastal.CA.gov. State of California,* 2012. Web. 21 Jun. 2014.

Cuddy, Bob. "Planned Seismic Tests Near Diablo Canyon on the Agenda for Tuesday's Board of Supervisors Meeting." *San Luis Obispo Tribune.* N.p., 25 Oct. 2012. Web. 30 May 2013.

Davis, Diane. *Breaking Up (at) Totality: A Rhetoric of Laughter.* Carbondale: Southern Illinois UP, 2000. Print.

Etling, Bert. "More Critics Decry Seismic Testing Off the Central Coast." *San Luis Obispo Tribune.* N.p., 18 Oct. 2012. Web. 30 May 2013.

Gorman, Quinn R. "Evading Capture: The Productive Resistance of Photography in Environmental Representation." *Ecosee: Image, Rhetoric, Nature.* Ed. Sidney I. Dobrin and Sean Morey. Albany: State University of New York Press, 2009: 239–256. Print.

Grabill, Jeffrey T. and Michelle Simmons. "Toward a Critical Rhetoric of Risk Communication: Producing Citizens and the Role of Technical Communicators." *Technical Communication Quarterly* 7 (1998): 415–441. Print.

Haraway, Donna J. *When Species Meet.* Minneapolis: U of Minnesota P, 2008. Print.

Lambert, Cynthia. "County Supervisors Vote to Oppose Seismic Tests at Diablo Canyon." *San Luis Obispo Tribune.* N.p., 30 Oct. 2012. Web. 30 May 2013.

Latour, Bruno. *We Have Never Been Modern.* Trans. Catherine Porter. Cambridge: Harvard UP, 1993. Print.

Maddow, Rachel. "The 'Diablo' in Nuke Plants Details." Online video clip. *The Rachel Maddow Show. MSNBC.* MSNBC, 22 Mar. 2011. Web. 21 Jun. 2014.

Michael, Mike. "Roadkill: Between Humans, Nonhuman Animals, and Technologies." *Society and Animals* 12.4 (2004): 277–298. Print.

Navarra, Daniele. "Conceptualising Risk: A Theoretical and Practical Agenda." *Innovation, Risk and Governance.* Giannino Bassetti Foundation, 29 Jun. 2004. Web. 4 Apr. 2014.

"Seismic Safety at Diablo Canyon." *PG&E.* Pacific Gas and Electric Co., 2014. Web. 21 Jun. 2014.

Polom, Cameron. "The Seismic Effect: Mysterious Dolphin Deaths in Peru." *KSBY News*. sott.net, 1 Nov. 2012. Web. 30 May 2013.

Sahagun, Louis. "PG&E Plan to Conduct Underwater Seismic Tests is Shot Down." *Los Angeles Times*. Los Angeles Times, 15 Nov. 2012. Web. 21 June 2014.

Sneed, David. "Nearly 3,000 Marine Mammals Will Be Harassed in Diablo Canyon Seismic Survey." *San Luis Obispo Tribune*. Legacy.com, 29 Sept. 2012. Web. 30 May 2013.

—. "PG&E May Still Pursue Permits for Seismic Testing Off Diablo Canyon." *San Luis Obispo Tribune*. 1 Dec. 2012. Web. 30 May 2013.

—. "Research to Track Otters' Response to Seismic Surveys." *San Luis Obispo Tribune*. Legacy.com, 20 Oct. 2012. Web. 30 May 2013.

Wolch, Jennifer and Jody Emel. *Animal Geographies: Place, Politics and Identity in the Nature-Culture Borderlands*. London: Verso, 1998. Print.

Zaragovia, Veronica. "Is Ocean Seismic Testing Endangering the Dolphins?" *Time Magazine*. Time Inc., 29 Sept. 2009. Web. 3 Apr. 2014.

TEACHING ACROSS DIVIDES

18 "What did you do in the war, Mommy?" Competing Constructs in the Women in Military Service for America Memorial

Amy Milakovic

At my Midwestern liberal-arts university, a colleague[1] and I have developed an interdisciplinary course titled "The 'Art' of War," which approaches a variety of war-related artifacts through the disciplines of graphic design and rhetoric. Students from many schools enroll in the course, which we have taught five times, most recently in spring 2015; few of them have any training in rhetorical principles beyond what my colleague and I introduce. The heart of the course is a jam-packed four-day trip to Washington, DC, where we visit as many memorials, exhibits, and government buildings as possible. Most of our students have never been to the capital city, so they are viewing its landmarks as tourists as well as fledgling rhetorical scholars. Of the average of eighteen students per course, typically two to three are military veterans.

This paper will focus on the class's interaction with the Women In Military Service For America Memorial ("Memorial"), located in Arlington, Virginia. I begin with my own interest in the memorial as a source of public memory. Next, I offer a brief history of its inception for those unfamiliar with its beginnings. Finally, I analyze the Memorial through the framework that Kendall Phillips calls "the publicness of memory" (6). My sense of the narrative that visitors receive from the Memorial is informed by students' reactions to the Memorial's location, design, and exhibits. This paper will show that despite the Memorial Foundation's intent to tell a story of women's heroism and military accomplishments, it instead positions them as ancillary actors on the margins of a masculine chronicle.

My interest in the Memorial lies in its intersection with continuing cultural battles in the US over women's appropriate place in society. For example, many conservative writers still decry the presence of women in combat, based on the premise that their participation will fundamentally change both military and civil society. Columnist Kathleen Parker contends that men would be trained to "ignore the screams of their female comrades" and thus carry that disregard back to civil society (Parker). In a similar vein, Gene Veith, Provost at Patrick Henry College, argues that women's child-bearing abilities mandate that men protect them, and thus allowing women in combat would "undermine the traditional role of women" and men (Veith). He further asserts that women lack a "macho . . . recklessness" necessary for combat, and therefore their combat involvement would "feminize" the military (Veith). The refutation of such myopic constructions of females was part of the impetus to found the Memorial; as its website notes, "[u]ntil recently, women who joined the military acted counter to cultural expectations of their appropriate place in society as girlfriends, wives and mothers" ("Mattel's Barbie"). Yet as Parker's and Veith's arguments illustrate, those cultural expectations are still very much with us.

A Mighty Effort, A Restrictive Response

A group of female World War II veterans established the Women In Military Service For America Memorial Foundation in 1985 with the goal of building a memorial to honor women's contributions to the US military. They obtained permission in 1986, and the Memorial was completed in 1997. It was a hard-fought battle: agencies with oversight[2] initially opposed the idea of a women's memorial based on three reasons: that "all memorials should honor both men and women" (James Clarity and Warren Weaver), that women were already sufficiently honored by the Vietnam Women's Memorial, and that the National Mall was becoming too crowded. Approval was eventually given for the memorial to be built at the abandoned Hemicycle site, just outside Arlington National Cemetery, with the Commission on Fine Arts (CFA) mandate that the design be "subtle" (Chairman J. Carter Brown, quoted in Kristin Hass 108). The design could not include statues, on the dubious concern that people would interpret Arlington National Cemetery as a cemetery just for women (Michael Kilian). The Foundation's first design choice was indeed rejected for calling too much attention to itself—the CFA ruled that glass prisms meant to evoke candles would be "too tall" and their light "would detract from the existing monuments" ("Women's Memorial Design Panned"). The prisms were removed.

Redesigned to be more horizontal, the completed memorial's near-invisibility drew wide praise: *Washington Post* architecture critic Benjamin Forgey declared that its "greatest strength" was the way in which it is "insistently respectful" of the Hemicycle and Arlington National Cemetery (Forgey, "Memorial Passes Muster"). Similarly, Maryland architecture professor Roger Lewis praised it especially for "not making waves" (Lewis). Such applause is jarring, given that the point of most memorials is expressly to be noticed. The irony of a memorial intended to honor "women whose achievements have for too long been unrecognized or ignored" being praised for its inconspicuousness echoes through the Memorial, as well ("History"). As this paper will show, the Memorial unfortunately does not offer a new narrative grounded in women's unheralded accomplishments, but reinforces cultural stereotypes about them, instead.[3]

The Memorial is built into the Hemicycle, shown in fig. 18.1, which lies at the west end of Memorial Drive, directly across the Potomac from the Lincoln Memorial.[4]

Figure 18.1. Highsmith, Carol. Women in Military Service to America. *Facebook.* Facebook. 12 Mar. 2012. Web. 6 Dec. 2014. Photograph by Carol Highsmith.

The Hemicycle, commissioned by Congress in 1924, was intended to serve as the ceremonial gate to Arlington National Cemetery. It was largely abandoned by 1938, however, and never used for that purpose. The main entrance to the Cemetery actually lies eight hundred feet east, in the direction of the Potomac, which means that most visitors never come across the Memorial. As fig. 18.1 illustrates, no visible signs identify it, and there is no indication that the Hemicycle is anything more than decorative. As Forgey wrote approvingly, "from a distance you would hardly know it is there, for the memorial has been subtly built in front of, on top of and behind an existing structure" (Forgey, "Stunning Surprise"). Likewise, professional photographer Stephen Brown calls it "one of the more significant yet invisible architectural triumphs in DC. Perfectly attuned to the cemetery's overall facade, it goes unnoticed" (Stephen Brown Studio). Such praise is unlikely to hearten those trying to weave women's military accomplishments more visibly into public memory.

When we first enter the building, students express surprise that this unassuming structure is actually the Women's Memorial. (Although it is listed as one site on our trip itinerary, my colleague and I do not preview the Memorial with students before their visit, so they approach it as they would any other memorial for the first time.) Having just come from the Tomb of the Unknowns, students are struck by the contrast between that site's richness and the meagerness felt at the Memorial. After we leave, many of them question why a woman's memorial didn't warrant a space on the Mall. They also compare its small size to the vast and prominent location of assumed masculine memorials. One student wrote that the "location seemed off to me. Arlington is a wonderful site in itself, but pairing this memorial with the world's most famous graveyard and the home of one of the most recognizable military figures in history [Robert E. Lee] didn't strike me as the best fit" (personal archive).[5] Although I relate the Foundation's story that they could not locate a suitable site on the Mall, female students in particular reject that explanation as a face-saving effort.

Compared to the massive World War II Memorial or the 7.5-foot-tall soldiers depicted in the Korean War Memorial, the women represented here feel dwarfed. Lacking grand monuments or heroic statues, the memorial's semi-circular gallery instead exhibits small personal artifacts such as photographs, diaries, and clothing, as seen in fig. 18.2. Students often remark on its "coldness" and what they perceive as its odd proportions. "Is this the whole thing?" is a frequent question. One of four alcoves where visitors may watch looped videos can also be seen in fig. 18.2, where a small television sits on a bare metal stand, tucked beneath a staircase. One student lamented that the memorial reminded him of a gymnasium where students' school projects are temporarily displayed. Another reflected later, "The space itself looked more like a storage area with exposed concrete, unfinished surfaces, and generally poor lighting." Undeterred by learning that critics praise the design, students come away with a clear impression that women are being honored far less than their male counterparts.

Figure 18.2. Parry, Donna. Women in Military Service to America. *Facebook*. Facebook. 22 Mar. 2011. Web. 23 Feb. 2015.

History Writ Small: a Domestic, Gendered Version

Many students are decidedly underwhelmed by the permanent exhibits; they see the display cases as too small, too crowded, and too concentrated on individual personal items. One wrote that the Memorial "lacks the artistry and scope" of men's memorials, adding that men's "focus more on the whole of the event instead of snapshots of a select few." Other displays include "song-books, holiday menus, and . . . items reflecting popular culture such as paper dolls, Barbies® and buttons" ("About Our Collections"). Such artifacts continue the long-standing narrative that both constructs, and locates, females outside of the masculine military narrative.

Although now removed, an exhibit showcasing the Memorial's groundbreaking displayed two mementos that feminized the site from its inception: a pink-handled shovel and a small teddy bear wearing a sweater. My own perception was that these items suggested a sense of childishness and make-believe, positioning women as young girls pretending to inhabit a world not actually their own. Students could not have articulated it in these terms, but they understood in general that the message worked against the normalization of women in the military. Some noted that the shovel reminded them of pink toy tools for girls. Another comment I heard repeatedly was, "You'd never see a teddy bear in a man's memorial."

Three other items from the exhibits similarly suggest that women are out of place in the armed forces. The first is a quote from US Marine Corporal Nichole Fuentes,excerpted from a longer narrative and highlighting the sorrow she feels at leaving her infant son as she deploys to Iraq. Calling it "the hardest thing I'll ever do in my life," she laments that "I will not see him again until he is a year and a half." Our students understand the sadness of a parent leaving his/her child for a significant amount of time, especially those students with children of their own. But many are also quick to point out that men's memorials never mention fathers leaving their children to go off to war; instead, men are framed as active agents moving decisively through the world while women remain anchored at home in their maternal roles. Additionally, the focus on Fuentes' emotions rather than her military accomplishments invites visitors to react to her as a mother, not a Marine veteran. It also opens to critique the choices that resulted in her bearing a child while deployable—choices which would go unnoted for males.

A second quote calls attention to women's hygiene, as US Army Sergeant Wendy Michelle Diestra asserts that "[t]here are sanitary issues for a female . . . [sic] and having to confront that while on long road convoys is difficult." Female veterans in particular express dismay over these quotes. One acknowledged that women's anatomy is more exposed than men's when urinating, but she saw that as a matter of privacy, not hygiene. Another, speaking of menses, said, "Yeah, we dealt with it. Soldiers deal with a lot of things. Why bring it up here?" Although my personal belief is that the curator probably intended for these quotes to elicit admiration for challenges women have overcome, students see them as focused on women's "problems," not their achievements. The narrative they receive is one of females bound to personal concerns in ways that males are not. As conceptions of women's maternal instinct or physical deficits are frequently cited by those who oppose allowing them in combat, granting those issues public legitimacy undercuts the Memorial's mission to "illustrate [women's] partnership with men in defense of our nation" ("Mission"). At the very least, they position that partnership as unequal. As one student remarked, "Some of these quotes did more to perpetuate stereotypes than to dispel them."

I turn now to a third significant artifact upon which almost all students comment: the large quilt hanging prominently in the exhibit hall. Military personnel deploying to the Persian Gulf in 2003 began the sewing project, which was later completed by women from a Virginia church guild ("The Comfort Quilt").[6] It is an impressive piece of handiwork, but one to which our students react negatively. "Upon entering I was genuinely shocked that the first thing I saw was a giant quilt. It was to me a direct contradiction to the whole purpose of the memorial to strike down the stereotypes of women." Students—many of them senior nursing students themselves—value the activities represented on the quilt. Proud of their own caregiving, they respect those who treat the wounded and applaud humanitarian efforts such as sewing clothes for needy children. What they object to is placing the quilt in the Women's Memorial, convinced that it would never hang at a men's memorial because it would be seen as wholly out of place in a male narrative.

Taken together, these artifacts—quilts, songbooks, feminine hygiene concerns—perpetuate a public memory of female domesticity, not fighting prowess. As former Army nurse Diane Carlson Evans stated of another memorial, "The images we're given in our country are the images we remember. If you only see men, you only think of men in warfare" (qtd. in Ruth Tam). Likewise, if you see aprons and statements about motherhood, you think of women in the home, even if they are physically located in a war zone. While the Memorial does contain a few uniforms, combat boots, and pictures of women serving in Iraq, these items are simply not powerful enough to overcome the site's weaknesses. One student summarized it this way: "Overall, I was disappointed in the memorial. In many ways, I felt it was more of a statement about why women don't belong in the military than it was a celebration of the contributions they have made."

LESSONS: KEEPING DISAPPOINTMENT IN PERSPECTIVE

As my experience with students demonstrates, the Memorial regrettably falls short of creating a public narrative that establishes women's "patriotism and bravery [as] . . . part of our nation's heritage" ("Mission"). One student christened it the "separate but equal" memorial, likening it bitingly to the Supreme Court decision that institutionalized segregation under the guise of fairness. In doing so, he suggests that military women have been robbed of their equal rights in the public memory of our nation.

But students' disappointment may also be read in different ways. One could view their reactions as a positive—an indication that students feel a righteous indignation for the women whom they perceive as having been unfairly marginalized. In that reading, the Memorial has effected a positive change in public memory by bringing to light the separate-and-unequal honor afforded female veterans. On the other hand, these students are not wholly casual visitors. They are educated college seniors experiencing DC through a lens at least partially constructed by their professors. They are also traveling with a female professor and so may feel some sensitivity to gender concerns that other visitors might not.

Even so, an occasional student carries biases that remain unaffected by the course. One young man, having visited the same museums and monuments as the rest of the class, saw the Women's Memorial as more evidence that men are "getting ignored in the equal rights movement." For him and others like him, female gains and increased recognition subtract from a dominant masculine narrative that he finds reassuring.

The women of the Foundation worked very hard to accomplish something good under significant constraints and they deserve praise for their efforts. The Memorial is less than I had hoped for. But so are the sentiments of Parker, Veith, Memorial opponents, and the occasional narrow-minded student. I cannot effect a nationwide cultural shift; by the end of our trips, however, my colleague and I can cultivate an awareness of gaps in our national stories; a way to talk about females as sites of ideological contest; and, I hope, the desire to share what they've learned with others.

In short, crossing the classroom border offers a way of knowing that would otherwise be unavailable. For all of our students, the experience of directly engaging with the Memorial allows them to see themselves as participants in communal civic life. For those who are crossing regional borders for the first time, such engagement often whets an appetite to venture across more borders on their own.

NOTES

1. Eric Winter, Associate Professor of Graphic Design, Department of Art + Design, Avila University

2. Groups which initially opposed the Memorial include the National Parks Service, Department of the Interior, and U.S. Senate.

3. After my presentation at the RSA Conference, a professor from George Mason University noted that she had never heard of the Memorial, despite living in Washington, DC, and having visited Arlington National Cemetery on several occasions. She also noted that the site does not appear in suggested outings listed by local news sources for patriotic holidays.

4. Fig. 1 is a recent view of the Hemicycle with the Memorial built into it. Photographs of the site in 1993, before Memorial construction began, show its facade uncompleted and overgrown with vegetation.

5. Student comments come from my archives, which consist of student journal entries and semester-end reflections and my notes from personal conversations with students.

6. The quilt is named for their carrier, the USNS Comfort.

WORKS CITED

"About Our Collections." *Womensmemorial.org.* Women in Military Service to America Foundation, Inc., n.d. Web. 3 July 2014.

Clarity, James F. and Warren Weaver, Jr. "Women in the Military." *The New York Times,,* 14 Nov. 1985. Web. 17 Jun. 2014.

Forgey, Benjamin. "A Memorial Passes Muster." *The Washington Post,,* 18 Oct. 1997. Web. 18 June 2014.

—. "Women's Memorial: Stunning Surprise." *The Washington Post.* 25 Jul. 1992. Web. 3 July 2014.

Hass, Kristin Ann. *Sacrificing Soldiers on the National Mall.* Berkley: U of California P, 2013. *ProQuest.* Web. 16 February 2015.

"History." *Womensmemorial.org.* Women in Military Service to America Foundation Inc., n.d. Web. 7 Dec. 2014.

Kilian, Michael. "Women in Uniform Get Their Due." *Chicago Tribune,,* 17 Oct. 1997. Web. 2 Jul. 2014.

Lewis, Roger K. "New Memorial to Women Is Artful Work." *The Washington Post.* 18 Oct. 1997. Web. 18 Jun. 2014.

"Mattel's Barbie® Joins the Military." *Womensmemorial.org.* Women in Military Service to America Foundation Inc., n.d. Web. 18 Jun. 2014.

"Mission." *Womensmemorial.org.* Women in Military Service to America Foundation Inc., n.d. Web. 2 Jul. 2014.

Parker, Kathleen. "Military is putting women at unique risk." *The Washington Post.* 25 Jan. 2013. Web. 17 Jun. 2014.

Phillips, Kendall. Introduction. *Framing Public Memory.* Tuscaloosa: U of Alabama P, 2004. *Google Books.* Web. 3 Jul. 2014.

Stephen R. Brown Studio. "Women in Military Service DC Photo Book." 16 Feb. 2014. Web. 10 Dec. 2014.

Tam, Ruth. "Vietnam Women's Memorial celebrates 20 years on the Mall." *The Washington Post,,* 8 Nov. 2013. Web. 2 Jul. 2014.

"The Comfort Quilt." *Womensmemorial.org.* Women in Military Service to America Foundation Inc., n.d. Web. 2 Jul. 2014.

Veith, Gene. "Against Women in Combat." *Patheos.com.* Patheos, 28 Jan. 2013. Web. 3 Jul. 2014.

Women In Military Service For America Memorial Foundation, Inc. "American Servicewomen in the Global War on Terror." Women In Military Service For America Memorial, Arlington National Cemetery. Arlington, VA. April 11, 2015.

"Women's Memorial Design Panned By Critics." *Manchester Union Leader.* 14 Dec. 1989. Web. 2 Jul. 2014.

19 Service-Learning in the "Borderlands" at an Hispanic Serving Institution in South Texas

Susan Garza

The institution where I teach, Texas A&M University-Corpus Christi, is one of several universities in the state of Texas with the designation of Hispanic Serving Institution. The Coastal Bend region where Corpus Christi is located is richly shaped by the Hispanic culture. I teach mostly technical writing courses in our Technical and Professional Writing program, and in those courses we often work on service-learning projects. In this discussion, I focus on borders I have encountered/navigated/ and perhaps moved away from, as I have engaged with my students in service-learning.

I begin with a funny story in order to provide a visual context, because those of you reading this article cannot see me physically as the audience was able to at the Rhetoric Society of America conference where I first presented this discussion. I previously directed a program on our campus that served low-income, first-generation and minority students. To help increase enrollment, one of the local news stations interviewed me about the program, which was not yet well known around campus. A Hispanic student who saw the interview had to inquire in several places before she found us. The student later shared with the program coordinator that when she came looking for us, she told everyone that a lady named Susan Garza runs the program, but she has blond hair and blue eyes. Although I have a Hispanic surname (claimed through a previous marriage), I am White, Non-Hispanic. The program coordinator was Hispanic, so the student felt comfortable sharing the story with her. I learned later about the story from the program coordinator.

I agree with Steve Zimmer when he says, "Anytime a White person assumes a position of authority in a community space that is used primarily by communities of color, problems of legitimacy, intention and practice emerge" (13). We need to examine the relationships that develop in service-learning engagements so that we are not unaware of the dynamics at play when people traverse community spaces, especially those different from our own. In this discussion, I will share my experiences as a "White service-learning leader" (Zimmer 7) in South Texas and how I have experienced borderlands, community spaces that are different from my own. I will look at my *place* in terms of some of the *spaces* that I have occupied while doing service-learning with my students. I use the term *space* to refer to the actual scenes/situations in which the service-learning occurred. I use the term *place* to refer to my position within a space.

Much of the scholarship on service-learning focuses on how to do service-learning, but less is available on the relationships between teachers and students and how those relationships are shaped, how they function, or how they may change as a result of engaging in service-learning. In her article, "Difficult Stories: Service-Learning, Race, Class, and Whiteness," Ann E. Green shares her experiences as a white person doing both service-learning and teaching service-learning classes. She emphasizes that we need to "break our silences around race, class and service" in order to begin to dismantle racism "by unpacking white privilege" (277). In her experience, unlike mine, she works mainly with White students, but like my experience, Green has found herself in situations that led to her analyzing her role as a White person leading service-learning activities.

Green describes doing service-learning while she was still an undergraduate. Coming from a working-class, rural background, her volunteer work at an after school program at the Prince George Welfare Hotel in New York City placed her for the first time in the position of being a minority, making her feel "displaced" and "very white" (279). As Green explains, she wants to share this experience with her students but doesn't because she thinks her "mostly middle class, white students tend to erase differences in stories" like hers, "and make them the same as their story—a story of a middle class, white person helping" (280-81). Nonetheless, she advocates telling such stories so that we can all better understand the complexities of race and class as we engage in service-learning. Green quotes Elizabeth Ellsworth who makes the point that "whiteness is always more than one thing . . . and never the same thing twice" (263). Green's experiences, similar to mine, show that even though it may be uncomfortable or difficult, it is possible and certainly necessary to talk about the difficulties we may encounter.

In my years of doing service-learning I have learned much from my students, and through this discussion I hope to share some of what I have learned about practicing service-learning as a White service-learning leader. When we encounter borders, we need to develop an awareness of the differences and dynamics at play, and we especially need to be aware of how differences may shape the experiences.

My Stories

I have chosen two scenarios to illustrate my experiences with borders and boundaries in the space of South Texas. The transitions have not always been smooth, as I have found myself in spaces where my place was questioned. My experience is similar to Green's, as she found that her "whiteness prevented anyone else at the Prince George from reading," her, "as other than middle class" (296). Steve Zimmer, in "The Art of Knowing your Place: White Service Learning Leaders and Urban Community Organizations," also shares how he has navigated as a White service-learning leader. Zimmer believes that such a role requires "legitimacy, intention and practice" (13). He explains that in order to establish legitimacy, intention, and practice, relationships must be based on trust that comes as a result of action. Among other things, leaders must have a presence in the community and be engaged with agencies over an extended period of time, engage without co-opting, and not make assumptions based on personal knowledge and experience, but rather, understand the problems through the knowledge of the community members. I find the concepts of *legitimacy*, *intention*, and *practice* applicable to my situation, so I build on them here to share my experiences.

Scenario One

A graduate student becomes upset while working on an assignment requiring students to analyze the visual elements of a colonia.

This scenario happened as part of a graduate class focusing on visual rhetoric. The class visited a colonia to experience the actual space after studying about the conditions in the community and opportunities to engage in service-learning. Colonias are "unincorporated, unregulated, substandard settlements that are burdened by the lack of environmental protection" (Neal, Famira and Miller-Travis 48). For example, the lack of a potable water system is often a problem. After working for several days on the visual analysis assignment related to the visit, a White student let me know that she felt bad because she had grown up in a home similar to those in the colonia. She had lived with her father in that home and they had faced many struggles along the way. This student felt that the colonia space represented her agency and that I did not/perhaps could not understand that, and she perceived my intentions to be driven from a colonial perspective. Or in other words, she saw me as someone who believed I was going into a "lesser" place in order to save the people, to bring them up to my "superior" level. She placed me in a middle-class status as one who would not understand her working-class experience. We work to help students understand the "other" as we prepare them to do service-learning, but I had not realized that I might be viewed as "other."

Even though I grew up in a low-income neighborhood in a very modest home, I did not have *legitimacy* in the space of the colonia. The student did not feel that I had a place in the space of the colonia. In contrast, she felt strongly about her connection to the the colonia—she had a place in that space. My *intentions* were the best, as I viewed working on the colonia project as a way to help students learn and also assist in finding ways to improve the conditions in the colonia. But in my *practice* of having the students work on this assignment, my place and my *intentions* were misunderstood.

One may ask why my background or experience matters, but it can be a common concern for those I work with. I began the service-learning project unaware that my background would make a difference. I now realize the importance of my background because of the student's perceptions of the situation. As Zimmer reveals, problems occur because feelings, perceptions, and beliefs shape the space and experience of learning. So while from one perspective it might seem that my background should not matter, it does matter because how students perceive situations is very important. If we as teachers cannot value those perceptions, we may very well fail at getting students to engage in service-learning in ways that fit our goals of action and reflection.

Since the encounter with this student, I have changed my *practice* in how I introduce service-learning projects. Now when we venture into areas similar to a colonia, a borderland very deeply shaped through the Hispanic experience, I share from my personal perspective why it is important to me to engage in these projects, and I make it clear that my role and my *intentions* are not guided by a colonial perspective. Later when I worked with a class on a similar project, I pulled up on Google a picture of the home I grew up in, and shared with the students that while I don't have a *legitimate* place in a space like a colonia, I am not as far removed from that type of experience as they might assume based on their visual analysis of my physical presentation. I try, as Green advocates, to tell my story, even if it feels like it may create an uncomfortable atmosphere, so that we can better understand the complexities of the different experiences we bring to the service-learning setting. I try to acknowledge that I, along with many of the students, am venturing into a borderland that may be different from our own places, but we venture nonetheless with good *intentions*.

Scenario Two

> An undergraduate student in a class working on a grant to build a community center in the colonia asks, "Why don't the people who live in the colonia just move to an area that has better services?" Another student asks why the people don't just put in their own water system?

This class was working on a grant for a local agency, the South Texas Colonias Initiative, so this group also visited the colonia. We talked to a few of the people who live there and we drove through the area for the students to gain a first-person perspective from which they could describe the needs of the area in the grant proposal. We visited the colonia after spending time reading about colonias and the economic, social, and political dynamics that help to create such conditions. The students had many questions and brought back information that would help them as they wrote the grant.

One day as we were discussing the colonia and going through a section of the grant, one student asked the first question, "Why don't the people who live in the colonia just move to an area that has better services?" We had previously discussed the population of the colonia and the dynamics, such as low income and language barriers, that make it difficult for some people who live in the area. I believe this student understood these issues from her own place, a very different place from the one the colonia residents occupy. The student's experience and the place she currently occupied, however, limited her from making stronger connections between the conditions in the colonia and the larger societal issues that help to create such a space. This is similar to one of Green's students, Brian, who produced a handout with information about preparing for college to help the students at the predominately African American school he was assigned to for his service-learning project. In spite of the feedback Green gave him to think more about the needs of the intended population and how those were different from his needs, Green tells that "Brian" still "produced a handout much like the ones he might have received in his suburban high school" (287). Reflecting on this experience, Green posits that she wasn't "sure whether he actually didn't want to acknowledge the differences he experienced or whether he didn't know how to talk about difference" (287).

During the same discussion, another student asked the second question: "Why don't the people just put in their own water system?" As they asked their questions, other students nodded in agreement. Most of the students in the class were traditional-aged college students, probably from middle-income families who grew up basically unaffected by the societal conditions that affect the population of the colonia. Also, the students were not asking these questions to indicate they did not care. They did care, as was evidenced by their interest in the project and their desire for the grant to be funded. In this situation, my experience was probably more similar to that of the colonia residents as I had more first-hand experience with and knowledge of such spaces; however, I had no *legitimate* place in that space, or in other words, I had not lived in such a space and was not culturally part of the Hispanic space. The students, although they shared the Hispanic culture with residents of the colonia, made the same move that Green finds her students make, in that they craft stories of others to fit into their middle-class stories.

We all know that we can't assume that students will be greatly interested in studying topics/issues related to their own backgrounds, geographical spaces, or cultures, or that they will understand how their situation is different. This colonia is in a sense right in our own backyard, the place of South Texas where many of our students have lived for their entire lives. And the two students who asked the questions were Hispanic. But even though I was aware that students will engage with topics in many ways, this discussion stuck with me and helped me to think about my role as I engage in service-learning with them. I changed my *practice* as a result of this experience because I became more aware of how students may or may not critically engage with the issues related to service-learning projects.

LEARNING FROM THE SCENARIOS

The critical perspective in service-learning can be the most difficult to navigate, and to develop, as evidenced by these two scenarios. While the students may definitely make progress in knowing how to write a proposal/how to communicate through emails with community partners, etc., they may still come away from such projects with a disconnect regarding the societal structures at play in terms of why a community like a colonia came to be and why colonias still exist. There is some discussion in the service-learning literature that looks at the issue of time in relation to how the arbitrary semester course structure can inhibit the service-learning experiences of students and even create a sort of artificial view of what it means to do service-learning, even though we are engaging in real world problems within real world spaces (Dubinsky 2002, Garza and Cardenas 2015).

The questions of the students point to the difficult nature of learning how to critically examine an issue such as a colonia. Part of learning to critically engage is enlarging and developing the contexts through which we examine ideas and issues, and this effort takes time. If students have limited critical frameworks through which to examine the spaces where we engage in service-learning, their ability to evaluate and effect change will be limited. Often, students get to the end of the semester and the focus is on finishing a project for a grade, not finishing a project to effect change. In terms of developing the critical frameworks needed to understand the issues related to service-learning work, there usually is not enough time for students to make much progress in developing these frameworks. Students instead tend to fall back to the strategies they have developed for solving problems, those strategies that come from their mostly middle-class backgrounds. So rather than the focus being on "completing" a project by the end of a semester, the focus and the reason for engaging in service-learning projects should be the overall development of the kinds of critical understanding the students in my scenarios were in the process of developing. Rather than trying to help students solve a problem in some way by the end of the semester, the goal should be to help students gain a deeper critical understanding of the spaces, the borderlands where we engage in service-learning.

A New Model for Engaging in Service-Learning

In addition to the changes in practice that I have made in my courses, our program faculty are currently in the process of implementing a studio model for our technical and professional writing program. One result of this new model will be a focus on developing the critical skills students need to understand a space like a colonia. Changes in the time element that will allow for a different way to engage in projects will be one focus of the new model. Armarego and Fowler describe modern studio learning as

> . . . being driven by industry demands for graduates who integrate and function effectively into organizations, developments in education theory towards considering education as active engagement and the learning expectations of current students. Considered a paradigm shift, Studio Learning involves confronting learners with situations modeled on professional practice. It is a group-based approach that requires the assistance of academics working as facilita-

tors to provide guidance in a richer, holistic learning environment. (Armarego and Fowler)

We are creating a Technical and Professional Writing Studio that will be coordinated by a committee of faculty who teach courses in our program and community partners we work with on service-learning projects. All of the service-learning work, from proposal to delivery, is coordinated through the Studio. Students enrolled in technical and professional writing courses choose projects from a service-learning website; however, projects are not separated by course.

In the Studio Model, students no longer try to complete a full project in one semester. They work instead on whatever the next step is in the project, and they may work on the same project over several semesters and in different courses. Students from different courses create teams to work on projects of their choosing, so projects span across courses rather than each course focusing on separate projects. Using this framework, we hope students will have the opportunity to see projects from more of a critical perspective, and since the period of engagement will be longer, we hope this approach will help students to better develop the critical skills they need to understand a space like a colonia as they engage in service-learning. This model will provide more time for students to develop critical frameworks, and they will not have to try to solve problems in one semester. When questions such as "Why don't the people who live in the colonia just move to an area that has better services?" come up, we will have more time to understand the answers and to allow students to develop the critical awareness that will help them understand within a broader perspective.

My Place as a White Service-Learning Leader

My position as a professor who teaches technical writing provides *legitimacy* in terms of the technical aspects of leading students as they work on projects. But when working on projects like the colonia project, which has very deep space connections, I had not been as aware of how my place in such spaces was being viewed, which in turn affected my *legitimacy*. However, these experiences I share have helped me to better understand how my *place* within certain spaces is being viewed. I don't have a legitimate *place* in the space of a colonia. I know my *intentions* are ethical and academically valuable, but I have become more aware that I have to better clarify my intentions so that no one has to guess. Knowing and examining my *legitimacy* and *intentions* has helped me to expand my *practices* in ways that hopefully provide better learning experiences for me and my students. Students are in the space of a "class," but engaging them in service-learning projects situates them in other spaces, and I have learned to better understand what I need to do as I try to lead students in doing service-learning. Because, as Green reminds us, "all stories about race and class are both partial and contradictory," it is important that we tell our stories so that "we can create a different kind of space for discussions about the social change work that service ideally creates," and in turn create "relationships, friendships" that "work to end racism and classism" (278, 277, 294).

WORKS CITED

Armarego, Jocelyn and Lynne Fowler. "Orienting Students to Studio Learning. *Proceedings of the 2005 ASEE/AAEE 4th Global Colloquium on Engineering Education.* Australasian Association for Engineering Education, 2005. Web. 9 December 2014.

Dubinsky, James. "Service-Learning as a Path to Virtue: The Ideal Orator in Professional Communication." *Michigan Journal of Community Service Learning* (Spring 2002): 61–74. Print.

Ellsworth, Elizabeth. "Double Binds of Whiteness." *Off White: Readings on Race, Power and Society.* 2nd ed. Ed. Michelle Fine, Lois Weis, Linda Powell Pruitt, and April Burns. New York: Routledge, 1997. 259–69.

Garza, Susan and Diana Cardenas. "Implementing the Studio Model in a Technical and Professional Writing Program to Build on Service-Learning Opportunities." Council for Programs in Technical and Scientific Communication Conference. Colorado Springs, CO, 2014. Unpublished Conference Paper.

Green, Ann E. "Difficult Stories: Service-Learning, Race, Class, and Whiteness." *College Composition and Communication* 55.2 (2003): 276–301.

Neal, Daria, Veronica Eady Famira, and Vernice Miller-Travis. "Now is the Time: Environmental Injustice in the U.S. and Recommendations for Eliminating Disparities." *Lawyers' Committee for Civil Rights,* June 2010. Web. 9 December 2014.

Zimmer, Steve. "The Art of Knowing your Place: White Service Learning Leaders and Urban Community Organizations." *Reflections: Writing: Service-Learning, and Community Literacy* VI (2007): 7–26.

20 Assessing the New Media Rhetoric: Crossing Disciplinary Boundaries

Kathleen Marie Baldwin

What, though, do these gestures to design seek to accomplish? What does it mean for writing studies practitioners to engage in design work? What can design offer writing studies?

—James Purdy

As multimodality and a pedagogy of multiliteracies increasingly become part of Rhetoric and Composition, the questions James Purdy asks have yet to be satisfactorily answered. Purdy's analysis of the multiple meanings evoked by *design* illustrates part of the issue I explore here: how are students supposed to interpret *design* when their instructors use the term so nebulously? More to the point, what are the questions about design's relationship to rhetoric that the field of rhetoric and composition should be asking in the first place?

While Purdy's article explores what "design thinking" can offer rhetoric and composition, he does not address what *design* offers that rhetoric does not. And that is the question we need to address. This question is not at first glance about assessment. But I would argue that before rhetoric and composition can develop valid multimodal assessment practices, these questions must be addressed: What is the relationship between design and rhetoric, especially in the context of assessing new media compositions, and which principles best serve writers across academic writing contexts?

INTERDISCIPLINARY BY NATURE

Rhetoric and composition is inherently interdisciplinary. The infusion of New London Group-inspired multiliteracies pedagogy into the K16 writing curricula by educational policies like the Common Core State Standards has further highlighted that interdisciplinary nature ("Common Core"). Drawing from rhetoric, new literacy studies, new media studies, graphic design, and technical writing, multimodality in the English Language Arts (ELA) and college writing classrooms continues to push writing instructors across disciplinary borders and into potentially unfamiliar waters. Although interdisciplinarity provides fertile ground for theorization, it simultaneously presents a potential minefield for classroom practice, and assessment in particular (Takayoshi 250; Zoetewey and Staggers 136-7; Yancey 90; Odell and Katz 198). The tangled relationship between design and rhetoric is one specific area within the existing scholarship that influences multimodal assessment. Restated, the question posed by the assessment literature is: How does an emphasis on rhetoric versus design, and vice versa, affect what a writing instructor values in a new media text?

DESIGN AND/OR RHETORIC?

A brief examination of the various uses of *design* by multiliteracies and multimodality scholars highlights just how muddy the waters are. For example, Gunther Kress and TheoVan Leeuwen define *design* as "the organisation of what is to be articulated into a blueprint for production" (50). Design is equated with planning/process and in opposition to distribution/product. Design as outlined within Kress's multimodality also suggests that our "blueprints" lack materiality, that the choices we make before production begins are not embodied and contextually rich (Kress and Van Leeuwen 56-7). This conception of design begs the questions: How can design be both contingent upon and independent from production? Don't the choices a student makes during the composing process happen as part of the production of the text? Even Kress and Van Leeuwen acknowledge the border between them is "blurry" (55). If the scholars who developed the theory struggle to parse meanings, then writing teachers surely must. But this is not the only aspect of *design* that holds multiple, sometimes overlapping meanings.

Kress also defines *design* as a " complex act" that is "about both the best, most apt representation," and, "the best means of deploying available resources" ("Design and Transformation" 158). This definition sounds incredibly similar to how Aristotle defines rhetoric: "Rhetoric may be defined as the faculty of observing [discovering] in any given case the available [appropriate] means of persuasion" (160). Bill Cope and Mary Kalantzis provide another definition of *design*: "Design . . . refers both to structure and to agency. [. . .] Design is the process in which the individual and culture are inseparable" (203). In other words, *design*, to use Jay David Bolter and Richard Grusin's term, is *remediation*, the recreation (or redesigning) of media (or available designs) to suit one's individual communicative purpose (Kress, "Design" 156; Cope and Kalantzis 203-5). So, what is it about design that distinguishes it from rhetoric? What does design offer that rhetoric does not? Or is design simply being used as a synonym for rhetoric or envisioned as part of rhetoric?

While Kress uses the term *design* in much the same way rhetoric and composition scholars use *rhetoric*, one is left guessing how he envisions the rhetoric's role in multimodality. Claire Lauer posits design happens within the context of a rhetorical situation: "Design is important to the composition classroom because it emphasizes the development of ideas (invention) and the engagement with a process by which students make choices, receive feedback, and revise those choices concerning arguments they are making within a particular rhetorical context" (236). However, Kress never uses the word "rhetoric." Whereas Lauer is assuming that writing teachers approach multimodality from the perspective of rhetoric and composition studies, in practice, the question of how teacher-scholars differentiate *design* and *rhetoric* remains. Are they using the terms as synonyms or in opposition to one another? In much of the literature, the authors assume a shared definition that may or may not exist (Lauer; Yancey; National Writing Project et al.; National Council on Teaching English). I argue that depending on how they are actually employing these terms, the emphasis in assessment shifts.

Writing teachers' rhetorical training, their understanding of the many factors and contexts that influence both the creation and reception of a text, promote having sensitivity to the materialities of all the texts they encounter and to teach their students to do the same. Writing teachers are, in fact, uniquely positioned to incorporate new media into the traditional writing classroom (Wysocki 8-9; Welch 13, 23). As described in influential works in new media studies by Bolter and Grusin, in *Remediation*, and Lev Manovich, in *The Language of New Media*, newmedia texts are importantly conceived of as materially aware texts. Adopting the notion that a new media text is a materially aware composition on the part of the writer allows writing teachers to both effectively and ethically employ an expanded notion of what writing is and does in the twenty-first century. It is writing teachers' rhetorical expertise, not necessarily their design expertise, that so positions them. As Collin Brooke argues, writing teachers' understanding of rhetoric is not made moot by digital technology, but it must be adapted to better suit twenty-first century rhetorical situations (41-7). For the average writing teacher, such adaptation is challenge enough. Perhaps a larger impediment to embracing and fully integrating multimodality into the writing curriculum is feeling inadequate, feeling the need to master an additional field—design (Odell and Katz 198).

Yet, an expectation that writing teachers expand their expertise to include design does exist. The NCTE Position Statement on Multimodal Literacies argues that "English/Language Arts teachers will need to become more informed about these [design] conventions because they will influence the rhetorical and aesthetic impact of all multimodal texts." But does the professional development and support to build writing teachers' design expertise exist? In many institutions, it does not. Where exactly is this new expertise supposed to be gained? When asked by a decidedly anxious writing teacher at a recent talk if writing teachers need to study design to teach multimodality, Kress answered yes ("Dartmouth Address"). Kress, among others, apparently sees design as offering something rhetoric does not, but *what* is not clear. Isn't design an integral part of rhetoric? Arrangement, also called at times design or organization, is one of the five canons of classical rhetoric after all.

The relationship between design in multimodal texts and rhetoric in alphabetic texts remains unclear. Further, the role such a relationship plays in assessment is also unclear. As Diana George points out, the relationship between rhetoric and composition and design is as yet unresolved (25). Scholars such as Cope and Kalantzis make the argument that it is the materialities of design that articulate the meaning made in visual texts. New Literacies scholarship argues a pedagogy of multiliteracies seeks to redefine writing to include multimodality not simply as an additive, as an "other," but instead as the natural extension of writing in the twenty-first century, an answer to the expanding writing technologies students already use and will be expected to use. For that to, in fact, be the case, assessment models need to reflect such a positioning (Bearne 22-23). The call for flexible assessment models made by scholars like Kathleen Blake Yancey, Diane Penrod, and Carl Whithaus emphasize the desire for transferability across media. In other words, for multimodality to fully take hold as part of writing instruction, students must be able to apply the same principles—the same habits of mind—to every writing situation they encounter (NCTE, Framework; NWP 5; Eidman-Aadahl et al.). By sidestepping the relationship between design and rhetoric through uncritical usages, we run the risk of positioning multimodality as simply an additive to traditional alphabetic texts, as a novelty to be considered under different terms and through different lenses.

Part of this lack of clarity results from the fact that *design* is used with multiple meanings in multimodal and assessment scholarship (Odell and Katz 204). For example, Kress and Van Leeuwen use *design* both as a synonym for *process* and in reference to the field of graphic design. Yancey also uses aspects of the field of design, such as alignment, in her assessment heuristic, but at the same time emphasizes that rhetoric is central to any communicative act. What precisely is meant when *design* is invoked as a consideration in multimodal assessment? Is using the language of design regarding new media texts a means of accessing the language of rhetoric? As Cheryl Ball points out, a "designerly" text is not the same as a "readerly" text (394). If the knowledge produced by assigning and assessing new media compositions is to be transferrable across writing situations, the relationship between design and rhetoric must be more clearly articulated. So, how is this relationship explained in the literature on multimodal assessment? As the following section demonstrates, it is not.

Design and/or Rhetoric in Multimodal Assessment

The amorphous relationship between design and rhetoric is most transparent in the budding field of multimodal assessment—even within works that emphasize the utility and ubiquity of rhetoric. Yancey's 2004 *Computers and Composition* article, "Looking for Sources of Coherence in a Fragmented World: Notes Toward a New Assessment Design," calls for "an assessment informed by intent, effect, awareness, and design" (93). Again, *design* is evoked. In this case, Yancey is borrowing from the language of the field of design, but only as it relates to the rhetoricity of the composition. Yancey begins outlining three assumptions. Of particular note, is her assumption that, "rhetoric is at the heart of our worlds [. . .]" regardless if a text is digital or print-based (90). Like Anne Frances Wysocki, Yancey argues that the visible materialities of a new media text offer new ways of communicating with the potential for increased intentionality on the reader's and composer's parts (100). Yancey's heuristic is at its core rhetorically driven: "1. What arrangements are possible? 2. Who arranges? 3. What is the intent? 4. What is the fit between the intent and the effect?" (Yancey 96). In this instance, design is subsumed in rhetoric.

Later in the same article, however, Yancey uses *design* to describe the composing process. Like Cope and Kalantzis, Yancey uses the language of design as a synonym for processes undertaken in the production and reception of a text: "The text has a design to it, a pattern, and to assess that pattern, we need assistance from the designer, much as we solicit information about the logic of a painting from an artist or about the interpretation of a novel from a novelist" (96). While she accounts for the different kinds of texts that may be produced, her heuristic is not a radical departure from the best practices for assessing a print-based text. The rhetorical situation in which a digital text is produced, distributed, and consumed may be more complex, but it is still an essentially rhetorical act, an ongoing process, on part of both writer and reader(s). This is only one example of the multiple meanings design is ascribed in multimodal assessment scholarship.

Penrod's *Composition in Convergence, The Impact of New Media on Writing Assessment* (2005) offers another example. Like Yancey, Penrod's work explicitly uses rhetoric as its anchor. Penrod calls for a "communicative assessment" model proposing four flexible criteria by which to evaluate student multimodal compositions: (1) critical analysis of audience and context, (2) rhetorical awareness, (3) the use of multiple media and genres, and (4) rhetorical and technological skill (55). Penrod's model is an example of a context-specific approach based upon the learning objectives set by the individual instructor. Penrod's emphasis on rhetoric, as opposed to design, also implies transferability across media. Moreover, Penrod is careful to point out the ways in which these "transformed assessment practices" easily mesh with the learning objectives of most writing programs. For example, in line with Wysocki, Penrod places importance on the materiality of texts and students' awareness of how networked writing is both produced and received (55). This material awareness is rhetorical awareness. Thus, a student must be aware of not only the options they have when composing any text, they must also be attentive to the effects those choices have on their prospective readers. Such awareness promotes the habits of mind central to effective writing in any medium or genre. By focusing on composing rhetorically effective texts, Penrod's approach makes writing and evaluating across media less daunting.

Nonetheless, Penrod (like Yancey) employs a multimodal assessment model that features design as a component of rhetorically effective texts. Students' design choices, such as which graphics to include and where, are made in relation to their communicative purpose and audience forming Penrod's fourth evaluation criteria: rhetorical and technological skills (31). Here again *design* and *rhetoric* share a complex and somewhat confusing relationship. *Design* for Yancey and Penrod does function as agentive in the same way that Kress and Cope and Kalantzis define it. However, they do not invoke *design* as the driving force behind the communicative act as Kress does. That is left to rhetoric. In Yancey and Penrod, design is employed as a synonym for rhetoric.

While Yancey and Penrod foreground rhetoric in their use of *design*, other scholars sidestep rhetoric all together. Troy Hicks begins his 2009 book *The Digital Writing Workshop* with the notion that digital writing is distinct in form, in practice, and in locality from traditional twentieth-century essay writing (2). Hicks organizes his book around the core principles of the writing workshop that inform, at least in part, most process-based pedagogies. He argues that by adapting these principles-in-practice to digital literacy writing, teachers can promote twenty-first century literacies in ways that maximize the potentials of collaboration and design offered by digital writing (Hicks 1-2). Like Kress, *design*, and not rhetoric, informs the composing process. Hicks offers a more narrow reading of *multiliteracies* or *new literacies* to speak specifically to teaching composing with digital tools, *digital literacy*. Hicks points out that the majority of the writing teachers and students do is digital in some form, in that it was most likely composed on a computer with software incorporating a variety of media sources on a networked device (Hicks 8-10). Today's students are, then, asked to be digital writers (Hicks 10-11). If all the writing students compose is digital, then what role does rhetoric play in digital literacy? Hicks leaves that question unanswered. In fact, he never uses the word "rhetoric." But he does use "design" in the layered, multiple ways outlined in the previous section. He uses it to speak to both the composing process and to the designer's agency—and he uses design as a stand-in for rhetoric. That is, design functions *as* rhetoric, as the process during which a composer makes complex choices driven by her audience and purpose. Hicks is emphatic throughout the book that digital writing should not be viewed as additive or less than traditional literacies. He argues for multimodal assessment practices that expand on and modify print-based assessments so writing teachers can maximize transferability across media. However, by ignoring rhetoric's role in digital literacy—a literacy that by his definition necessarily includes traditional word-processed alphabetic texts—he risks undermining that goal.

Conclusion

In the end, the question of whether a focus on rhetoric or design should guide multimodal assessment practices must be more fully explored. The best answer should derive from what best serves students. As the NCTE, National Writing Project, and *Digital Is . . .* initiatives make clear, multiliteracies pedagogy must include transferability across media so that students can apply the same core concepts to all the writing they do and encounter. Writing teachers also need that transferability to effectively assess new media compositions without having to reinvent the wheel for each text students produce, including the potential for receiving a variety of texts in response to the very same assignment. That's not to say a one-size-fits-all assessment model is possible or even desirable. But writing teachers at all levels deserve some clarity (Eidman-Aadahl et al.; Moran and Herrington). If rhetoric and composition scholars truly embrace multimodal writing, they must also fully embrace assessment challenges that arise in response. Before rhetoric and composition can know how an emphasis on design or rhetoric affects what writing teachers value in new media texts, they must first decide what those terms mean and their relationship to one another.

Works Cited

Aristotle. *On Rhetoric, A Theory of Civil Discourse*. 2nd ed. Trans. George A. Kennedy. New York: Oxford UP, 2007. Print.

Ball, C. "Designerly !≠ Readerly: Re-Assessing Multimodal and New Media Rubrics for Use in Writing Studies." *Convergence: The International Journal of Research into New Media Technologies* 12.4 (2006): 393–412. ERIC. Web. 13 Jan 2011.

Bolter, Jay David and Richard Grusin. *Remediation, Understanding New Media*. Cambridge, : The MIT P, 2000. Print.

Brooke, Collin Gifford. *Lingua Fracta : Towards a Rhetoric of New Media*. Cresskill, NJ: Hampton Press, Inc., 2009. Print.

"Common Core State Standards." *Common Core State Standards Initiative*. Common Core State Standards Initiative, 2014 Web. 30 Jan 2014.

Cope, Bill and Mary Kalantzis. "Designing for Social Futures." Bill Cope and Mary Kalantzis, eds. *Multiliteracies, Literacy Learning and the Design of Social Futures*. New York: Routledge, 2000. Print. 203–34.

Eidman-Aadahl, Elyse et al. "Developing Domains for Multimodal Writing Assessment: The Language of Evaluation, the Language of Instruction." Ed. Heidi McKee and Dànielle DeVoss. *Digital Writing Assessment and Evaluation*. Utah State UP/Computers and Composition Digital P: 2013. E-book.

George, Diana. "From Analysis to Design: Visual Communication in the Teaching of Writing." *College Composition and Communication* 45.1 (Sept. 2002): 11-39. *JSTOR*. Web.15 Oct 2008. Ebook.

Hicks, Troy. *The Digital Writing Workshop*. Portsmouth, NH: Heinemann, 2009. Print.

Kress, Gunther. "Dartmouth Address." Dartmouth College. 25 April 2010. Public Talk.

—. "Design and Transformation." Ed. Bill Cope and Mary Kalantzis. *Multiliteracies, Literacy Learning and the Design of Social Futures*. New York: Routledge, 2000. 182–202. Print.

—. "Gains and Losses: New Forms of Texts, Knowledge, and Learning." *Computers and Composition* 22 (2005): 5–22. *ScienceDirect*. Web. 5 May 2009.

—. "Multimodality." Ed. Bill Cope and Mary Kalantzis. *Multiliteracies, Literacy Learning and the Design of Social Futures*. New York: Routledge, 2000. 179–200.

Kress, Gunther and Theo Van Leeuwen. *Multimodal Discourse, The Modes and Media of Contemporary Communication.* New York: Oxford UP 2001. Print.

Manovich, Lev. *The Language of New Media.* Cambridge, MA: The MIT P, 2001. Print.

Moran, Charles and Anne Herrington. "Seeking Guidance for Assessing Digital Compositions/Composing." *Digital Writing Assessment & Evaluation.* Ed. Heidi A.McKee and Dànielle Nicole DeVoss. Logan, UT: Computers and Composition Digital Press/Utah State University Press, 2013. Web .

National Council on Teaching English. "NCTE Framework for 21st Century Curriculum and Assessment." *NCTE.org.* National Council on Teaching English, Feb. 2013. Web. 12 Feb 2013.

—. "Position Statement on Multimodal Literacy." NCTE.org. National Council on Teaching English, Nov. 2005. Web. 10 Sept 2008.

National Writing Project et al. *Because Digital Writing Matters, Improving Student Writing in Online and Multimedia Environments.* San Francisco: Jossey-Bass, 2010. Print.

New London Group. "A Pedagogy of Multiliteracies: Designing Social Futures." *Harvard Educational Review* 66.1 (Spring 1996). *ScienceDirect.* Web. 10 Sept 2008.

Penrod, Diane. *Composition in Convergence, The Impact of New Media on Writing Assessment.* Mahwah, NJ: Lawrence Erlbaum Associates, Inc., 2005. Print.

Purdy, James P. "What Can Design Thinking Offer Writing Studies?" *College Composition and Communication* 65.4 (June 2014). 612–641. Print.

Takayoshi, Pamela. "The Shaping of Electronic Writing: Evaluating and Assessing Computer-Assisted Processes and Products." *Computers and Composition* 13 (1996): 245–251. *ERIC.* Web. 2 Dec 2008.

Welch, Kathleen. *Electric Rhetoric, Classical Rhetoric, Oralism, and New Literacy.* Cambridge: MIT P, 1999. Print.

Whithaus, Carl. *Teaching and Evaluating Writing in the Age of Computers and High-Stakes Testing.* Mahwah, NJ: Lawrence Erlbaum Associates, Inc., 2005. Print

Wysocki, Anne Frances. "Opening New Media to Writing, Openings and Justifications." Wysocki, Anne Frances et al. *Writing New Media, Theory and Applications for Expanding the Teaching of Composition.* Logan, UT: Utah State U P, 2004. 1–41. Print.

Yancey, Kathleen Blake. "Looking for Sources of Coherence in a Fragmented World: Notes Toward a New Assessment Design." *Computers and Composition* 21.1 (2004): 89-102. *ERIC.* Web. 30 Sept 2013.

Zoetwey, Meredith and Julie Staggers. "Beyond 'current-traditional' Design: Assessing Rhetoric in New Media." *Issues in Writing* 13.2 (2003): 132–152. *RAPID.* Web. 20 August 2014.

21 Positioning Rhetoric at The Heart of the Matter: Engaging Faculty, Engaging Students

Jane Detweiler, Margaret R. LaWare, Thomas P. Miller, &
Patti Wojahn

We live in a world characterized by change—and therefore a world de-
pendent on the humanities and social sciences. . . . How do we understand
ourselves if we have no notion of a society, culture, or world different from
the one in which we live? A fully balanced curriculum—including the hu-
manities, social sciences, and natural sciences—provides opportunities for
integrative thinking and imagination, for creativity and discovery, and for
good citizenship."

—The Heart of the Matter (2013)

The humanities and social sciences—the liberal arts disciplines where
rhetoricians commonly reside—are, to put it bluntly, not doing so
well. In the recently released report, *The Heart of the Matter*, the
Commission on the Humanities and Social Sciences sounds a number of
alarms for these disciplines. At the moment and for the foreseeable future in

higher education, the humanities and social sciences are undermined by political, social, and economic changes, including a narrow focus on job training, drops in educational funding, poor teacher training, and declines in reading. The report recommends that universities renew efforts to invest in research on "grand challenges," expand efforts to strengthen the civic infrastructure by partnering with schools and nonprofits, and prepare politically active citizens with a full set of literacy skills. Rhetoricians are trained and well positioned to advance such efforts. We can do so by engaging faculty and students in crossing a range of borders, those between one discipline and another, between university and community, between a professional curriculum and the liberal arts, and between knowledge consumption and knowledge creation. As rhetoricians and educators, we are uniquely situated to address a renewed interest in undergraduate education and outreach by advocating for and leveraging rhetoric's civic vision and institutional position to address broader educational trends.

In the sections that follow, we consider how those affiliated with rhetoric have a critical role to play not just in advancing the value of rhetorical study but also in realizing the promises of such study. We begin by discussing "grand challenges" that students and educators can work together to address, challenges that require the specific theoretical and methodological lenses to be found in the humanities and social sciences. Next, we address the need for educational institutions to not just value but promote civic engagement among students as well as educators themselves. We then stress the important role of the liberal arts in education and in public life. Finally, we highlight the value rhetoric and related fields bring to enhancing literacy, the foundation for all learning.

SETTING OURSELVES THE GRAND CHALLENGES AT THE HEART OF THE MATTER

A first border we need to dismantle is our overly partitioned system of education. It is time for rhetoricians and others to move out from behind disciplinary divisions and work together to be more engaged in the challenges of our day. *The Heart of the Matter* recommends that "foundations, universities, research centers, and government agencies draw in humanists and social scientists together with physical and biological scientists to address major global challenges such as the provision of clean air and water, food, health, energy, universal education, human rights and the assurance of physical safety" (44). *The Heart of the Matter* also recommends that liberal arts disciplines engage their students in collaborations on "grand challenges" that can energize interdisciplinary research. Such challenges can not only prompt the next generations to consider problems facing their world but also entice students to connect what they are learning across many disciplines, strategies that enhance learning and engagement.

The field of rhetoric has expansive potentials to strengthen these types of interdisciplinary collaborations and community engagements. Toward that end, we need to leverage our leadership in general education and optimize our bridge position to deepen and expand rhetoric's traditional concern for political leadership, ethical problem solving, and critical thinking. The challenge is to promote the skills we teach in terms that connect with broader cultural and social issues. Given the pervasiveness of rhetoric and the need for rhetorical considerations, we should be up to the challenge.

In discussing such issues, *The Heart of the Matter* identifies the liberal arts with its roles in exploring values and fostering communication and problem-solving skills. This is the critical nexus that gives rhetoric its power and our discipline its *kairos*. As James L. Applegate and Sherwyn P. Morreale point out, "broad change can be accomplished by a few people properly placed, promoting the idea of engagement adapted to disciplinary culture, in a context where society's expectations and need for our energy is growing daily" (np). We need to stop acting as though only biologists can address challenges such as global warming and only rhetoricians can change the world through language.[1]

INVESTING IN COMMUNITY ENGAGEMENT

A second border we need to cross is one between the academy and the communities in which educational institutions exist. One frame that can help us think about what David J. Coogan and John M. Ackerman refer to as "doing rhetoric" (2010, 1) is the concept of the scholarship of engagement. This framework connects with the rising attention to translational research, to community and business partnerships, and to efforts to enhance the undergraduate experience. In an article introducing what he referred to as the "scholarship of engagement," Boyer argues for a "climate in which the academic and civic cultures communicate more continuously and more creatively with each other" (20). He calls on the academy to "become a more vigorous partner in the search for answers to our most pressing social, civic, economic, and moral problems" (11). To raise the standing of our service work and respond to forces undermining the liberal arts, we need to apply our collective efforts to leverage points where interdisciplinary collaborations converge with institutional needs and broader social changes. To address public misperceptions about "rhetoric," we suggest focusing not so much on what rhetoric *is* as much as what rhetoric does, what rhetoric can do. The scholarship of engagement can help us with that.

The *Heart of the Matter* argues that we "can maintain scholarly integrity even while engaging a variety of audiences" such as the general public, schools, and non-profits. Such engagements can, the report says, "remind Americans of the meaning and value of the humanities and social sciences" (19). *The Heart of the Matter* also places the humanities and social sciences, or, in our case, rhetoric itself at "the heart of the matter," as "keeper of the republic—a source of . . . civic vigor" (9). Yet, we have to ask whether preparing students to be active citizens is enough. Might we not also benefit as researchers, scholars, practitioners if we ourselves also become more active and engaged with civic life?

The historic increase in the political engagement of the generation sitting in our classrooms (Schwab) challenges us to reflect upon how rhetoric can contribute to such engagements. These reflections can be enhanced by considering rhetoric's holistic vision of the politics of civic life and its practical engagement with collective action. We agree with Coogan and Ackerman, who argue that making such connections is in fact "vital to rhetoric's ongoing efforts to renew itself and to demonstrate our relevance locally and for a changing world" (1). As they state, "communities can benefit from the increased attention of rhetoricians in pursuit of democratic ideals, but rhetoric can also benefit from community partnerships premised on a negotiated search for the common good" (1-2). How might we develop those community partnerships, and what will it take to reach out to and integrate new publics into our scholarly and pedagogical frameworks?

One obstacle has traditionally been the lack of reward that universities assign to public engagement, service, or outreach. We need to work with others to find ways for educational institutions to identify, value, and reward the ways our engagements productively connect to critical issues in the world. As one example, the National Communication Association has drawn positive attention for making efforts to engage publics through community partnerships over the last two decades. This and other examples display what can be possible through developing partnerships and outreach with community members, bringing our knowledge and skills to conversations and communication around contemporary issues, which becomes more and more significant as we see our democracy grinding to a halt in the halls of Congress.

RHETORICAL ENGAGEMENTS: THE ROLE OF THE LIBERAL ARTS IN PUBLIC EDUCATION AND PUBLIC LIFE

A third border we need to cross is the one between the liberal arts and the professionally oriented curriculum. *The Heart of the Matter* underscores how liberal education is losing its public currency and needs strong, timely, well-crafted advocacy. This situation, including rhetorical scholars' involvement, is not new. In the middle of the last century, the "New Rhetoric" emerged amidst broad debates over the place of "liberal education" in modern society, bringing attention to language as a mode of social action and the rhetorical underpinnings of the liberal arts curriculum itself. Rhetoricians helped to develop the general education programs established in response to exploding enrollments of less-prepared adults returning to the classroom; the New Rhetoric was shaped by critical engagements in public debates and general education.

A panoply of articles from the postwar period on rhetoric and general education speak to primary issues raised in *The Heart of the Matter*. For example, Everett Hunt's "Rhetoric and General Education" from *QJS* in 1949 argues for educating citizens in cross-disciplinary skills and aptitudes needed to debate issues of the day. Then as now, scholars expressed anxieties in identifying the discipline of rhetoric with "service courses," fearing an undermining of the disciplinary status of "content" courses (see also Bryant). James Beasley reviews the history of these debates, underlining how they justified broader efforts to enlist the New Rhetoric in teaching critical analysis, public speaking, and persuasive writing in general education.

Certainly the New Rhetoric, associated perhaps most prominently with Kenneth Burke, sought to achieve many aims outlined in *The Heart of the Matter* through the study of rhetoric as symbolic action and through developing an understanding of persuasion as identification. As interconnectivity engenders greater possibilities for identification and influence, rhetoric invites us to actively engage in popular discussions and policy debates about what it takes to build a democratic, truly deliberative society. To contribute to that work, we need to leverage our pedagogical involvement in general education to make the case that rhetoric provides the skills, civic engagements, and modes of leadership vital to democracy.

Reasons abound for maintaining a critical distance from discussions of our role in general education, the values of the liberal education, or the role of the humanities and social sciences in public education. For one, general education courses have little status; they often rely upon temporary funding and contingent faculty. In addition, for those of us carrying heavy service loads administering large communications or composition programs, it can be a real struggle to prevent those commitments from completely defining our work. General education is also a struggle because it has often operated as an unfunded mandate based on the dubious proposition that all incoming undergraduates can be taught "generalizable" oral and writing skills in a course or two. Nonetheless, if we think more strategically, more rhetorically, about our engagements in these programs, we may be able to leverage institutional investments in them to address the transformative challenges facing higher education, the humanities and social sciences, and the field of rhetoric in particular.

RECLAIMING RHETORICAL SKILLS AND APTITUDES

A final border we need to cross is that separating knowledge consumption from knowledge making. As teachers of rhetoric, we likely see ourselves committed to the first item *The Heart of the Matter* lists for connecting the liberal arts to civic purposes: preparing students to be active citizens by inviting them to expand their critical thinking, literacy, and analytical abilities. As rhetoricians, we are well positioned to enlist *The Heart of the Matter*'s emphasis on *supporting literacy as the foundation for all learning*. However, we have shied away from talking about what we teach, in part because we have been put upon by the disabling dualism of skills and content courses.

Our work with the craft of argument, critical analysis, close reading, and style is part of a liberal tradition that can be enlisted to break down the disabling dualisms that lead to rhetoric being placed on the down side of the sciences and arts. To advance that work, we can strengthen pedagogical collaborations across communications and composition. Working together, we can publicize the theory and research involved in rhetorical studies, something we have not always positioned as a primary aim.

In considering how to publicize the values of rhetoric, we have some outstanding models for advocating the value of both public writing and speaking courses, along with the need to ground those courses in shared theories and history. One key figure is the late Michael Leff, who played a leading role in the efforts of the Rhetoric Society of America to bring together rhetorical scholars from English and Speech (Zarefsky). We can build on Leff's commitment to connections among rhetoricians by encouraging integration of both theory and pedagogy in communication and public speaking. Whether we work in English, composition, or communications departments, we share a general concern for the pragmatics of deliberating upon collective needs and purposes.

Other efforts could address the second goal outlined in *The Heart of the Matter*: "Educators should focus new attention on the 'qualities of mind'—problem-solving, critical analysis, and communication skills—that are embedded in all disciplines" (11). We need to open conversations about learning goals and pedagogy and be more public about our research and theoretical groundings, advocating for the importance of research and theory in both the teaching and the practice of effective communication, composition, and critical thinking skills. Making our disciplinary frameworks more public invites us to consider how we might better use the resources of rhetoric to engage the community and garner support for liberal arts and general education. Further, helping others to recognize and understand the rhetorical nature of the general education curriculum itself may help us deepen conversations across divisions within the institution.

Conclusion: Engaging Faculty, Engaging Students

If institutions of higher education do begin to re-envision "academic work," if universities recognize and reward work informed by our academic expertise—work often relegated as little respected service and outreach—it is a perfect time to strengthen the public as well as the academic standing of rhetoric. As *The Heart of the Matter* states, "the public valuation of the humanities will be strengthened by every step that takes this knowledge out of academic self-enclosure and connects it to the world" (43). In a time of heavy attention on science, technology, engineering, and mathematics, the scholarship of engagement can help us strengthen rhetoric's public standing in ways that are meaningful for academics and the public alike.

The late Stuart Brown's motto "Have Rhetoric, Will Travel" (199) argues the value of not just studying rhetoric but also applying it widely and well. Yet when we as rhetoricians find ourselves solely speaking to and among ourselves, writing to and about ourselves, we are not traveling far. We have learned much from analyzing rhetoric at play in the world, among publics, and in our society. We have much more to learn by actually engaging with and among those publics, traversing what Coogan and Ackerman (2010) describe as "'lost geographies' of public life that hold within them the political and ethical dimensions of real events and social relations that [could] make our disciplinary identity newly possible" (8). As rhetoricians, we can invest our disciplinary capacities and leverage our disciplinary power toward changing how academic work can be envisioned. We can work toward changing institutional hierarchies to increase value for applying professional expertise within real world, public realities.

This essay has responded to those challenges by outlining rationale for the specific ways that rhetoricians can take a lead in advocating for the humanities and liberal arts in students' education. As rhetoricians and as educators, we know that such advocacy needs to integrate reflection and action across individual, departmental, institutional and community borders. We also know that rhetoric can provide an integrative framework drawing upon our work with ethos, politics, identity, social movements, and collective action to speak to such challenges as the privatization of public education, the imposition of assessment regimes on learning, and the subordination of liberal education to career preparation. To respond to these challenges, we need to embrace rhetoric's fundamental role and critical potentials in general education, and we need to reevaluate the marginalization of outreach and service by traditional research hierarchies. In short, we can put rhetoric at the heart of the matter through engaging faculty and engaging students.

NOTE

1. Although conversations and efforts between scholars in rhetoric and scientists, for instance, have begun within organizations such as the International Environmental Communication Association and the Health and Science Communications Association, so much potential remains untapped.

WORKS CITED

Applegate, James L., and Sherwyn P. Morreale. "Engaged Disciplines: One Association's Efforts to Encourage Community Involvement." *AAHEA Bulletin. American Association for Higher Education and Accreditation, May 2001. Web. 30 Jun 2014.*

Beasley, James. "The Journal of General Education and an Institutional Return to Rhetoric." *The Journal of General Education* 61.2 (2012): 126–140. Print.

Boyer, Ernest L. "The Scholarship of Engagement." *Journal of Public Service & Outreach*, 1.1 (1996): 11–20. Print.

Brown, Stuart. "Have Rhetoric, Will Travel." In *Living Rhetoric and Composition: Stories from the Discipline.* Ed. Duane Roen, Stuart Brown, and Theresa Jarnogi Enos. New York: Routledge, 1998. 199–206. Print.

Bryant, Donald. "Rhetoric: Its Functions and its Scope." *Quarterly Journal of Speech* 39.4 (1953): 401–424. Print.

Commission on the Humanities and Social Sciences. *The Heart of the Matter: The Humanities and Social Sciences.* Cambridge: The American Academic of the Arts and Sciences, 2013. Print.

Coogan, David J. and John M. Ackerman. "Introduction: The Space to Work in Public Life." *The Public Work of Rhetoric: Citizen-Scholars and Civic Engagement.* Ed. John M. Ackerman and David J. Coogan. Columbia, SC: U of South Carolina P, 2010. 1–16. Print.

Hunt, Everett. "Rhetoric and General Education." *Quarterly Journal of Speech* 35.3 (1949): 275–279. Print.

Zarefsky, David. "Remembering Michael Leff," *Rhetoric and Public Affairs*, 13.4, 2010. 669–678. *Academic Search Premier (EBSCO.)* Web. 15 May, 2014.

In Conversation: Fragments and Provocations

22 Fragments from "In Conversation: Critical Rhetorics of Race"

Keith Gilyard & Kent A. Ono

Keith Gilyard: Race is, as many of us would argue, a social construct or a social construction. But of course we also know that even though it is a social construction, it is real in its effects. People confuse that sometimes. This hotel is socially constructed; it's not natural. It's socially constructed. But if it collapses, we *going* to be in trouble. So the idea that something is socially constructed, people declare that as though it ends the conversation, you know. To me it begins the conversation, right. So if race is socially constructed, what are its effects? What are its effects in life, culture, etcetera? We have had critical race theorists, you know, David Roediger, the late Ted Allen, Ruth Frankenberg, and Toni Morrison in that wonderful little monograph *Playing in the Dark*. They have talked about the formation of racial identities, in particular whiteness identities, as well as others. Other scholars like Zeus Leonardo talk about race as a continuing project of construction. So not only is it constructed; it's not finished. It is continually under construction. So race is continuing to shift in American culture, and we continue to grapple with how to define it, with what it means. In addition to that, I would say that racism, as distinct from race—we might talk about why I see them as different later—but racism as distinct from race is also a project of continuing construction. How do the structures of racial inequality, in other words, those mechanisms that produce unequal racial results, which is the imperative of racism, continue to operate? And how do they continue to produce inequality, somewhat efficiently? Which *is* the question. Of course, folks here know that it is largely a rhetorical project.

Kent Ono: Keith already said this, but I will say it a little differently. I think rhetoric is really important in thinking about race, and the role of rhetoric has been understated both in academic terms and political terms. One of the things that makes rhetoric so important to trace, and Keith alluded to this, is that race is there and not there at the same time. When something happens—let's say a racist event or even a racist history—it's almost as if it's not there, it doesn't exist, it hasn't happened unless someone calls attention to it. Rhetoric is absolutely essential to making race real. Someone has to witness it. Someone has to say it. It has to be out there for it to actually be acted upon, for people to know and to be that episteme. There has to have been a statement first. As a result, people who want to talk about race, critique it, and maybe change things are a little bit at a disadvantage because the media get to set the agenda for what is and is not race. If you look at the preponderance of media discourse, you see that race is sort of on the sideline of the conversation, and when it is not on the sideline, then it's characterized in particular ways. So there are those who have the power to use rhetoric and those who are on the margins responding to it. So those who talk about it determine how it appears, and those on the sidelines who respond are often either marginalized or ignored. Or race is obscured. It's covered over. It's made less visible by what is said. And there are psychological dimensions to it, such as suppression and repression. So with suppression, people purposely push it down and hide it. With repression, they don't want to acknowledge that it is there and that it is happening and that it is existing all of the time. So I think a whole lot more rhetoric has to happen—but by whom?

23 Fragments from "In Conversation: Rhetoric and Activism"

Dana Cloud & Seth Kahn

Dana Cloud: I had long been in a socialist organization and been an activist. I started in 1990 and just never quit doing what I was doing. People would say, "Aren't you afraid you won't get tenure?" My position was this: if a place won't tenure me because I am outside demonstrating against the death penalty then maybe it's not the kind of place I want to be. But that is a flippant answer when you live in this economy and you have to get a job. So many of the jobs are precarious now, and I totally get that. At the same time, what kind of life do people want to live? I mean, I have to live a *whole* life, and if I had to squelch that part or keep it secret in any sustained way, I would really not feel like myself. So, I give sort of bifurcated advice. If you want to be super practical and be really responsible, and if I wanted to give you really good advice, I would say wait until you are in a secure place—maybe not just until you get tenure but until you feel like there is symbolic, intellectual, and physical space for you to do things. But the other side of me is, the academy is just one expression of the kind of fucked up social relations that characterize our world. We can't be living in those social relations and not be struggling against them..

Seth Kahn: I think my answer to that is a little different. Not particularly inconsistent, but a little different. That is to say, as a graduate student, as a junior faculty member, if you're going to do activism, I think there are two things that need to happen along with it that are simultaneously good for you and also offer protection. One of which is to write about it and make it an explicit part of your identity. So that if you're publishing about activism and you're out there doing it, it doesn't look weird, it doesn't look like a distraction from what you're supposed to be doing. The other reason to do it in that way is because it makes both of them better, right? My activism got a whole lot better when I took the time to actually think really carefully and really analyze what I was doing. So that, I don't want the word "synergy" here because it is really corporate, but that overlap is a really important one. The other kind of line of advice here, and those of you who were in the session earlier are probably sick of hearing this word already, but I take the Hart and Negri metaphor of "network" very, very seriously. As a graduate student or junior faculty member, you need to understand that you don't have to be a leader to be an activist. You come to people like Dana and me. Part of what we do as senior people with tenure is make sure that you don't get in trouble for doing the work. I take it very seriously as part of my ethical responsibility when I work with adjunct faculty who are agitating for better working conditions or what have you.

24 Fragments from "Coalitional Gestures, Third Spaces, and Rhetorical Imaginaries: A Dialogue in Queer Chican@ Feminism"

Karma R. Chávez & Adela C. Licona

Karma Chávez: We came together last spring at the following points of connection (among others): coalition, third space, Chican@ feminism, queer theories, activism, and intersectionality. Though we weren't as familiar with each other's work as we should have been given the similarities and resonances within our work; as we read, we quickly discovered so many of these convergences. While many people in rhetorical theory across English and Communication return to scholars such as Aristotle, Cicero, Burke or Marx to develop and inform their knowledge-making, our own rhetorical theories and practices emerge from a particular lineage of women of color feminism, one that materialized from the struggles of the 60s, 70s, and 80s within liberation and feminist movements. These scholars include Gloria Anzaldúa, Audre Lorde, Cherríe Moraga, María Lugones, and others. We are invested in continuing to read these theorists and thinkers deeply and understand their relevance to our scholarly and activist knowledge-making practices, while remaining acutely aware of the contexts out of which those struggles emerged.

Adela Licona: The differences that constitute our present moments and those of the writings that animate our work span more than just the turn of a new century. For one, at least in the context of our present academic work on this dialogue, we engage our struggle within a discipline grounded on all of the premises that a field such as women's and feminist studies sought to uncover and rupture—patriarchal and individualistic norms, narrow forms of civic engagement, and producing a cohesive citizenry. Even if we speak more broadly about the academy, other differences exist. We engage our work from margins that have perhaps been codified more permanently now than they were then—those who maintain the power structures have let us in the doors, offered us their gifts of tenure and journal pages and a national stage. They've told us they understand our critiques of their sexism/racism/homophobia/imperialism and the like. They nod their heads in pace with the rhythm of our indictments, and then they carry on with their days. They have learned our languages. Sometimes they even write in them. In letting us in, bringing us from margin into the center (at least at its periphery), our marginalization is less visible, less palpable. Our contexts as queer women of color who study rhetoric are different than those of Anzaldúa and Lorde. Context is important. Without context, how do we make meaning? Without context, would we make—work from only assumptions and universalisms?

Karma Chávez: These fragments we are going to share with you reveal the various ways we are wrestling with our past and present contexts and the insights we have gained by putting our contexts in conversation with the theories that resonate with us most . . . We are not putting forth a coherent argument. We put these out as offerings, *ofrendas*, which we hope can enable a conversation with all of us at these intersections and interactions among, between, and within queer Chican@ feminisms.

Adela Licona: This video ["A Swarm of Vitalities/Swarms of Affiliates: Possibilities for (Coalitional) Action"] emerged after a series of conversations and exchanges with Karma and after having just read Jane Bennett's *Vibrant Matter: A Political Ecology of Things*. At the same time, I had been working with Tucson youth around issues related to youth sexuality and rights, and I had been taking care of my elderly mother in Arizona. In other words, in the midst of populations of people actively overlooked and marginalized, if not criminalized and pathologized. In her discussion of the human/thing divide, Bennett offers a reminder of the ways in which particular humans are positioned in that divide as humans and others as things. She acknowledges "human-on-human instrumentalization (as when powerful humans exploit illegal, poor, young, or otherwise weaker humans)" (12). This acknowledgement, together with Bennett's exploration of resistance to categorization (which I read as always a queer endeavor) and active engagement with humans/things as vital materialities, leads to the introduction of the concept of a *swarm of vitalities.*

> This concept stayed with me as I continued to reflect on the ideas Karma and I were discussing from coalition to agency to identity. It also stayed with me as I experienced shifting temporalities in myself and in my contexts. I was becoming mother to my mother as her vitality was disbursing and producing new assemblages of energy and matter. As the next oldest in our multi-generational household, I was slipping and sliding into the position that highlighted my own mortality. Impermanence and continuation, not at odds but in tension—productive, creative tension . . .

> Ghosts. Ingested knowledges, penetrating histories, disintegrating body, reintegrations

> My own vitality shifting in ways unfamiliar . . . Re-organ-izing myself . . .

> I worked as my mother's caretaker all day, every day, in a state that was privatizing care and incarceration. Invisible labor, con amor.

> I was also and at the same time working with young people during a time of state-induced panics around race, migration status, sex, and gender and when youth were being vilified in the media for wanting/demanding access to their own histories—whose access to information about sex and sexualities was being denied, who were experiencing and witnessing racialized profilings and deportations. They were spitting and slamming in response.

> Precarity.

> Different ghosts. Disappearing knowledges, invisibilized bodies . . . violences, silences

> Distinct temporalities, vitalities but a swarm of affinities, affiliates, vitalities . . .

I buzzed like a bee.

Swarms.

Watching the frenzied dance of lights and mirrors across my mother's body did something to me, for me . . . I imagined tiny fragments of her being spinning off—chaotically—into the universe and penetrating our beings and bones, doings and things . . . Reconstituting, reassembling, reproducing . . . Agentive? Coalitional?

I lost the words but felt it, heard it . . . I sent the video to Karma who made beautiful sense of it and offered it to an audience who continued to make meaning of it.

Karma Chávez: This short video, "A Swarm of Vitalities/Swarms of Affiliates: Possibilities for (Coalitional) Action" is comprised mostly of video footage taken during one of Adela's participatory media projects with Tucson's queer youth and their allies. The voices and images from the remixed videos—a metaphor Adela briefly offers for coalitional gestures—are framed by images of her mother, on a particularly good day. The film of Grannie, lying in her hospice bed, oxygen tube under her nose, is sped up, embodying a queer temporality as we watch her in conversation with an unknown interlocutor while these amazing and vibrant squares of sunlight dance across her body. The only sound is a sort of meditating hum that vibrates in odd contrast to the images of Grannie. In the transition, the temporality shifts to a slower tempo and the sound abruptly turns from peaceful to playful as we hear the voices and see the images of the youth talking and laughing in an art gallery. The voices and images are purposely remixed, as the identities being claimed by the voices and the bodies featured in the images don't always seem to match. Through the remix, we get several senses of what it might mean to gesture toward coalition through art and across issues of identity, health, and bodies. Creating together, confirming each other's positionalities and social locations, and learning to empower ourselves and protect our bodies. After the last youth announces their identity, and as the faces of the youth flash across the screen, the meditating hum re-enters the soundscape, and for only a moment, Grannie Dottie returns, as the words, "vital material conjunction: locating possibilities for action" appear, flicker in rhythm with the checkers of sunlight, and finally disappear.

Grannie Dottie died Friday, February 21ˢᵗ. I spoke with Adela that day as we had a Skype date scheduled, and she told me that they were in the final hours. A few hours later, I saw the announcement on her partner Jamie's facebook page. And this is the stuff of real life, the precarity, the pain, the transitions. It is also the intimacy developed and shared between two people who were strange to each other just a year ago, but who have been on a journey together of discovery and creation. I think it is appropriate that the differences in our lives over the last year and now the newness and rawness of her mother's death frame our encounter. After all, this is how we come to coalition—across generation, from different life circumstances, with differing health conditions, and in our cases, and in the cases of so many before us who have theorized coalition, through our own racialized queerness.

25 In Conversation: The Rhetoric of Disability and Access

James L. Cherney & Margaret Price

This is an excerpt from the actual Communication Access Realtime Translation (CART) transcript that was projected onto a screen in large font during the conversation to improve access to attendees. CART transcription has become an important technology used for making presentations accessible. Since the panel emphasized access, we feel that retaining the transcript style provided the best experience of how many of the participants understood the conversation. Minor edits have been made in the form of bracketed inserts to clarify or correct information.

>> *Price:*

[. . .]

Our fourth question and I think this is the first one we actually got really excited about.

Is it more useful to say that disability studies is a disciplinary approach; that is, that it is a discipline?

We talked a fair amount about disciplinarity while we were having this our our prep conversations.

Or would it be more accurate to say that it is a kind of rhizomatic cluster of approaches that tend to go under one name. Disability studies scholars approach many parallel ideas circulating in the field in substantially different ways.

For example, methods of studying ableism which we've mentioned, or how, quote, unquote, the normal is conceived and studies. For example, we could examine the normal from a historical literary stance as Leonard [Lennard] Davis has, or from a contemporary or political argument stance as many people who identify as rhetoricians do, and each of these would reflect different assumptions about rhetorical theory and practice.

Because we're closing in on on our selfappointed time for us to sit here and jaw, I'm just going to mention I'm going to mention what I wanted to talk about here very briefly.

I think we can very loosely agree that disability studies has arrived in English studies, this year, 2014, in a way that it had not arrived in 1999.

Now, that doesn't mean that studying disability studies is easy, or easily rewarded.

It doesn't mean that graduate students going on the job market don't agonize over how to position themselves, but, you know, to some degree it is as Rosemary [Rosemarie] Garland Thompson has said a field emerged.

In that emergence, I have perceived some gaps in resources that concern me, and we can talk more about these during the open discussion if people are interested, but very briefly, first of all, I'm I'm concerned about the gap between scholars who identify as doing disability studies. I feel compelled to put scare quotes around "doing".

And the people who identify the Society for Disability Studies as their home discipline.

Now, maybe this is a sign of the robust interdisciplinarity that marks academia today or maybe it's a sign that disability studies now confers enough cultural capital within the within academia that people perhaps don't need the Society for Disability Studies anymore.

And that's a genuinely troubling question for me.

It's an open question, and I'm not sure what to do with it.

The second resource gap that I perceive and again this is a very personal and a very open question for me.

I perceive a gap between the people who discuss access and exhort accessible practices and the number of people who actually do this in everyday life or in everyday academic practice.

Again, I'm not sure what to do about that.

I mean, I I don't want to like just sort of be like "What's wrong with people!!??"

But I wonder what why does that why does that gap occur?

Why is it that it is relatively easy and I'm speaking here largely of my experiences within rhetoric and composition. Why is it relatively easy to sort of say that access is a good thing, but then perhaps not to get as specific about how to practice access as as we might.

That's all I'll say on that for now.

>> *Cherney:* Well, and I think that the speech rhetoric position has been or tradition has also had a similar response to access, that it's it's something that there's been widespread agreement, this is a good idea, this is something we need to be thinking about, but then the move to it is often, okay, let's set out a series of guidelines and prescriptions that we have to follow, and that these are the right ways to make access, and and that this is accessible, and that this isn't, and and it makes all I mean, essentially it looks at able access from an ableist perspective, I think, and I really like the idea that we need to find sort of new ways of thinking about ableism, and access, and and I mean, we keep picking on Jay [Dolmage], sort of glad that he's here, but the idea of it as a way to move, right, which is that thinking about articulating, you know, access as a kind of movement.

Becomes not just a way to move in terms of flowing from one room to another, and having the ability to go through the door, but also vary, right, movere, MOVERE, Movement of the mind, right, moving how we think and how we imagine others and what motivates us to act. I think that's a useful conception that that speech rhetoric needs to adopt, it's like you said, at conferences, in my case, the National Communication Association, the NCA conferences, access has been something that we've been working on for a long time, and there's been we've always had widespread agreement from the the executive council and the people that run the NCA that this is something that needs to be done, but what gets done over the years has been well, it's been an ongoing process.

I've actually sort of informally been kind of liaison for a number of years. I chair the Disability Studies Caucus I'm sorry, Disability Issue Caucuses [Caucus's] Accessibility Committee, which essentially means that over the years when there's been an access problem, I'm the person that they go find and then I go find the people who are running NCA and we try to deal with it, and it's NCA has always been open to it, but they haven't been very perceptive of the kinds of things that need to be done beforehand. I think that's been the experience for a lot of people. SDS [Society for Disability Studies], one of the things I think we will always get out of SDS is probably the most accessible conference you can go to, at least in the United States. There's been more attention to access I think at SDS than anywhere else that I'm aware of. I mean, and I think they've done a really good job.

26 Fragment from "What Role Can/Should Academic Journals Play in the Future of Rhetoric Scholarship"

Barbara Biesecker, James Jasinski, & Kelly Ritter

Baraba Biesecker: It has been my genuine pleasure and honor to serve as editor of the *Quarterly Journal of Speech*. I have learned a great deal, already, from the experience. About it, on this occasion, I wish to make [a couple of] points or, perhaps better put, provocations—provocations to submission, provocations to thought, provocations to action . . . What am I seeing? A lot of work on material memory. A lot of work on affect, the body, and articulation. Very little work on Public Address. Very little work on the history of Rhetoric. Very little on economics. Very little work on war, except in the context of public and collective memory—and I think that is significant. Even less feminist work and queer work. Almost no work on rhetoric pursued from a trans-national or global frame. And almost nothing that is not on or about the US. Nothing that is not about the US, is not US-centric, almost. There's been no disability studies submissions. And to date, no retranslations of primary texts with commentary, although I issued a special invitation for such submissions. All of this takes me to my second point: What we will see in our journals has a relationship to what we teach in our graduate courses and what we require of our graduate degrees. The desire for work, for new kinds of work, work about, say, China, the Middle East (not the US in the Middle East, but Middle Eastern rhetoric). rhetoric in Cuba, rhetoric in India, etcetera is predicated on that—on a different kind of graduate training. So I wish to begin by issuing a call to graduate programs to tighten up their tool requirements (serious instruction in languages as well as advanced coursework in other other disciplines). Old fashioned, I know, but if Warren Buffet can see the new in the train, I can see the new in the return to studying languages.

James Jasinski: *RSQ*'s mission speaks directly to the question of its role, which is the topic of our conversation. That mission, originally articulated on the back, inside cover of the journal, stipulates that *RSQ* hopes to offer new knowledge or advance the discussion of significant issues across the multiple disciplinary homes of rhetorical studies. I take the final prepositional phrase seriously. *RSQ*'s role is to produce cross or interdisciplinary scholarship in rhetoric. If you can't engage those literatures, you are not coming close in my judgment to meeting *RSQ*'s role. Second, I think that specific projects, whether they are analyses of Presidential rhetoric or histories of pedagogical practices, need to advance and contribute to larger conversations on rhetoric. I had a really interesting experience as I was making the transition to the *RSQ* editor role. I was talking to a colleague who had just recently published a piece in *RSQ*, which I liked very much, and I said, "You know, I would have liked more history." He said, "That's really interesting you said that because that is what I thought but Carolyn [Miller] had said no. No more history. No more case. Talk more broadly about things rhetorical." And a light bulb went off. Carolyn was right. She was absolutely right. I wanted more history. I would have found it more interesting, but that wouldn't have served *RSQ*'s mission. And I have tried to take that lesson to heart. So, again, whatever the specific case might be, if all you're doing is advancing knowledge of that particular case, odds are small that I and other *RSQ* reviewers are going to want to accept that piece for publication. You have to engage an issue, topic, controversy, (etc.) with broader rhetorical significance outside of the case.

Kelly Ritter: [A] final hypothesis that I will make is a positional one on what I think I am calling rhetoric and how that has been lately perceived as being endemic to what my own journal (*College English*) has termed English Studies. We don't have time or the occasion to get into the place that rhetoric has in English departments. Nor can we parse out the differences, if you believe there are any, between rhetoric and composition, though I would be happy to talk about that at another time with anyone here. I have classified *College English* submissions as rhetoric-related if they specifically evoke rhetoric in the title or elsewhere, if they employ an analysis of the power of persuasion in some systematic way throughout their argument and use evidence, and if they use rhetoric as a classifying means for an object, people, or phenomenon. What I often call the rhetoric of X or Y, or how X or Y subsequently makes meaning in the world. When you think about how capacious my definition of rhetoric is already, I wonder if I could actually go back to my statistics and find that I have been conservative in my tallies of how much rhetoric-related scholarship gets published in the journal. Or is it likely that everything that I plan to publish or have already published, maybe, actually *is* rhetoric? To potentially turn my own data around forces me to next ask the question of whether, on these terms, rhetoric is the master discipline. If it is, it's rather pointless for the three of us [editors] up here to differentiate ourselves or make distinctions about whether any of our journals is more or less influential in the relationship of publishing to the future of rhetorical scholarship. We could back that up even further, and ask, since our journals are where rhetorical scholarship happens, is that happening truly a dialogic one? Are the readerships of journals porous enough? Do they cross-pollinate in all of the ways we want them to? Or do we want something different from the rhetorical scholarship that actually gets published? Do we want to further that in a way that our editors up here have yet to articulate?

27 Fragments from "Rhetorical Theory: Questions, Provocations, Futures"

Bradford Vivian & Diane Davis

Bradford Vivian: Countervailing forces of *retention* and *protention* have significantly shaped late-modern research in rhetorical theory. Recent generations of theorists have sought to acknowledge some manner of continuity with their forked disciplinary lineage (itself a synthesis of various classical and modern intellectual traditions) while simultaneously demonstrating how and why rhetorical theory is an independent mode of inquiry distinct from cognate theoretical endeavors—such as philosophy, sociology, critical theory, and psychoanalysis—to which their work is conspicuously indebted. Such energetic topical and intellectual promiscuity poses a challenge to answering the question: What is called rhetorical theory?

That which is called rhetorical theory investigates the nature of a manifestly mercurial phenomenon whose defining properties may be radically altered by the process of theoretical examination, like particles that appear as waves or waves that appear as particles during empirical observation. What is called rhetorical theory appears to exert a force akin to a twofold chemical change in which self-attuned saying—neither "speech" nor "writing," but *saying*—becomes a worldly thing, and in which worldly things exhibit properties of saying. The dynamic chemistry of that which is called rhetorical theory—its inherent *dynamis*—allows greater clarity as to its own-most conditions of possibility.

That which is called rhetorical theory *describes* according to the etymologically refined sense in which Cormac McCarthy uses the term. Consider this sentence from *Blood Meridian*: "In the predawn dark the sounds about describe the scene to come" (109). This sentence lacks an agent: the sounds *describe* the scene *to come*. The scene is described before it is visible, apparent; that scene, not yet seen or known for purposes of conventional description, is described in the sense of being sounded out. This manner of description concomitantly *inscribes* and, by the same gesture, *circumscribes* that which it *de*scribes: a description that calls its object into being and delimits its contours so as to suggest that the object in question always existed as such, prior to the description that called it into being. That which is called rhetorical theory describes rhetorical problems, questions, concepts, or phenomena in this sense of sounding out their rhetorical nature, calling them forth as if for the first time from that place where allegedly they have always been, awaiting their fitting articulation. Hence, science is (and apparently always was) rhetorical, capitalism is (and apparently always was) rhetorical—just as bodies are likewise rhetorical, history is rhetorical, archives are rhetorical, deconstruction is rhetorical, disciplinary power is rhetorical, and so on. Ergo, *retention* and *protention*: a power of description that elaborates its intended object anew so as to retain its ostensible inceptive essence.

Rhetorical theory describes *modes of communication* between *language* and *world*, between world and language. This account exploits the etymologically rich senses of *communication*, its fundamental connotations of sharing something substantial in common, an exchange of properties, of physical contact or connection (rather than historically recent connotations of information exchange). *World* refers not only to individual phenomena, situations, or material conditions but to the appearance of full and round ontological, historical, and existential depth that composes the objective conditions of subjective experience and interaction. *Language* connotes neither individual linguistic phenomena nor a conventional category that encompasses customary mediums of rhetorical expression (speech, writing, discourse, textuality, signification); it connotes, rather, the very medium of *self-attuned saying* in which saying appears as a worldly thing and in which worldly things exhibit properties of saying. That which is called rhetorical theory describes modes of communication in which speech is force, writing is creation, and hard things vibrate with suasive sense—modes of communication between world and language, between language and world.

Agon incites and conditions modes of communication between language and world insofar as world is agonistically at stake in the saying that language allows. *Political world, social world, technological world, ethical world, intersubjective world,* and *biophysical world* (to name a few permutations) are at stake in such modes of communication. That which is called rhetorical theory de-scribes agonistic forces of competition, strife, and crisis, forces of power and resistance, conducted through efforts to bring world into true with language and to bring language into true with world—including the incessantly agonistic relations among beings within. Those modes of communication—of substantial sharing, substantive exchange, or physical contact—that obtain between world and language, between language and world, embody the *agon* which renders them available for investigation as pertinent objects of rhetorical theory. Hence, rhetorical theory describes modes of communication between language and world, between world and language, which are incited and conditioned by the forces of *agon* that obtain among beings.

Diane Davis: Brad noted in our discussions that many of these responses seem to point to the issue of empiricism. The question of rhetoric's relation to the sciences, on the one hand, or to affect, on the other, may be two symptoms of the same underlying condition, one that drives rhetorical theory to search for an empirical base or substance (whatever it's called: affective, corporeal, natural) to which it might hitch itself, however contingently or provisionally. That's an astute observation, one I have no intention of challenging. However, I'd like to suggest that something else, too—something very different and possibly more defining—may *also* be getting exposed here. Most every rhetorical theorist we approached articulated some dissatisfaction with rhetorical theory today because of something it's *leaving out*, something that we're not yet able to account for or assimilate, something that's been hanging around the edges, harassing without making itself available to cognition.

I'd like to suggest that theoretical reflection, when it manages to distinguish itself from method or critique, catches traction (or at least skids around) on what is *as yet* unthinkable, what remains unaccounted for: it catches traction on the remains of the thinkable. Theory involves a way of seeing, and as such it can, and typically does—maybe even must—succumb to a totalizing impulse. So we get *the* theory of X or Y, which becomes this or that specific method of critique or pedagogical practice: Marxist criticism, post-structuralist criticism, feminist criticism, psychoanalytic criticism, or methodology or pedagogy, and so on. But theory is also that which keeps a little part of itself on the lookout, straining toward the testamentary whimper of whatever has been and must be sacrificed for the sake of a clearly articulated and teachable concept. What is called theory is indeed *called*; all theory *as* theory is *called* theory. In this way, theory both is and is not tied to critical, political, ethical, and pedagogical praxis: it *is* inasmuch as theory grounds praxis, but theory is also that which is *called* to interrupt praxis. Its task, if it has one, is provocation rather than explanation [. . .]

As rhetoricians, our theorizing begins within the purposeful if protean confines of what is called "rhetoric." Rhetorical theory is, maybe, at least a kind of theorizing that begins within the realm of whatever one might consider to be rhetorical concerns. However, many of the responses we got to our inquiry were less interested in where rhetorical theory begins than in where it should land. Some of you proposed that rhetoric's major concern is democratic politics, and that rhetorical theory needs to find more effective ways of intervening in contemporary political issues. Others suggested that rhetorical theory's most pressing concern right now is how it will protect rhetorical studies from the "numbers driven" mentality of the university. And still others argued that the most pressing task for rhetorical theory right now is to come up with a way to think about agency that doesn't precisely cancel out the possibility *for* rhetorical theory, defined as the study of strategic symbolic interventions in public life.

So there is some sense in these responses that rhetorical theory should be fairly goal oriented, responsible for intervening in pressing issues and contemporary concerns. And I certainly don't want to argue against or take lightly the important work these pragmatic responses aim to prompt. I would, however, like to suggest that if rhetorical theory is to remain theory and so distinguishable at some level from method, critique, or approach, it cannot get underway with an end goal already prescribed, however valuable or imperative that goal may be. That is to say, though theorizing would not begin without some provocation and intention, it also *could* not begin, at all, if its destination were dictated in advance. Rhetoric can and does inspire theory, but rhetorical studies cannot circumscribe or plot the destiny of theory's theorizing and still call it theory. Rhetorical theory typically *begins* within the accepted—or possibly stretched—confines of what is called rhetoric. It may indeed set out to think through the tortured question of agency, for example. But it may end up crashing through the gates, which may then be recognizable as *gates*. And theory that is not given the right or the freedom to veer off unexpectedly in this way is no longer active; it becomes applied theory, sleepwalking theory [. . .]

Let me say again that theory may be indissociable from a certain praxis: not only because all praxis is grounded in some theory, but because theory cannot become operational without articulating itself and so already giving itself over to application or method. Theory and praxis are probably, maybe, indissociable in that sense, but they are also heterogeneous—they are not and cannot be the *same* thing. What I'm trying to suggest is that one of theory's fundamental qualities, and what distinguishes it from method or critique— from *applied* theory—is something Derrida called "destinerrance," which tries to name a kind of destiny of errant circulation, a destiny of wandering without the promise of return. For theory to be what it is, it must have room to wander, to follow its leads wherever they take it. That never prevents it from being interrupted and put to use, but it does mean that *that* interruption will also be interrupted, and that the terms of use will be challenged, refined, disarticulated, or dissolved. That's both the hope and the challenge of theory *as* theory: it won't ultimately settle or allow for recuperative moves, neither in criticism nor in pedagogy. Theory will not bow to mastery; or, at least it won't bow for long. It will quickly return to its post, snapping again and again the presumed link between rigor and certitude, interrupting certitude by listening for and attending to what it's sacrificing—so that it might sacrifice that sacrifice.

Works Cited

McCarthy, Cormac. *Blood Meridian*. New York: Vintage, 1992. Print.

Contributors

Lora Arduser is an Assistant Professor in Professional Writing at the University of Cincinnati. She has published in journals including the *Journal of Technical Writing and Communication, Women's Studies in Communication, Technical Communication Quarterly, Computers and Composition*, and *Narrative Inquiry*. She is also the author of several chapters in edited book collections. She is currently working on a book project about rhetoric, agency, and chronic illness.

Maha Baddar is writing faculty at Pima Community College in Tucson, Arizona. Her research interests include medieval Arabic rhetoric, cultural rhetorics, and translation studies.

Kathleen Marie Baldwin is a doctoral candidate in Composition and Rhetoric in the Department of English at the University of Massachusetts Amherst, where she developed writing programming to support graduate student and postdoc writers across disciplines. Her dissertation, "Multimodal Assessment in Action: What We Really Value in New Media Texts" explores what kindergarten through higher education writing teachers value in students' new media compositions and how teachers' classroom practices are informed by - and speak back to - the emerging body of scholarship on multimodal assessment. Kathleen's scholarly interests also include WAC, multi/translingualism, and issues of race and writing.

Barbara Biesecker is Professor and Department Head of Communication Studies at the University of Georgia. Throughout her career, Professor Biesecker has explored the role of rhetoric in social change by working at the intersections of rhetorical theory and criticism and continental philosophy, psychoanalysis, feminist theory and criticism, and cultural studies. She serves as the editor of the *Quarterly Journal of Speech*, and she continues to serve on the editorial boards of *Communication and Critical Cultural Studies Journal*, *Philosophy and Rhetoric*, and the University of Alabama's Rhetoric, Culture, and Social Critique book series.

John Angus Campbell is Professor Emeritus in the Department of Communication at the University of Memphis: twice recipient of the National Communication Association's Golden Monograph award, recipient Distinguished Teaching Award, University of Washington, the James Madison Freedom of Speech Division award, Southern Communication Association; twice President Association of the Rhetoric of Science, Technology and Medicine and currently Vice President of the North Mason School Board in Belfair, Washington. Professor Campbell gave the 2014 Thomas Scheidel lecture at the University of Washington. With David Henry and Anthony DeValesco he co-edited, *Living Art: Rethinking Rhetorical Theory, Criticism and Pedagogy*, by the late Mike Leff forthcoming from Michigan State Press.

Karma R. Chávez is an Associate Professor in the Department of Communication Arts and affiliate in the Program in Chican@ and Latin@ Studies and the Department of Gender and Women's Studies at the University of Wisconsin, Madison. She is co-editor of *Standing in the Intersection: Feminist Voices, Feminist Practices* (with Cindy L. Griffin, SUNY Press, 2012), and author of *Queer Migration Politics: Activist Rhetoric and Coalitional Possibilities* (University of Illinois Press, 2013). Karma is also a member of the radical queer collective Against Equality, an organizer for LGBT Books to Prisoners, and a host of the radio program, "A Public Affair" on Madison's community radio station, 89.9 FM WORT.

James L. Cherney is an Assistant Professor of Communication Studies at Wayne State in Detroit. His primary area of research is the rhetoric of ableism, particularly as it operates around sport and visibility. He's published articles such outlets as the *Western Journal of Communication*, *Disability Studies Quarterly*, and *Argumentation and Advocacy*. He frequently coauthors with Kurt Lindemann of San Diego State University and he's currently working on a book manuscript entitled *The Rhetoric of Ableism*. He's also writing about the Web-based grassroots "Battling Bare" campaign that seeks to increase awareness of PTSD, in order to outline a "rhetorical model" of disability.

Dana L. Cloud is Professor of Communication and Rhetorical Studies at Syracuse University. She writes and teaches in the areas of rhetoric and critical cultural studies; the critique of race, gender, sex, and class in popular media; and resistance and movements for social change, particularly the labor movement. She has two books, *Control and Consolation in US Politics and Culture: Rhetoric of Therapy* (Sage, 1998) and *We ARE the Union: Democratic Unionism and Dissent at Boeing* (Illinois, 2011). She has published articles in the journals *Communication and Critical/Cultural Studies*, *Quarterly Journal of Speech*, *Rhetoric & Public Affairs*, *Management Communication Quarterly*, *Rhetoric Society Quarterly*, *QED: Journal of GLBTQ Worldmaking*, *Western Journal of Communication*, and others, in addition to numerous book chapters. A longtime socialist activist, she lives in Syracuse, NY with her family and pets.

Diane Davis is Professor of Rhetoric & Writing and English at the University of Texas at Austin and holds the Kenneth Burke Chair at the European Graduate School in Saas-Fee, Switzerland. She is the author of *Breaking Up [at] Totality: A Rhetoric of Laughter* (2000) and *Inessential Solidarity: Rhetoric and Foreigner Relations* (2010), coauthor of *Women's Ways of Making It in Rhetoric and Composition* (2008), and editor of *Reading Ronell* (2009) and *The UberReader: Selected Works of Avital Ronell* (2008).

D. Robert DeChaine is Professor of Liberal Studies and Communication Studies at California State University, Los Angeles. His research engages rhetorical and cultural theory to explore productions of humanitarian discourse, civic identities, and social imaginaries. He is author of *Global Humanitarianism: NGOs and the Crafting of Community* (Lexington, 2005) and editor of *Border Rhetorics: Citizenship and Identity on the U.S.-Mexico Frontier* (University of Alabama Press, 2012). He is current editor of *Communication and Critical/Cultural Studies*. His work has appeared in the *Quarterly Journal of Speech*, the *Journal of Communication Inquiry*, *Text and Performance Quarterly*, and the *Western Journal of Communication*.

Antonio Tomas De La Garza is a PhD candidate at the University of Utah. His research focuses on the ways that communication reifies and/or resists white supremacist power relations. His current work focuses on the US/Mexico borderlands as an anchor for discursively produced violence. His interest in theory derives from a desire to explore the ways that scholarship can become relevant to political struggle. He most recent work can be found in the book *Racial Battle Fatigue: Insights from the Front Lines of Social Justice Advocacy* (Praeger, 2015).

Anne Teresa Demo is an Assistant Professor in the Department of Communication Arts and Sciences at Pennsylvania State University. A past recipient of the National Communication Association's Golden Monograph award, her articles have appeared in the *Quarterly Journal of Speech, Critical Studies in Media Communication, Rhetoric and Public Affairs*, and *Women's Studies in Communication*. She is the coeditor of *Rhetoric, Remembrance, and Visual Form: Sighting Memory* (Routledge, 2012) and *The Motherhood Business: Communication, Consumption, and Privilege* (University of Alabama Press, forthcoming).

Jane Detweiler is an Associate Professor of English, and currently serves as Associate Dean for the College of Liberal Arts at the University of Nevada, Reno. She has pursued a variety of inquiries into writing in academic, professional, and public fora, with special emphases on narrative as a means of inventing, composing and delivering arguments. She has published in the rhetoric of health care disciplines (*Written Communication*), composition pedagogy (*Composition Studies*), writing program assessment (*Organic Writing Assessment*, ed. Bob Broad) and environmental discourse studies. More recently, her work has centered on public moral argumentation and political deliberation, and on leadership in higher education.

Rasha Diab is an Assistant Professor of Rhetoric and Writing at The University of Texas at Austin. Her work focuses on comparative and peacemaking rhetorics and the history of rhetoric. Her book *The Shades of Ṣulḥ: A Study of the Rhetorics of Interpersonal, Civic/Communal, and Diplomatic Arab-Islamic Conciliation* is currently under contract with Pittsburgh University Press. Her publications include a co-authored chapter in David Fleming's book *From Form to Meaning*, articles in *Praxis* and *Across the Disciplines* and forthcoming chapters in edited collections on writing for social justice and the economies of writing.

Keith Gilyard is Edwin Erle Sparks Professor of English and African American Studies at Penn State. He has written and edited numerous publications, including *True to the Language Game: An African American Discourse on Language, Cultural Politics, and Pedagogy* (2011). He is a former chair of CCCC and a past president of NCTE.

Susan Garza is Haas Professor of English at Texas A&M University-Corpus Christi. She is the editor of *Adding to the Conversation on Service-Learning in Composition: Taking a Closer Look* (2013). Her work has also appeared in *Kairos, Reflections*, and the *Journal of Border Educational Research*. She has presented her work internationally, including the Writing Research Across Borders conference.

Peter Goggin is an Associate Professor in Rhetoric (English) and a Senior Scholar in the Global Institute of Sustainability at Arizona State University He is the editor of *Environmental Rhetoric and Ecologies of Place* (Routledge, 2013), *Rhetorics, Literacies, and Narratives of Sustainability* (Routledge, 2009) and author of *Professing Literacy in Composition Studies* (Hampton, 2008). His articles on literacy, environmental rhetoric, and writing include publication in *Composition Studies, Community Literacy Journal*, and *Computers and Composition*. He is founder and codirector of the annual Western States Rhetoric and Literacy conference, which features themes on sustainability, culture, transnationality, and place.

Jeffrey B. Holmes is a Ph.D candidate in Rhetoric and Composition (English) at Arizona State University. He is a Founding Graduate Fellow at the Center for Games and Impact. His research and teaching focuses on videogames and digital media, literacy, informal teaching, and collective learning. His work has appeared in *Terms of Play: Essays on Words That Matter in Videogame Theory* (McFarland, 2013) as well as conferences including the *Games+Learning+Society, Association of Internet Researchers, Rhetoric Society of America*, and *American Educational Research Association*.

James Jasinski is Professor of Communication Studies at the University of Puget Sound. He is best-known for his 2001 book *Sourcebook on Rhetoric: Key Concepts in Contemporary Rhetorical Studies* (Sage). He has authored or co-authored over two dozen essays, monographs, and book chapters on such topics as Martin Luther King's (1967) Riverside Church speech against the Vietnam war, Henry Highland Garnet's (1843) "Address to the Slaves," and language and voice strategies in *The Federalist Papers*. He serves as the editor of *Rhetoric Society Quarterly* and has served as an associate editor for four journals in rhetoric and communication.

Seth Kahn is Professor of English at West Chester University, where he teaches courses primarily in rhetoric and writing. He is currently serving as Co-Chair of the CCCC Committee on Part-time, Adjunct, and Contingent Labor and as Chair of the newly convened CWPA Labor Committee. Recent publications include "What Is a Union?" in *A Rhetoric for Writing Program Administrators;* "'Never Take More Than You Need': Tenured/Tenure-Track Faculty and Contingent Labor Exploitation" in *Forum: Issues about Part-Time and Contingent Faculty*; and a co-guest-edited special issue of *Open Words* on «Contingent Labor and Educational Access.»

Amy Koerber is Professor and Associate Chair in Technical Communication and Rhetoric, Texas Tech University. Her book *Breast or Bottle: Contemporary Controversies in Infant-Feeding Policy and Practice* (University of South Carolina, 2013) was recently awarded the 2015 Conference on College Composition and Communication Award in the category of Best Book in Technical or Scientific Communication. She has published articles on women's health, medical rhetoric, and related topics in journals such as *Women's Studies in Communication, Technical Communication Quarterly*, and *Health Communication*.

Jeffrey A. Kurr is a doctoral candidate in the Department of Communication Arts and Sciences at Pennsylvania State University and a Dissertation Fellow in the Center for Democratic Deliberation at Pennsylvania State University. He received his master's degree at Baylor University in 2013. His research focuses on presidential rhetoric, public address, economic rhetoric, digital media, and argumentation theory.

Margaret R. LaWare is an Associate Professor in the Department of English and the Program in Speech Communication at Iowa State University. She is also an affiliate of the Women's and Gender Studies Program. Her articles have appeared in *Argumentation and Advocacy, Women's Studies in Communication, Women and Language, NWSA Journal* and in edited volumes including two volumes of the *Urban and Suburban Communication Reader*.

Adela C. Licona is an Associate Professor & Director, Graduate Program, Rhetoric, Composition, and the Teaching of English at the University of Arizona. Affiliations: Gender &Women's Studies, Family Studies, Institute of the Environment, & Mexican American Studies. Serves on Faculty Advisory Committee, Institute for LGBT Studies, and Center for Critical Studies of the Body. Co-edited *Feminist Pedagogy: Looking Back to Move Forward* (JHUP 2009) and authored *Zines In Third Space: Radical Cooperation and Borderlands Rhetoric* (SUNY 2012). Co-director, Crossroads Collaborative. Co-founder, Feminist Action Research in Rhetoric, FARR.

Board service: *Women's Studies in Communication, QED: A Journal of GLBTQ Worldmaking, Tucson Youth Poetry Slam,* and *Orion Magazine.*

Bruce McComiskey is Professor of rhetoric and writing in the English department at the University of Alabama at Birmingham. He is the author of *Dialectical Rhetoric* (Utah State University Press, 2015), *Gorgias and the New Sophistic Rhetoric* (Southern Illinois University Press, 2002), and *Teaching Composition as a Social Process* (Utah State University Press, 2000). He is also the editor of *English Studies: An Introduction to the Discipline(s)* (National Council of Teachers of English, 2006) and the co-editor of *City Comp: Identities, Spaces, Practices* (State University of New York Press, 2003).

Amy Milakovic is an Associate Professor and Chair of the Department of English and Foreign Languages at Avila University in Kansas City, Missouri. An affiliate member of the Women's Studies Advisory Council and the Center for Global Studies and Social Justice, her research focuses on the rhetoric of modern war.

Keith D. Miller is Professor of English at Arizona State University and author of *Voice of Deliverance: The Language of Martin Luther King, Jr., and Its Sources* and *Martin Luther King's Biblical Epic: His Great, Final Speech.* His scholarly essays about African American rhetoric have appeared in *College English, College Composition and Communication, Rhetoric Society Quarterly, Rhetoric Review, Publication of the Modern Language Association, Journal of American History, Rhetoric and Public Affairs,* and elsewhere. He recently co-authored (with Nicholas Behm) an essay included in the collection *Race and Writing Assessment,* which the Conference of College Composition and Communication named as the best scholarly collection of 2012. He is currently writing a book about *Autobiography of Malcolm X.*

Thomas P. Miller is Professor of English and Vice Provost for Faculty Affairs at the University of Arizona. He has won awards for teaching, mentoring, diversity leadership and advocacy for shared governance. His research focuses on rhetorical theory and history, faculty development, the history of higher education, and the teaching of writing. He received a national book award from the Modern Language Association for *The Formation of College English Studies: Rhetoric and Belles Lettres in the British Cultural Provinces.* The second part of his history of college English appeared in 2011 as *The Evolution of College English: Literacy Studies from the Puritans to the Postmoderns.*

Kent A. Ono is Professor and Chair in the Department of Communication at the University of Utah. His articles have appeared in such journals as *Communication Monographs*, *Critical Studies in Media Communication*, *Communication and Critical/Cultural Studies*, *Rhetoric and Philosophy*, *Cultural Studies*, *Amerasia Journal*, and *Journal of Asian American Studies*. He is author and/or editor of numerous books. Most recently, he co-edited (with Michael Lacy), *Critical Rhetorics of Race* (New York University Press, 2011).

Lisa L. Phillips is a doctoral candidate and teaching assistant in the Department of English at Illinois State University. Her area of concentration is feminist rhetorical theory. Her research areas include sensory rhetorics, environmental justice, material ecocriticism, and feminist materialism(s). Phillips is the 2013 recipient of a $45,000 National Science Foundation Project InTe-Grate grant entitled: "Mapping the Environment with Sensory Perception," a peer-reviewed, open-source project uniting interdisciplinary geoscience and environmental justice initiatives with humanities research. Her work has appeared in *JAC: A Journal of Advanced Composition*, *Sage* reference publications, *Women and Gender Studies* program papers, and the *Grassroots Writing Research Journal*.

Alexis F. Piper is a dissertator at the University of Wisconsin-Milwaukee in the Rhetoric and Composition program and an instructor of Rhetoric and Composition at Marian University and Lakeland College. She specializes in Environmental Rhetoric, Environmental Discourse Analysis, and Composition Pedagogy. Her past publications include a review published in *Kairos: A Journal of Rhetoric, Technology, and Pedagogy (2013)*, and a chapter published in *Colors of Nature: Culture, Identity, and the Natural World* Online Teaching Guide (2012).

Margaret Price is Associate Professor at Spelman College, where she teaches rhetoric, creative nonfiction, and disability studies. Her book *Mad at School: Rhetorics of Mental Disability and Academic Life* (University of Michigan) won the Outstanding Book Award from the Conference on College Composition and Communication. Margaret is now at work with Stephanie Kerschbaum on a study of disabled faculty and the rhetorics of disclosure. In addition, she serves as current chair of the Composing Access Project (http://composingaccess.net). If you see her at a conference, she will probably be knitting.

Amy D. Propen is faculty in the Writing Program at the University of California, Santa Barbara. Her research has appeared in *Technical Communication Quarterly*, *Written Communication*, and *ACME: An*

International E-Journal of Critical Geographies, as well as *Rethinking Maps: New Frontiers in Cartographic Theory* (Routledge, 2009), and *Environmental Rhetoric: Ecologies of Place* (Routledge, 2013). She is coauthor of *Victim Advocacy in the Courtroom: Persuasive Practices in Domestic Violence and Child Protection Cases* (Northeastern University Press, 2011), author of *Locating Visual-Material Rhetorics: The Map, the Mill, and the GPS* (Parlor Press, 2012), and coeditor of *Design, Mediation, and the Posthuman* (Lexington Books, 2014).

Kelly Ritter is Professor of English and Writing Studies and Director of the Undergraduate Rhetoric Program at the University of Illinois at Urbana-Champaign. She is the author of *Before Shaughnessy: Basic Writing at Yale and Harvard, 1920-1960* (Studies in Writing and Rhetoric/Southern Illinois UP, 2009), *Who Owns School? Authority, Students, and Online Discourse* (Hampton Press, 2010), *To Know Her Own History: Writing at the Woman's College, 1943-1963* (University of Pittsburgh Press, 2012), and the forthcoming *Reframing the Subject: Postwar Instructional Film and Class-Conscious Literacies* (University of Pittsburgh Press, 2015), as well as co-editor of *Exploring Composition Studies: Sites, Issues, Perspectives* (Utah State UP, 2012) and *Can It Really Be Taught? Resisting Lore in Creative Writing Pedagogy* (Boynton/Cook, 2007). She is the current editor of *College English*.

Patrick Shaw is an Associate Professor of English and Director of Composition at the University of South Alabama. His research centers on twentieth- and twenty-first-century rhetorics of identity and of identification. He has published on Richard Weaver and Kenneth Burke, as well as Gertrude Stein. He currently is working on a book on Stein.

Bradford Vivian is an Associate Professor of Communication Arts and Sciences at Pennsylvania State University. He is the author of *Public Forgetting: The Rhetoric and Politics of Beginning Again, Being Made Strange: Rhetoric beyond Representation*, and co-editor, with Anne T. Demo, of *Rhetoric, Remembrance, and Visual Form: Sighting Memory*. His work has appeared in such journals as the *Quarterly Journal of Speech, Philosophy and Rhetoric, Rhetoric and Public Affairs, History and Memory*, and the *Journal of Speculative Philosophy*. He is a recipient of the Winans-Wichelns Award, the Karl R. Wallace Memorial Award, and the B. Aubrey Fisher Award, and his research grants include a National Endowment for the Humanities Summer Stipend.

Ron Von Burg is an Assistant Professor in the Department of Communication and Core Faculty in the Interdisciplinary Program in Humanities at Wake Forest University. His research interests include rhetoric of science, public argument, public discourses on religion and science, and science fiction film studies. His work has appeared in *Critical Studies in Media Communication, Southern Journal of Communication, Journal of Public Deliberation*, and *POROI.*

Rosemary Williamson is a Lecturer in English and the Convener of Writing in the School of Arts, University of New England, Australia. Her articles have appeared in *Media International Australia, TEXT: Journal of Writing and Writing Courses, Social Alternatives*, and other journals. She is the coeditor of two special issues of *TEXT: Journal of Writing and Writing Courses*: *Australasian Magazines: New Perspectives on Writing and Publishing* (Australasian Association of Writing Programs, 2014), and *Supervising the Creative Arts Research Higher Degree: Towards Best Practice* (Australian Association of Writing Programs, 2009).

Patti Wojahn recently concluded her seventh year as Writing Program Administrator (WPA) at New Mexico State University, where she has taught for sixteen years in the Rhetoric and Professional Communication program. As WPA, her work focused on exploring characteristics of successful and less successful students in composition courses; exploring students' access to computers and the internet within the impoverished area in which NMSU resides; examining first-year students' research practices; as well as identifying language preferences and practices among first-year students. She is also interested in communicative technologies, collaboration, and peer review.

Elizabethada A. Wright is Writing Program Administrator and Associate Professor of Writing Studies at University of Minnesota Duluth. She is also the Chief Reader Designate for the College Board's Advanced Placement English Language and Composition Exam. With articles published in *Rhetoric Society Quarterly, American Journalism, Markers, Studies in the Literary Imagination* and several collections, she focuses on understanding how marginalized peoples find voice in a world that tries to silence them.

Index